ROUTLEDGE LIBRARY EDITIONS: ALCOHOL AND ALCOHOLISM

Volume 17

DRINK

DRINK

An Economic and Social Study

HERMANN LEVY

LONDON AND NEW YORK

First published in 1951 by Routledge & Kegan Paul Ltd

This edition first published in 2024
by Routledge
4 Park Square, Milton Park, Abingdon, Oxon OX14 4RN

and by Routledge
605 Third Avenue, New York, NY 10158

Routledge is an imprint of the Taylor & Francis Group, an informa business

British Library Cataloguing in Publication Data
A catalogue record for this book is available from the British Library

ISBN: 978-1-032-59082-0 (Set)
ISBN: 978-1-032-61569-1 (Volume 17) (hbk)
ISBN: 978-1-032-61575-2 (Volume 17) (pbk)
ISBN: 978-1-032-61572-1 (Volume 17) (ebk)

DOI: 10.4324/9781032615721

Publisher's Note
The publisher has gone to great lengths to ensure the quality of this reprint but points out that some imperfections in the original copies may be apparent.

Disclaimer
The publisher has made every effort to trace copyright holders and would welcome correspondence from those they have been unable to trace.

DRINK

AN ECONOMIC AND SOCIAL STUDY

by

HERMANN LEVY

LONDON

ROUTLEDGE & KEGAN PAUL LIMITED

BROADWAY HOUSE, 68-74 CARTER LANE

First published in 1951
by Routledge and Kegan Paul Limited
Broadway House, 68-74 Carter Lane
London

Printed in Great Britain
by Western Printing Services Limited
Bristol

EDITOR'S PREFACE

When Professor Levy died early in 1949 he left an unfinished draft of a book on alcoholic drink. I knew that he had been working on this but no more: we had never talked about it in any detail. It was characteristic of the Professor's keenness to help his younger friends that, whenever we met, we talked about my work rather than his.

The draft lacked the concluding chapter and some of the figures to bring the report up to date. But otherwise the material was as complete as Professor Levy seemed to want it. In preparing the draft for publication I have therefore restricted myself to rearranging the existing data and to editing the text; and where the draft indicated it I have inserted recent statistics. I have added no data. Even the last chapter, for which there were no notes of any kind, consists of arguments and material found elsewhere in the draft.

I have been conscious of the possibility that, even though I was interpreting my function in this restricted way, I might significantly influence Professor Levy's argument; and, conscious of it, I hope I have avoided it. I have interfered most in the chapters relating to methodology, that is Part I, Chapter IV, *Complexity and Severity: Some Case Evidence*, and Part II, Chapter V, *Scope and Method of Statistical Enquiry*: but there were corresponding chapters in the draft and I do not think that I have done more than clarify Professor Levy's theme through extensive rearrangement of the material. I have also reduced the number of chapters. The first fourteen chapters of the book correspond to the eighteen of the draft; and I have somewhat changed their order, particularly in the last part. But the present division into three parts—in brief: what is the drink problem and what are its effects, how widespread is its incidence, and what can be done about it—was indicated in the draft.

Altogether, though subsequent work on it has been substantial, this is certainly a book by Professor Levy—alas, his last.

R. P. LYNTON

CONTENTS

PART ONE

THE ANATOMY OF THE PROBLEM

CHAPTER I

MEDICO-SOCIAL ASPECTS

THE problem of drink, by which in this treatise is meant alcoholic drink, is difficult to define. The economic and social investigator can derive little benefit from merely technological or chemical descriptions of alcohol, although these may well enter his considerations now and then. He may direct his particular interest to the medical side of the problem as a fundamental starting-point of further enlightenment, but he will soon discover that the doctor is in principle concerned only with the effect of drink on the individual. Medicine is not concerned with economics; and it is for social hygiene and social medicine to state and analyse the general social impact of medical discoveries as they relate to many matters, among them to drink. As a German authority on the subject, Professor Alexander Elster, rightly observes: 'It is the sociological aspect of the problem, i.e. that of social hygiene, which puts the study as well as the attempts at counteraction into modern perspective. This modern scientific attitude is due to a better distinction between the analysis of the individual and the social aspects of the problem, and transforms the question of alcoholic drink into a problem of national economy, state policy and social reform.'[1] As such, the problem has naturally and considerably gained in complexity as well as in importance. The Scientific Committee of the Research Council on Problems of Alcohol in America has recently expressed the opinion that 'the alcohol problem has become one of the major complexities of civilisation. On top of the intrinsic difficulties of the situation, there have been superimposed emotional and political elements that have produced still further complications.'[2] But little attention

[1] See Professor Alexander Elster, '*Alkoholismus*' in *Handwörterbuch der Staatswissenschaften*, 4th ed., n.d.

[2] Quoted by Karl M. Bowman in his introduction to the interesting American publication *Alcohol Addiction and Chronic Alcoholism*, edited by E. M. Sellinck, New Haven, 1942.

has yet been paid to the subject even in medico-social handbooks.[1]

Valuable as the scientific investigations of the Medical Research Council in Britain have been, the strict demarcation between, on the one side, a body interested in the discovery of the medico-social effects of drink as they result from the action of alcohol on the human organs, and, on the other, organisations from which the application of these findings are to be expected, has prevented the immediate and practical utilisation of our increased knowledge.[2] It is here, probably, that science and politics are allowed to clash.

Scientists are extremely reluctant to express an opinion on the political action to be taken as a result of their studies: it apparently seems to them unfortunate that the problem of drink entails so many political implications. Thus, in the excellent publication, *The Action of Alcohol on Man*, to which such authorities on the subject as Professor Ernest H. Starling, Robert Hutchinson, Sir Frederic W. Mott and Professor Raymond Pearl contributed valuable essays, no attempt whatsoever was made to draw conclusions as to the social, economic or sociological implications of the problem, except that the Editor, Professor Starling, expressed the view in a few introductory sentences that 'the abolition of all alcoholic beverages from among our midst even if carried out by universal consent' would be a mistake and that legislation to that effect enforced against the wishes and convictions of the members of the community would be 'little short of calamity'. (*The Action of Alcohol on Man*, 1923, pp. v–vi.) Any discussion of the possibilities lying between uninhibited freedom to drink and legislation to abolish its patent evils was carefully avoided; and no suggestion was made in the various chapters so nearly bordering on matters of sociological significance as 'Alcohol as a Food', or the 'Effects of Alcohol on Fatigue', or the 'Influence of Alcohol on the Community', concerning the legal measures required to translate the results of the study into a programme of social reform.[3]

[1] No mention is made of the problem, e.g., in the two stout volumes *Health and Social Welfare*, 1944–5 and 1946–7, which cover a great variety of topical medico-social problems.

[2] Important publications of the Medical Research Council on the medico-social aspects of drink are: *Alcohol: its Action on the Human Organism*, 1918; Sir E. Mellanby, *Influence of Alcohol on Manual Work*; in connection with other investigations on industrial fatigue: W. McDougall and May Smith, *Effects of Alcohol on Fatigue*, 1932.

[3] The authors even contradicted themselves: while Professor Starling contended, on page vi, that the abolition of all alcoholic beverages 'would not result in the long run

'Teetotalism', says Eric Gill, 'is a comic version of the virtue of Temperance.'[1] When giving evidence before the Royal Commission on Licensing,[2] the Secretary of the Royal Society and Director of the National Institute for Medical Research, Mr. (later Sir) Henry Dale, was anxious to make it clear that the famous treatise *Alcohol: its Action on the Human Organism* (see above, footnote 2, p. 4) was purely 'scientific' and that his evidence based upon this book should be understood as not advocating any 'policy' (see Amulree Commission A. 11,437). With the same view it is quite understandable that Sir George Newman gave a definition of 'alcoholism' which limited the word strictly to the 'medical term': 'I am not talking about habits or customs, but about something which I think I may say is of the nature of a morbid condition' (ibid., A. 11,273).

How very different to this is the definition of 'alcoholism' given by Professor Alexander Elster, the economist, who urges that the term should comprise and, indeed, presupposes, the consumption of alcoholic drink as a general social phenomenon, and that it should consequently be immaterial whether drink is taken 'regularly or irregularly, in exaggerated or moderate quantities', and that 'only then the term alcoholism should not apply, when the taking of alcoholic beverages is due to medical prescription'. (See Elster, op. cit., p. 208.) It was probably the undue limitation of the problem of drink when viewed exclusively from the medical angle which led Lord D'Abernon, in his evidence before the Amulree Commission, to recommend with great vigour the setting up of a committee which would be given the widest possible terms of reference to 'enquire into every aspect of the problem' (see Amulree Commission, A. and Q. 32,289 and sqq.).

There can be no doubt that the reluctance of 'scientific' circles to commit themselves to any political or socio-political programmes has been largely due to the fact that the problem of drink had been hitherto dealt with by two directly opposing sides, the one linked up with the temperance movement and largely backed by the Churches, the other connected with purely private

in the improvement of national health and efficiency', the author of the chapter on 'The Influence of Alcohol on the Community' emphasised—see pages 166–7—that 'there is no doubt that, if we could abolish "industrial drinking", the efficiency and health of much of the labouring part of the community would be improved'.

[1] See Eric Gill, *Christianity and the Machine Age*, 1940; *The Christian News Letter Books*, No. 6, p. 48.

[2] The Commission will from now on be referred to as the Amulree Commission and its Report as the Amulree Report.

interests and designed to fight the former—the 'two hostile camps, Trade and Temperance', as they have been called.[1] 'Scientists' wanted to dissociate themselves from any movement with either a purely 'moral' or a purely 'capitalist' aim. As George B. Cutten put it as long ago as in 1907, 'Men of science who have spent years in investigating the subject look upon it as a disease of body and mind, which may or may not have had a beginning in sinful indulgence' (see George B. Cutten, *The Psychology of Alcoholism*, 1907, p. 277). So strong was, and perhaps still is, the feeling among doctors that they should not allow moral approaches to colour their attitude towards the problem of drink, that the late Lord Dawson of Penn, who was certainly aware of the narcotic function of drink, ventured to suggest in the House of Lords that 'anybody who refers to alcohol as a narcotic is a scientific Philistine'.[2] This once again shows how specific attitudes towards the term may narrow its analysis: for if it should really wish to segregate the moral aspect from the physical one, modern medical science would have to ignore the close interaction between the psychological conditions of man and his physical structure, and thus place itself outside the ever-growing progress of psycho-physical knowledge. The reluctance of doctors and scientists to take a wider view has meant that hitherto it has been left to authors writing about drink from a non-medical or at any rate not from an exclusively medical angle to pay regard to the very heterogeneous components of the problem; among them George B. Wilson deserves the front place. (See George B. Wilson, *Alcohol and the Nation*, 1940.)

THE EFFECTS OF ALCOHOL ON MAN

The general effects of alcohol on the human organism arouse no disagreement in medical circles. Alcohol is not a 'stimulant'; evidence before the Amulree Commission emphasised that in point of fact it has no such property: its action is almost entirely narcotic. The Report explained that alcohol first selects the delicate nerve centres of the brain, retarding and sometimes paralysing the action of the higher inhibitory controls. Its first results, accordingly, are a feeling of comfort and self-confidence and the temporary disappearance of cares and worries; and the dulling of the faculties of self-criticism and self-control may lead progressively on to incautious and, eventually, disorderly behaviour. Alcohol is 'thus

[1] See H. M. Vernon, *The Alcohol Problem*, preface by Lord D'Abernon, 1928, p. vii.
[2] See for a discussion of this remark, Amulree Commission, Q. 25,025 sqq.

definitely a drug, in that its effect is to modify, for the time being, the action of parts of the mechanism of the body. (See Amulree Report, pp. 14–15.)

These results take place very quickly. For alcoholic drink is a rather singular type of 'food', in that, unlike the common foodstuffs, it is already soluble and can be absorbed without change. It has been estimated that about one-fifth of alcoholic drink is absorbed directly through the wall of the stomach while practically all the other substances eaten or drunk—with the exception of water—pass through the stomach into the intestine before they are absorbed (see *A Review of the Effects of Alcohol on Man*, 1931, p. 13).

Alcoholic drink has, in addition to its drug action, a food value, in the limited sense that it contributes to the supply of 'fuel' necessary for the generation of energy for the use of the body (see Amulree Report, p. 16); in this respect it distinguishes itself from its rival narcotic, tobacco. But the food or fuel value of drink 'is strictly circumscribed by the disadvantages of its drug action' (Amulree Report, p. 17). It is so well realised in scientific circles that alcoholic beverages cannot be taken into account from the point of view of nutrition that a technical committee of the Health Section of the League of Nations, in a report on the *Physiological Bases of Nutrition*, published in Geneva, 1935, ignored alcoholic beverages altogether and made no mention of them in its different models of nutrition. (See *The Alliance News* of July–August 1946, p. 31.) Recently, Dr. Charles Hill, the General Secretary of the B.M.A., was reported to have said that 'It is farcical to speak of alcohol's food value. It has about as much calorie value in a glass of beer as a knob of bread or a lump of sugar'.[1]

A limited amount of alcohol taken with a meal may have beneficial effects: Sir Adolphe Abrahams, Physician of Westminster Hospital, pointed out recently that a concentration of 15 per cent or less of alcohol in the stomach (which is as high as that ordinarily resulting from the moderate imbibition of wine or beer or dilute spirits with a meal), is unlikely to cause damage to the mucosa. And he added that 'anything which adds to the enjoyment or the anticipatory enjoyment of a meal or to the removal of disturbing states of mind, which in man will include

[1] See *Alliance News Summary*, 10th May 1948. See also Sir W. Crawford and H. Broadley, *The People's Food*, 1938, p. 284; A. L. Bacharach and T. Rendell do not mention alcoholic drink at all in *The Nation's Food*, a survey of scientific data, 1946; see also Courtney C. Weeks, M.R.C.S., L.R.C.P., *Alcohol and Human Life*, 1938, the entire chapter 'Is Alcohol Food?' and also p. 204.

worry, anxiety, intellectual over-activity—anything in short which promotes a sense of ease and well-being—will increase appetite and be favourable to the normal physiological process of digestion'. But he also said that there was always 'the danger of dependence upon the assistance and the possible cultivation of a habit', and that the appetising effect of alcohol might well be a legitimate boon or a danger.[1]

Between chronic alcoholism and vitamin deficiencies there is a direct interaction; it has been found that the vitamin intake attendant upon inebriety is insufficient, and that changes occur in vitamin assimilation and utilisation resulting from liver damage and gastric anomalies in chronic alcoholics.[2] These important effects and interrelations are ignored in the brewers' press, which exalts the latest discoveries of vitamin content in beer.[3] The point which is of such importance to the drinker's health is not solely what the beer may contain in vitamins, but how it is utilised by his body.

There can be no doubt that alcohol has its medicinal qualities. It may be an aid to digestion. It may be a useful medicament during convalescence from serious disease. It may be beneficial to some extent in disorders of the circulation and heart. In aged persons certain actions of alcoholic drink may be beneficial and even counteract a tendency to senile gangrene. Alcohol has no appreciable direct action upon the heart, but may indirectly affect the circulation and be of benefit in some disorders of the cardio-vascular system, notably where peripheral vasodilatation and depression of venous pressure are advantageous.[4] All this may readily be granted at once. But the result of these possible medicinal effects has been that alcoholic drink has gained a popular reputation as a drug which it certainly does not deserve. Doctors agree that alcoholic drink may be a valuable drug, but at the same time emphasise very important provisos: when the physician orders a drug in an amount which will minimise its toxic qualities and allow as full an activity as possible to its therapeutic qualities, he has to consider not only how much he will order, but to whom it

[1] See *The British Journal of Inebriety*, July–October 1945, p. 8; also, for many details, *The Action of Alcohol on Man*, pp. 170 sqq. on *Alcohol as a Medicine*.

[2] See Jellinek, *Alcohol Addiction* as cited above, 1942, p. 241 and entire chapter III.

[3] See, e.g., *The Brewers' Journal*, 21st April 1948, p. 129, where it is said that 'considerable progress' has been made in our knowledge of the nutritional value of beer from the point of view of its vitamin content.

[4] See *The Effects of Alcohol on Man*, pp. 198–222, 'Alcohol in the Practice of Medicine'

is to be given; how it is to be given; when it is to be given; in what form; and by what route. Moreover, as Dr. Robert Hutchinson has emphasised, it is often a difficult matter in an illness to be sure whether a medicine that was given has contributed to the patient's recovery or not, and this is specially so in the case of an agent such as alcohol, where a good effect in one direction is often balanced by an unfavourable influence in another.

SOME ILLUSORY EFFECTS

Alcohol gives the body no direct help in fighting the most common cause of high fever, namely infection. It follows that a person attacked by infectious fever might be led to believe that by taking a large dose of alcoholic drink a beneficial result might be achieved. Actually such self-medication may merely prevent the necessary immediate consultation of the doctor. While alcoholic drink is expected to give warmth—the body may, in fact, react as it does to a hot bath (see *Effects of Alcohol*, p. 214)—it has become a recognised fact that any such effect is mere illusion: even moderate doses of alcohol will tend to increase the loss of heat from the body in consequence of dilatation of the blood vessels of the skin. The 'feeling of warmth' induced by moderate doses of drink is merely evidence, not of the body being warmer, i.e., of increased heat production, but of the skin being warmer, and therefore of increased loss (see *Action*, pp. 137–8). This being so, alcoholic drink may be beneficial when there is excess heat production, as in fever, and may be advantageous when vascular congestion needs to be reduced, as in catarrh or the common cold. In other conditions, however, the risk of a fall of body temperature is a grave danger, especially before any exposure to cold; and a feeble individual may have his powers of resistance lowered in that way so that he may readily contract disease, especially chills and pneumonia (see *Effects*, p. 214). Everybody is aware of the danger of catching a chill after exercise; the reaction of the body to alcohol is similar, and a chill contracted after drinking alcohol, as is emphasised by medical authorities (see ibid., p. 215), is often the starting-point of an acute infection. The 'feeling of warmth' is therefore deceptive. Arctic explorers are forbidden the use of alcohol by leaders of their expeditions because it causes a loss of heat which is especially dangerous in cold climates, and because it lessens strength and endurance (see for this John A. Hunter, *Alcohol and Life*, 1935, p. 45).

The belief that alcohol increases efficiency is equally mistaken. It may be beneficial where one short effort is all that is required, for instance, to mountaineering parties: 'It is well known by mountain climbers, and confirmed by a man like Durig, who is at the same time a trained mountaineer and physiologist, that when a member of a party is utterly exhausted and can proceed no further, two methods are open: either he must rest for a couple of hours before he resumes his journey, or, if the effort which remains to be done is a short one, he can be made to accomplish it by a dose of brandy. The effect of this dose is temporary, but may be sufficient to get the man into a place of safety where he can be allowed to rest.' (*Action*, p. 99). But this case does not arise where continuous work has to be done. Eminent medical authorities, after fully reporting on the experiments made, came to the conclusion that alcohol does not exert any great influence on muscular power except in large doses: 'Probably the output of work is unaffected.' On the other hand: 'Even small doses definitely diminish the power of the body to carry out manœuvres demanding precision.' No evidence exists that alcoholic drink increases output (see *Effects*, pp. 30–6). To the contrary, it has been stated that 'whenever a man . . . is required to put forth his maximum efforts over a considerable time, as in the strenuous hill-climb . . . or where fine adjustment of muscular movements is necessary, as in feats of skill or acrobatic performances, alcohol is unsuitable from the point of view of food'. Alcohol, the authors expressly say, 'should be taken, not before or during work, but when the labours are over' (see *Action*, p. 69), a suggestion which stands in sharp contrast to advertisements showing workers with their beer bottles while performing hard work. Further they observe: 'Few educated people would be found now to champion the old idea that the more beer a man was supplied with, the more work could be got out of him' (see ibid., p. 67). Moderate doses of drink may dull the sensations of fatigue and thus may increase the pleasure of work; but the proviso is expressly made (ibid., pp. 69–70) that drink can improve the quality and amount of work only if it does not interfere with the execution of work. The question immediately arises as to what checks there are to be applied to prevent even slightly excessive drinking while at work: alcoholic drink cannot be prescribed in doses like medicine.

The Buckmaster Committee (see *Alcohol, Social and Economic Aspects*, p. 85) mentioned the statement of an ex-miner, who had formerly worked on the face, that the effect of drinking on efficiency was largely conditioned by the constitution of the individual worker: 'Some men would not be much good for about two hours on the morning after a drinking bout. Others would be quite alright. In fact, they would work harder to sweat it out.' The term 'excessive' is definitely relative; the claim of the authors of *The Action of Alcohol on Man* that an 'inquiry seems justified as to the quantitative definition of these terms, moderation and immoderation' still remains valid, but the attempt may be futile. (See p. 174 and *passim.*) The safest general statement would be that any dose is immoderate which diminishes a man's efficiency and powers of performing his normal avocations (this definition is used in *Action*, p. 174). For the psychopath, for the man of nervous tendencies, or one who has suffered from head injury, any use of alcohol would from this viewpoint be immoderate. Even transitorily alcohol cannot, as a matter of fact, ward off fatigue (see *Action*, pp. 99–100) while a person is at work; for the use of alcohol in ordinary circumstances has the tendency to promote repose and so allow recovery from fatigue. 'In exceptional circumstances a moderate dose of alcohol may for a time abolish the sensation of fatigue, or create an emotional drive which will enable the individual to overcome temporarily the effects of fatigue, so making him capable of continuing his efforts beyond the period at which they would otherwise have come to an end. This increased work is in the nature of a call upon capital, which must be repaid later by a prolongation of the period of rest.' (Ibid.)

The most serious effects of excessive drinking, it is believed, lie in reduced resistance to disease rather than in actual alcoholic complaints; additional evidence suggests that it has a deleterious influence on the chances of recovery from illness. Sir Humphrey Rolleston, sometime President of the Royal College of Physicians in London, has pointed out that if a chronic alcoholic is attacked by an acute disease, or, as he is liable to be, damaged by an accident from which an ordinary person would soon recover without incident or danger to death, the effect may be more serious. A body, and especially a nervous system, which is continually under the influence of drink, cannot stand up to an additional poison or to the shock of an injury. Clinical experience shows that addiction to alcohol impairs the power of the body to resist infection. From an analysis of 3,422 cases of pneumonia, Dr. Courtney

Weeks found that the mortality was 50 per cent among excessive drinkers, 34 per cent among moderate and only 23 per cent among occasional drinkers and total abstainers.[1]

Finally, while the consumption of alcoholic beverages up to an amount and frequency which in 'common parlance' is called moderate does not sensibly shorten the mean duration of life or increase the rate of mortality, as compared with that enjoyed by total abstainers from alcohol, the weight of the pertinent and significant evidence indicates, according to Professor Raymond Pearl, that the excessive use of alcohol as a beverage 'definitely diminishes the duration of life and increases the rate of mortality'. (See *Action*, pp. 277–8.) The possible pitfalls of statistical comparisons are, as we shall see in greater detail later, very numerous in this as in other connections; and Professor Pearl's conclusion regarding abstainers and moderate drinkers provoked criticism from statistical and actuarial investigators.[2] But the effect of heavy drinking is not in doubt, and it is probably significant that several insurance companies decline the risks of whole-life insurance from publicans, and others insure these risks only upon payment of extra charges; a considerable number of insurance offices charge an extra premium also for licensed grocers (see Wilson, op. cit., p. 267). An official publication of the Swedish Royal Social Board sums up by saying that 'theoretically' the teaching of temperance stands on a firmer basis now than ever before; for, firstly, medical progress has proved 'beyond doubt' that alcohol even in small quantities has 'a paralysing effect on the system'. Secondly in 'our modern technically progressive era, with its life of intense strain . . . greater demands are made on personal self-control and presence of mind than formerly. Since alcohol in particular benumbs the faculties, its abuse may have even more disastrous effects nowadays than ever before.'[3]

WHY PEOPLE DRINK

Yet, despite all the medical stress on the 'disastrous effects' of alcoholic drink, people do in fact drink: that is the crucial fact for

[1] See Sir Humphrey Rolleston, 'Alcohol and Morbid Conditions', in *The Alliance Year Book for 1939*, pp. 45 sqq.; see also Weeks, op. cit., pp. 331–2: 'That alcohol predisposes to pneumonia has long been recognised'; this important study contains a great number of statements illustrating the ill-effects of alcoholism on health.

[2] See for a detailed statistical comment Courtney C. Weeks, *Alcohol and Human Life*, 1938, pp. 366–78; for actuarial comment, see the *Transactions of the Actuarial Society*, 1938, p. 344: '. . . Pearl's material is of little value for determining the question of the effect on longevity of the consumption of alcohol'.

[3] See *Social Work and Legislation in Sweden*, as cited above, 1938, pp. 208–10.

the sociologist and the economist. There are, in the first place, those who wish for the full effect of the narcotic function of alcohol, to 'drown their sorrows', to obtain, by means of alcoholic drink, a sense of well-being or 'euphoria' (see *Effects of Alcohol on Man*, pp. 106 sqq.). The terms used in this connection are 'mental relief and relaxation', 'soothing', 'troubles seem to fly', 'freedom from care', 'oblivious to worry', and many others. Medical authors explain that 'the euphoria or happiness is accompanied by a pleasing sense of freedom, due to a relaxation of normal inhibitions' (see ibid., p. 107). McDougall tries to analyse this narcotic phenomenon more profoundly and suggests that it should be viewed in connection with Professor Jung's well-established distinction between introverts and extraverts.[1] He believes that alcoholic drink, in common with some other drugs, shifts the position of the individual, so that the introvert may become or tends to become extraverted: 'His reserve and reticence are broken down: he gives expression to his emotions, talks freely, and falls on the neck of his neighbour or comes to blows with him with equal ease. This is the charm of alcohol for the introvert, that for the brief period it lifts him from the burden of his introspective reflections and lets him live freely in and for the moment.' McDougall also states that the introvert has a strong head and is not easily intoxicated, while the extravert is upset with very little alcohol.[2]

But alcohol is mostly consumed, neither mainly for its narcotic function, nor, for that matter, for being a liquid food: to a large extent it is taken as a refreshment. The belief that alcoholic drink is 'used primarily for its psychological effect as a means of escape from unpleasant reality'[3] clearly leaves out of consideration that, as a refreshment, drink may not be and usually is not in the least to be regarded as serving such a purpose. Drink is certainly not just narcotics taken in the pleasant form of food. Famous vintages of Continental origin, the beer of Munich and Pilsen, and the liquors produced by the Benedictine and other monasteries, have become known and cherished because of their special flavour which appeals not to the 'drinker' alone, but to everyone with a refined palate.

Modern physiology has probably been apt to overrate the

[1] See W. McDougall, *Outlines of Abnormal Psychology*, 1926, p. 442 and *passim*.

[2] See also *Effects of Alcohol on Man*, pp. 120–1, and also the interesting observations under the heading of 'Psycho-analytical Explanations', pp. 121–9.

[3] See, e.g., Haven Emerson, *Alcohol, its Effects on Man*, n.d., p. 13, and elsewhere.

real significance of a diet based exclusively upon scientific elaborations of energy value (calories) and protein. We could not live on a few foods alone, whatever their scientific nutritional function, without impairing our health. We are dependent for our nutritional contentment on a variety of food—a necessity varying with occupation and environment. Moreover the factor of 'satiety' plays its part in the composition of our intake of food quite independent from the nutritional factor.[1] Yet little attention has been paid to the 'refreshment' element in alcoholic drink,[2] where the narcotic effect, though it is always present and may be harmful, plays a quite subordinate role compared with the enjoyment of the exquisite taste and flavour of drink, which depends on the skill of the producer and, as in the case of wine, on the weather of the season.

The refreshment element in drink has had the most far-reaching effects. For it is the element out of which drinking customs, as distinct from the drinking habits of individuals, have largely grown. Certainly, these customs have originated with generally using at meals, and particularly offering guests, liquid which would not only quench their natural thirst, but also please the palate. Through this usage, as Professor Elster rightly argues (see op. cit., p. 209), drink develops into an important subject in social psychology and sociology; for if it is sometimes argued that drink should be left to the free decision of the individual, it should be realised that, where such etiquettes prevail, the individual is hardly in a position to make his decision as independently as would be the case if there were no drink customs. The customs may immediately lead to excessive drinking on the part of people who otherwise would not be heavy drinkers at all. In Germany, for instance, excessive drinking among students has been greatly fostered by the drinking rules of the fashionable students' corporations—*Korp* and *Burschenschaften*—which consider heavy drinking as a test of gallantry and good comradeship. Lady Bell, again, mentions in her classic work, *At the Works*, that the stevedores, or stowers, who load iron ore vessels are practically obliged by public opinion to 'stand drinks round' with all those who have been employed in the work when the vessel is finally laden. She recalls the story of a very respectable woman who told a visitor

[1] See Otto Kestner and H. W. K. Knipping, *Die Ernährung des Menschen*, Berlin, 1924, Brit. Museum 7390 bb. 34.

[2] There is no mention of it in an otherwise very full chapter on 'Alcohol as Food' in *A Review of the Effects of Alcohol on Man*, as cited above, pp. 208 sqq.

that her husband had never drunk in his life until, at first to her delight, he was promoted to be stevedore; then this custom 'was the ruin of him. The pressure of opinion was too strong for him to withstand it, and having once begun, he took to going out of his home and drinking regularly' (see Lady Bell, *At the Works*, ch. x).

Finally, apart from being an attraction as an intoxicant or as a refreshment, and thus satisfying the consumer's want, drink may be taken for reasons which have no basis in fact. As we have seen, this is generally the case, for instance, when the layman expects drink to improve or maintain his health. The dangers of self-medication are obvious, and so also should be the dangers of self-medication through alcoholic drink. Perhaps one of the greatest dangers lies in the impression, which people who believe in the curative effect of alcohol are apt to have, that the beneficial effect of drink in some particular connection is responsible for their well-being in general. For instance, a drinker who finds that beer is having a beneficial effect on reducing constipation may come to the conclusion that 'the more he drinks the better he feels' (see for a drastic example of this kind: Mass Observation, *The Pub and the People*, 1943, p. 43). Sir George Newman, then Chief Medical Officer of the Ministry of Health and the Board of Education, observed before the Royal Commission on Licensing (see A. 11,277) that, though he did not know of any scientific evidence in support of the view that alcohol increased or fortified the natural powers of resistance of the human body to infective processes, nor that alcohol directly strengthened the tissues of the body, yet 'people say they take alcohol because it strengthens them against sickness, that it strengthens them against an oncoming disease, that it enables them to resist the oncoming of disease better than if they were without it'. This belief may be constantly fortified by the purely narcotic effects of alcoholic drink.

Similarly, the idea that alcoholic refreshment increases their working capacity is widespread among the working classes. Of this Mass Observation has given some striking illustrations (see op. cit., p. 46). Workers of all kinds seem to be genuinely satisfied that beer, far from hampering their efficiency for work, is driving it to a high pitch. Again, the transitory narcotic effect of alcohol may be partly responsible for the belief. Workers may also base their view on the belief that alcoholic drink has a particularly high nutritional value.

As all of us know, and as we shall have occasion to illustrate on later pages, there are other sorts of reasons which determine people's drinking habits. But these three—the desired narcotic effect, the support of social customs, and the illusions concerning the effects of drink—present probably the most fundamental factors determining an individual's consumption of drink. We will return to them after examining briefly some general socio-economic conditions.

CHAPTER II

THE DRINKING HABIT

The three fundamental factors which are, in the main, responsible for the consumption of alcoholic drink—drink as a narcotic, drink as a beverage, and drink for imagined invigorating and curative purposes—cannot explain, either singly or together, the variations in consumption as they exist in society. Little is said about these in books which deal with the action or effects of alcohol on man. A study of these variations cuts across any but the most special social groups and divisions, as, perhaps, groups which have problems particularly significant for medicine or physiology—the aged, or the neurotic, or persons employed in heavy muscular occupations.

So far we have done no more than disclose that the problem of drink has a wide and important sociological background: the mere existence of the narcotic factor does not explain why some people or some sections of the population fall in with the desire to have narcotic refreshment more than others; the refreshment factor as such does not explain why the refreshment may be taken in larger and smaller amounts by one or other section of the population and thus lead to greater or smaller consumption of drink; nor does the last of the three factors indicate why people believe in imaginary properties and effects of alcoholic drink when scientific knowledge is all against them.

The unfolding of this background cannot, of course, ever be quite complete. Individual motives are innumerable; they are just as differentiated as life itself. Somebody may be induced to take drink as a narcotic because he feels worried about his home life, about some financial or personal loss, because of his state of nerves, because he just wants to 'forget' for a while; there may be dozens of similar motives. But where such motives acquire a more general aspect, a certain regularity with groups of people, where they seem to be related to certain general or frequently recurring conditions in a community, they become of interest to the sociologist and may provide the clues to more general conclusions. And no variety is wholly miscellaneous: it allows always some classification.[1] It is just in this classification of variety in human affairs that social scientists are interested when they attempt to assess specialised factors as they affect the community, for instance, in its consumption of alcoholic drink.

As is general in the diagnosis of social problems, it is difficult and often impossible to disentangle the intricate web of causes and effects. The problem of drink is no exception. Even in relation to disease, the consumption of drink may be effect as well as cause: it may, in other words, be also a symptom of disease. It may similarly at once be a result and a cause of poverty. And destitution may in its turn lead to disease and further drink. The interdependence of these and other aspects is not simple but highly complex. Within that complexity, there are traits of varying generality, as well as others specific, say, to the consumption of drink as a narcotic.

INTERNATIONAL COMPARISONS

In a comparison of national drink habits, there can be no doubt that the United Kingdom has always been characterised by heavy drinking. Daniel Defoe said of the 'true-born Englishman' (see Daniel Defoe, *The True-Born Englishman*, 1701):

> 'In English ale their dear enjoyment lies,
> For which they'll starve themselves and families.
> An Englishman will fairly drink as much
> As will maintain a family of Dutch.'

These were the words, not just of a satirical critic of his times, but of a man whose labours were directed towards many social reforms designed to improve the conditions of what then were called the 'labouring poor'. There were frequent comparisons of this kind in those days, for the way the persecuted immigrants from Western Europe lived in their newly formed communities in England contrasted rather sharply with that of the native British workman.[2] In fact so important seemed the problem some eighty years later to Adam Smith that he gave some detailed attention to it in his *Wealth of Nations*. The price of drink was not the

[1] See some interesting observations on this in William F. Ogburn and M. F. Nimkoff, *A Handbook of Sociology*, 1947, p. 39 and *passim*.

[2] See Hermann Levy, *Economic Liberalism*, 1913, ch. 'The Protestant Immigrants

criterion. He was apparently impressed by the fact that 'the cheapness of wine seems to be a cause, not of drunkenness, but of sobriety'. (See Adam Smith, *The Wealth of Nations*, Book IV, ch. iii, ed. 1822, p. 162.) He noted that 'The inhabitants of the wine countries are in general the soberest people in Europe; witness the Spaniards, the Italians, and the inhabitants of the southern [*sic*] provinces of France. People are seldom guilty of excess in what is their daily fare. Nobody affects the character of liberality and good fellowship by being profuse of a liquor which is as cheap as small beer. On the contrary, in the countries which, either from excessive heat or cold, produce no grapes, and where wine is consequently dear and a rarity, drunkenness is a common vice, as among the northern nations, and all those who live between the tropics, the negroes for example, on the coast of Guinea. When a French regiment comes from some of the northern provinces of France, where wine is somewhat dear, to be quartered in the southern, where it is very cheap, the soldiers, I have frequently heard it observed, are at first debauched by the cheapness and novelty of wine; but after a few months of residence, the greater part of them become as sober as the rest of the inhabitants.' Adam Smith was anxious to show that 'the vice of drunkenness', as he termed it, is by no means one mainly prevalent among the rich who can afford to buy any amount of alcoholic drink. On the contrary, in his opinion, people take to drink who can least afford it and without much regard to the price that it costs them. Cheapness of drink is in his view not necessarily a temptation to excessive drinking.

Some hundred and fifty years after these observations about the particularly high consumption of alcoholic drink in England, the comparative position had scarcely altered.[1] The late Lord D'Abernon, who as a diplomat had a wide opportunity of studying national traits in many countries, spoke in 1928 about the abuse of alcoholic liquor 'which marred the English efficiency and gave this country a bad pre-eminence' (see H. M. Vernon, *The Alcohol Problem*, 1928, preface, pp. v–vi). This observation is also confirmed by the contributor on drink problems in the *Encyclopædia Britannica*, where the differences in international strength of the temperance movement are explained by the differences in drink consumption that exist between nations (see *Encyclopædia*

[1] See also Dr. Arthur Shadwell before the Royal Commission, A. 32,602: 'On the Mediterranean there is practically no drunkenness.'

Britannica, 1945 ed., vol. 21, p. 920): 'The organised agitation against the abuse, and, in many cases, also the use of alcoholic liquor, is a very interesting feature of social life in those countries where it is mainly carried on. These are the United States of America, the British Islands and Dominions and the northern countries of Europe, particularly Scandinavia and Finland. It is largely a matter of climate. In the wine-producing countries it is either weak or non-existent. In France alcohol means spirits, and that is generally the case on the Continent. In Spain, Portugal and also the Mediterranean there is no need to check drunkenness, because the people are naturally sober. But in the countries first mentioned this is not the case.'

But to give climate as the simple explanation for these differences is not convincing even if the word 'largely' is cautiously added. Adam Smith noted in his interpretation of the facts that the climate of the western and southern parts of the U.S.A., for instance, does not differ materially from that of Spain or Italy; nor does the winter in northern France differ decidedly from that in the New England States of the U.S.A. Evidently conditions other than climate, in the first instance socio-economic factors, play an important part in these territorial differences.

Clearly the kind of alcoholic drink normally consumed is a factor which may have a significant influence on drunkenness. Sir Edgar Sanders, formerly General Manager of the Carlisle and District State Management Area, stated in his Memorandum to the Royal Commission that it was spirit drinking which was responsible for a great part of the drunkenness in the North of England (see A. 20,033. Statement, para. 5). In the year ending 31st March 1939 the *per capita* consumption of spirits in England and Wales was 0·20 gallon, but in Scotland, 0·37 gallon. (See *The Alliance Year Book for 1947*, p. 149.) G. B. Wilson suggests this as the main explanation for the similar ratio of proceedings for drunkenness, (see G. B. Wilson, *Alcohol and the Nation*, 1940, p. 287)—the 'national drink of Scotland has for centuries been spirits, not beer', and, with most people, intoxication with spirits is very direct and rapid. The ways in which alcohol is consumed, and other habits, also vary widely between countries, and are also likely to be significant. The British custom of perpendicular drinking at the bar, for example, which is highly conducive to heavy drinking, is virtually unknown on the Continent.

DRINK AS A NARCOTIC: DISEASE

The narcotic, the refreshment, and the deceptive attractions of alcoholic drink play a varying part within these broad variations. As regards the narcotic value, it is only recently that alcoholism has begun to be regarded as 'a symptom rather than a cause of disease' (Dr. Arthur Guirdham, *Disease and the Social System*, 1942, p. 75). This is the case with dipsomania, which is, in brief, the intermittent compulsion to get drunk. 'Epileptics . . . are liable to fly to alcohol, which in turn worsens their attacks.'[1] The relevant diseases are best regarded as of the nature of a metabolic crisis, paroxysmal in nature and expressed principally through the central nervous system, but essentially total reactions of the total personality with profound mental and physical effects. 'Insomnia is both a motive for drinking and a result of it. The "nightcap" to send one to sleep is all too common. Usually it will send one to sleep, but not for long. Its soporific effect soon passes off. Then he has another nip and another sleep and so on until he becomes a confirmed alcoholic.'[2] This is agreed in the same way by other writers. For instance, John H. Ewen says (see John H. Ewen, *Mental Health*, 1947, pp. 92–3): 'Alcohol is more frequently a symptom than a cause of mental disorders, and its aetiological significance in the causation of mental disorder has been overestimated in the past.' It is probable, again, that some 'moods', and notably the despondent moods, which may lead to a strong desire to take refuge in alcohol, have their roots in the person's organic condition, such as an excess of thyroid activity.[3]

It is doubtful whether alcoholism can be directly inherited. In their Memorandum to the Amulree Commission, Mr. Roche Lynch, Senior Official Analyst to the Home Office, and Mr. W. Hurst-Brown said (see *Evidence*, p. 653A) that: 'There is little evidence for the conclusion that drunkenness in the parents is an inheritable characteristic, but persistent drunkenness is often associated with symptoms of mental instability which is definitely inheritable.'[4] But the position with regard to indirect inheritance

[1] Dr. H. Pullar-Strecker, Physician of the British Hospital for Functional Mental and Nervous Disorders on 'Collateral Uses of Benzedrine', in *British Journal of Addiction*, July 1947, p. 56.

[2] See, for some interesting observations on the drinking habit being the cause and effect of sickness, Dr. Walter E. Masters, *The Alcohol Habit and its Treatment*, 1931, ch. iii, 'Motives and Predisposing Causes', in particular p. 48.

[3] See Professor W. McDougall, *An Outline of Psychology*, 5th ed. 1931, pp. 359 sqq.

[4] The same opinion is to be found in *Effects*, p. 72: 'There is little evidence that the offspring of drunkards are themselves, necessarily, or indeed, in any direct way, predisposed to become drunkards.'

seems to be different. Dr. Guirdham states (see op. cit., p. 75) that dipsomania as well as epilepsy have 'a strong hereditary factor' in their aetiology. Mental defects caused or aggravated by drinking may be inherited by the children and sooner or later lead to alcoholism on their part. The passing on, somehow, of the drinking habit is certainly significant: as Dr. Russell Brain observes (see *Diseases of the Nervous System*, p. 663), 'a parental incidence of alcoholism is frequently present, and there is a history of alcoholism in one or both parents of 30 per cent of patients admitted to institutions for inebriates'.

UNSATISFACTORY HOMES

Many social writers of the past and present have recognised that an unsatisfactory home life led in many instances to the formation of the drinking habit. Smiles, who was fully aware of the fact that the drinking habit and its disproportionate expense were ruining many homes, emphasised quite rightly that it was as often as not the neglect of home economy and comfort which led to drinking. 'Men themselves', he said, 'attach little or no importance to the intelligence or industrial skill of women; and they only discover their value when they find their homes stupid and cheerless . . . if the substantial element of physical comfort be absent from the home, it soon becomes hateful; the wife notwithstanding all her good looks, is neglected; and the public house separates those whom the law and the Church have joined together. Men are really desperately ignorant respecting the home department. If they thought for a moment of its importance, they would not be so ready to rush into premature house-keeping. Ignorant men select equally ignorant women for their wives; and these introduce into the world families of children, whom they are utterly incompetent to train as rational domestic beings. The home is no home, but a mere lodging, and often a comfortless one.' He does not hesitate to regard this as one of the 'chief causes of drunkenness'. Once Mr. Edwin Chadwick, Britain's classic social reformer, remonstrated with an apparently sensible workman over the expenditure of half his income on whisky; the worker replied: 'Do you, sir, come and live here and you will drink whisky too.' (See Smiles, *Thrift*, pp. 362–3.)

It should not be assumed that Smiles in his aim to extol the benefits of thrift and wise spending exaggerated the point. It permeates observations on drink to our days. Lady Bell made the point that 'in many cases' the craving for drink on the part of men was 'enhanced by the miserable unpalatable food, often cold and half-cooked, that the workman finds in his home, sending him out to seek elsewhere something with warmth and cheer in it'. (See Lady Bell, op. cit., p. 346.) Lord Askwith, writing in 1928, mentioned bad housing and poor food and 'various forms of wants of amenities of life' next to 'lack of education' as the main social causes of the excess in drink (Lord Askwith, *British Taverns*, p. 259). Professor Zweig wrote in 1948 that 'The women "regulars" are chiefly lonely women who have no interests outside the pub'—and in all probability no comfortable and satisfactory home. The regular male drinkers, according to Professor Zweig, consider to a large extent the 'home' as a joyless alternative to the pub: 'they prefer to stay at home' mostly and sometimes only when they just have not the money to spend on drink.[1] Professor Zweig came to the conclusion that it was the lack of entertainment at home which leads the worker to prefer to meet his friends and acquaintances in the pub rather than in the home. 'He would not think of inviting friends to his home, because it would be dull for him.' And 'when his home is slummy and full of noise and dirt, he is obviously driven out more frequently than otherwise'. He continues (see ibid., p. 30): 'Family relations are a very important factor in that respect. Most regulars are middle-aged married men, more or less bored at home. A happy family man would not go to a pub, but would stay at home, but the staler a man becomes in his work and family relations, the more escapes he wants and finds in drink.'

The pioneers of the Peckham Health Centre took pains to collect instances of early married life in working-class districts, which were repeated with 'monotonous regularity'. In one recorded case,[2] 'the husband came home to a hotted-up meal, stood for half an hour or more beside the cot of the elder child—who refused to go to bed or to sleep if he were not there. So at 9.30, or later, he went off to the billiard hall for a little recreation or to the pub till closing time, leaving his wife to see that the children came to no harm.'

It is certainly difficult to generalise and assess the various circumstances which make bad homes. But one factor about which

[1] See *Labour, Life, and Poverty*, p. 27.

[2] See Innes H. Pearse, M.D., and Lucy H. Crocker, *The Peckham Experiment; a study in the Living Structure of Society*, 1943, pp. 250–1.

there is little doubt is bad housing. The Amulree Commission took a great deal of evidence on the point—no less than nineteen witnesses expressed their view in the matter. Mr. Henry Riches, Chief Constable of Middlesbrough, was among them: 'The lack of accomodation in the majority of workmen's dwellings, owing to more than one family in many instances occupying the same house, accounts to some extent for men seeking the well-lighted and comfortable rooms in a public house, or at their club, in preference to spending the evening in their own place of abode' (see A. 7,752 (23)). Nothing had changed since Lady Bell had given the same description of Middlesbrough twenty-five years before. The evidence of the Bishop of Barking was perhaps the most impressive (see Index *sub* Housing; in particular A. 34,801–2 (3) and 34,836). The Amulree Report did not fail to emphasise its particular significance (see Amulree Report, para. 101): 'We recognise . . . the undoubted fact that, particularly where housing conditions are bad, the public house may represent the main chance of comfort and social enjoyment which is open to the worker and his wife. Here, however, the danger of a vicious circle needs to be reckoned with. By seeking refuge in the public house a man or woman may become tolerant of bad conditions at home, and *pari passu* the means to remedy those conditions may be seriously prejudiced by the amounts spent on intoxicants. We were impressed by the evidence put before us in this regard by a number of witnesses from their own experience and observations of social conditions in the poorer districts of large cities.'

A sample survey of a single street carried out during the war by the London Diocesan Church of England Temperance Society concluded that 'houses and atmosphere alike constitute a tremendous obstacle to decent family life' (see *Our Street*, 1943, p. 5). The dismal characteristics of such conditions include overcrowding, dirt and filth, lacking amenities, lack of proper sanitation, dilapidation. From his great practical experience, Dr. Alfred Salter came to the conclusion that 'the poorer the borough, the worse the housing conditions, and the worse the general environment, the greater the expenditure on alcoholic drink'. (Amulree Report A. 26,042.)

Allied to bad housing conditions is the wife's neglect of the home. In many cases this is due to lack of appreciation and consequently of application on her part. Sometimes it is due to poverty and loss of heart; to this extent poverty, and unemployment and other conditions leading to poverty, may lead also to drinking. But sometimes it is due to the attempt of women to combine the function of housewife with full-time employment outside the home. The modern separation of home and workplace, as PEP suggests (*PEP*, Broadsheet of 23rd August 1946, 'Mothers in Jobs', p. 4), makes it 'very difficult . . . for mothers to combine housework and gainful occupation, and those who attempt to do so usually fail to do justice to either'. Even for married women without children, full-time work is often incompatible with adequate care for home and husband. Yet it is accepted in several large areas and large sectors of industry that women naturally go to work, and altogether about one million and a half married women are in paid employment. Though improved economic conditions would in many cases lead to a happier home life, and a reduced consumption of alcohol, the employment of married women seems a doubtful method of improving them.

ATTRACTIONS OF THE PUBLIC HOUSE

The pub is the 'home from home', the place where the downcast goes to drown his sorrow, but mostly where people go for the social life and entertainment, often in agreeable surroundings, which they lack at home. The drinking habit comes with this attempt to meet the home's deficiencies. Club life, in the sense that 'My house is my castle—but my home is my club', is a peculiarly British institution; and, as Mass Observation put it, 'the pub is the only free, non-esoteric, non-exclusive, weather-proof meeting-place for the ordinary worker' (op. cit., p. 165). This has been so for some centuries. The early friendly societies and trade unions met in the inn. Sir Frederic Eden observed at the end of the eighteenth century that the members of friendly societies not only secure for themselves 'a competent support in old age and sickness', but also have a regular opportunity 'to spend a convivial hour with their neighbours and to hear what is often, as Goldsmith says, "much older than ale",—the news which has been collected by rustic politicians'.[1] As Sidney and Beatrice Webb have pointed out, the drinking on such occasions was sometimes more significant than the business done.[2] Social entertain-

[1] See Sir Frederick Eden, *The State of the Poor*, 1798; also Sir Arnold Wilson and Professor Hermann Levy, *Industrial Assurance*, 1937, p. 15; see for interesting documentary material also Sidney and Beatrice Webb, *English Local Government*, vol. I, 1906, pp. 56–7.

[2] See also Lord Askwith, *British Taverns*, 1928, pp. 102–3, and history of clubs, pp. 250 sqq.

ment outside the home on some of the evenings of the week is thus an established tradition with the British working classes, and to some extent the middle classes as well.

Mass Observation give a vivid account of the elements which make this 'home' in our age. In some pubs regular customers are regarded as 'our chaps' and their relationship of publican and customer is that of friends. Frequently the connection between the pub and its regular customer is similar to affiliation to a political organisation. But even when meeting strangers, regulars feel that they are 'participating in the same pleasures at the same time and place' (see Mass Observation, *The Pub and the People*, pp. 133–4). The familiarity between the regular customer and the staff is a pseudo-home characteristic. Most regulars are known to the staff by their Christian names, and mostly they address each other that way. They tend to sit or stand in the same places every night; this is, as Mass Observation says, 'particularly noticeable with regular groups who stand at the bar'. They further observe: 'The degree to which the regular pub-goer can come to look upon his pub as a kind of second or alternative home is shown by a friend of ours, a spinner, who spends almost every evening in a small beerhouse. He goes home after work, has his tea, then comes down to the pub, about 7.30 as a rule. When he comes into the taproom he goes to the cupboard in the wall, opens it, and takes out his spectacles. Then he puts them on, spreads the evening paper out on the table, and reads it. He always stays until closing time.' Professor Zweig's recent study bears out these experiences. He states that 'some houses, especially off the main road, resemble a workmen's club, with almost an exclusive membership where everybody knows everybody else'. The idea of the 'regular pub-goer is to have company'. In Zweig's experience, the 'regulars who go every day or nearly every day' are mostly elderly men. 'They form a sort of club in the pub, and if, as sometimes happens, a regular does not turn up one night, he must make excuses on his next visit.' They are the backbone of the pub, at least of a certain kind, the drinkers who seek a home from home (see Zweig, op. cit., pp. 25, 27).

The 'personality' of the landlord and the friendliness of the atmosphere are, according to *The New Survey of London Life and Labour*, almost as great attractions as the beer itself. In this respect, and in that of physical amenities, public houses do not lag behind other distributive establishments in using 'every inducement open to the store proprietor to reach the customer' (Lawrence E. Neal,

Retailing and the Public, 1932, p. 17). Landlords and bartenders with well-known talents attract people specially to their place. Particularly in England, the management of public houses can often be undertaken with success by retired boxers, wrestlers, vaudeville artists, billiards or football players, who 'are not necessarily good business people, but have an automatic working-class following of their own'. (See *New Survey*, op. cit., also reprint as cited above, p. 17.) On the Continent, and in particular in wine-producing countries, the owner of an establishment may be known as a particularly well informed and well supplied 'connoisseur' of vintages; his house may be frequented for meals with drink in the first instance for that reason, all the more so if he knows how to combine good cuisine with wines of distinction.

Increasingly, public houses have comfortable equipped lounges and spacious rooms with chairs and tables, facilities for games and gambling, wireless and television. Women are more and more accepted even in the socially more exclusive establishments, and many women who previously had their refreshment with their evening meal now join their husbands in their relaxation.[1] The pub as 'a home from home' is no longer restricted to the individual member of the family; it has become a family affair.

SOCIAL DRUNKENNESS

A large number of people are prone not merely to drinking, and perchance heavy drinking, in a crowd of like-minded folk, but to systematic 'group intoxication'. Mass Observation regard 'social drunkenness' as a significant species of drunkenness. 'In the life of the ordinary town-worker no occasion arises when he is officially sanctioned and encouraged to dance in the streets, unless the Monarchy is involved in some ritual climax. But it is all right for him to do it at Blackpool, and he often does, not necessarily because he has drunk a lot, but because a lot of people have got drunk and don't care any longer for the social conventions which forbid them to dance in the streets' (see *The Pub and the People*, pp. 245–54).

THE ILLUSIONS

The belief in the health- and strength-giving properties of alcoholic drink, finally, has a variety of immediate causes. With some people it derives primarily from faulty deductions from ex-

[1] See Sir William Crawford and H. Broadley, *The People's Food*, 1938, p. 74 and *passim*.

perience, passed down, occasionally, from generation to generation. Mass Observation, for instance, found a woman who referred to the drinking habits of her grandmother in connection with the fact that she died at ninety-two, and a man who recollected with satisfaction the time of his childhood when 'a horn of beer before breakfast was the foundation for the day' (see *The Pub and the People*, 1943, p. 43). The illusion may be promoted by the immediate feeling of ease and relaxation after some drink which the unknowledgeable may readily accept as a symptom of improvement of his health, in much the same way as the same effect after a dose of some patent medicine, which does no more than temporarily relieve pains and uneasiness, creates the conviction of greater strength or of cure.

The possibility of just this effect has led to the advertising of drink for its strength- and health-giving properties, just as, in the words of the Secretary of the Pharmaceutical Society, many advertisements of patent medicines 'are couched in scientific or semi-scientific terms, often meaningless, designed to impress and deceive uneducated and credulous people'.[1] Self-medication by alcoholic drink is often fostered by advertising. The very existence of such terms as 'medicated spirits' and 'medicated wines' has reinforced the popular belief that there must be a close interrelation between alcohol and health. A witness before the Amulree Commission spoke of 'psychological suggestion'. 'The advertisement of a jolly-looking nurse leaning over a patient with a bottle of Wincarnis in her hand is very suggestive to a girl not feeling strong' (see Royal Commission, A. 25,155–6). We shall have cause to revert to the question of advertising drink, to see, for instance, to what extent it is practised today. It is worth stressing at this point that it may lead to a small beginning, but that habits often stem from small beginnings. This applies to all the aspects sketched in this chapter and to many more. In this as in other connections 'one drink will lead to another'—and to the lasting habit of drinking.

[1] See Hugh Linstead, M.P., *Patent Medicines* (pamphlet), 1946, p. 24. The pamphlet was published by National News Letter.

CHAPTER III

SOME SOCIAL IMPLICATIONS

A. THE DOMESTIC BUDGET

THE causal connections between the factors that make up a social phenomenon, like the drinking habit, are very complex. They are often, as we have seen, in the nature of vicious circles: excessive drink causes disease, but disease can also lead to drink; drink often entails destitution, but a destitute man can also take to drink; or, more complicated, drink can lead to sickness, thence to unemployment, on to poverty, and so on to more drink. But one difference in the quality of these relationships is perhaps worth stressing: in terms of health, excessive drink is bound to cause disease, but disease need not by any means cause drink; similarly in terms of wealth, excessive drink means destitution, but destitution need not, and often does not, lead to drink.

There are few writers on social subjects since Adam Smith who have not heavily criticised the high proportion of working-class incomes spent on alcoholic drink. In times when there was less understanding of social and medico-social problems than in ours, the disproportion between income and expenditure on drink was simply explained and criticised as the result of vice and plain immorality. Smiles, who was shocked by the fact that 'many spend a third, and others half their earnings, on drink' suggested that 'it would be considered monstrous, on the part of any man whose lot has been cast among the educated classes, to exhibit such a degree of selfish indulgence, and to spend even one-fourth of his income upon objects in which his wife and children have no share' (see Smiles, op. cit., pp. 58–9). He explained that 'it must be the hereditary remnant of the savage: the savage feasts and drinks until everything is gone, and then he hunts or goes to war. Or it may be the survival of slavery in the State.' Slaves 'were never required to save for any purpose, for they had no right to their own earnings', and in England 'the last serfs were emancipated' not earlier than in the reign of Queen Elizabeth (see ibid., p. 61).

This analysis can hardly apply now that there is no lack of opportunities to spend the money for other and better purposes and when the motive to drink is constantly fostered by those interested in its sale: heavy consumers of drink among the working classes cannot be accused of indulging in alcohol simply through reckless passion—or thus excused. But the impact of drink on domestic budgets remains the same. Lady Bell describes the situation at the beginning of the century: 'Time after time one finds a household ruined, children growing up half fed, because the husband is drinking away half his money, and his family are struggling with the rest.' In an investigation after the first World War it was found that of 1,375 cases requiring outdoor relief in Edinburgh, 181 cases or 13·2 per cent could be mainly ascribed to drink; and a classification of 93 indoor relief cases showed that as much as 38 per cent of destitution was due to drunkenness.[1]

The Amulree Commission did not seriously consider the question of the proportion of family income spent on drink, perhaps because it seemed outside their terms of reference. But a good deal of evidence was given on the point. It was stated by a witness with information on a number of working-class budgets that industrial workers earning at that time about £2 15s. a week spent from 5s. to 15s. a week on drink.[2] Others put the matter into another form: Mr. G. B. Wilson observed that 'if a man drinks a quart of beer a day, he is spending a shilling a day on drink, and therefore spending £18 a year. If he is a man earning £3 a week, six weeks of his earnings have to be entirely devoted to the paying of his beer bill.' (See A. 25,072 and 25,075). Dr. Alfred Salter, M.P., gave the Commission a very detailed Memorandum on the drink problem in his constituency, the West Bermondsey Division of the Borough of Bermondsey, from which it emerged that 16s. to £1 a week was spent by adults in families earning between £2 and £3 a week. His evidence, which has not been forgotten by economists writing about the problem (see Robert Sinclair, *Metropolitan Man*, 1937, p. 123) also threw light on how working-class families

[1] *The Social and Economic Aspects of the Drink Problem*, 1931, pp. 118, 123; this book, generally called the Buckmaster Report, represents the results of an investigation made by a committee which included Professor A. L. Bowley, Sir Alexander Carr-Saunders, and Mr. B. Seebohm Rowntree.

[2] See A. 26,547 and 26,599, evidence of Miss Christabel Hulbert Sewell; see also her comprehensive Memorandum, ibid.

were managing to balance their other and more necessary expenses with this heavy optional item. Dr. Salter, speaking 'from intimate knowledge of personal visitation to the homes as a doctor', made it quite clear that this balancing was made up by 'the deprivation of actual necessities of life to most of the family'; he stressed the point that, for instance, 'an entirely insufficient quantity of fresh milk is consumed by the average family because after this large expenditure on drink there is insufficient money left in the family exchequer to pay for the necessary quantity of fresh milk' (see A. 26,093–5; also A. 26,126–7). This agreed with the information of another witness, experienced in nursing: 'I have consulted a good many district nurses on the point, and they agree with me that one of the first things to fail in a drinking home is the milk ration' (see A. 26,528 and 26,547).

In view of the rather slight way the problem of drink and the domestic budget was treated in the Amulree Report, it was fortunate that, five years later, *The New Survey of London Life and Labour* devoted a particularly searching review to this very problem (see *The New Survey of London Life and Labour*, vol. IX, pp. 246 sqq.). It concluded that, just before the first World War, as much as one-quarter of the average poor family's income was spent by the husband and wife on drinking, while by 1933–4 the proportion had fallen to one-sixth. But when real wages were also considered, little alteration had really taken place in the proportion of income spent on drink, at any rate since 1913–14. And the apparent reduction was largely due to the rise in the standard of living, which had caused the very poorest class with the highest alcoholic expenditure largely to disappear, so that the poorest class in the early nineteen-thirties could be compared only with the second-poorest class in 1913, whose proportionate expenditure had always been less. 'Moreover,' the Report went on, 'apart from this very poorest class of families, the average expenditure on drink, and the average proportion which it represents of the family income, would almost certainly show an increase during the last twenty years. Where before the war it was possible to say that of all working-class and family incomes—other than the poorest—from 10 per cent in the better-off to 15 per cent in the less prosperous was spent on drink, it could now be said that, including the whole working-class of London, an average of about 15 per cent of family income is spent on drink, and this applies roughly to all families whose head is in employment' (see *New Survey*, pp. 246, 263); and, '15 per cent is a fair figure to take as a high-average proportion of the family income spent on drink by wage-earning classes'.[1]

The *New Survey* emphasised that the working-class family could more easily bear the domestic drink bill in 1934 than formerly: 'money wages have risen, so that a reasonable amount of drinking can be done without putting an impossible strain on the normal wage-earner's means'. Consequently, less poverty was caused by drink, though the expenditure on drink, and its average proportion of the total money income, had not been reduced. But London's 15 per cent in 1934 compared with 5 to 6 per cent given for German working-class families in the lowest income bracket ten years earlier.[2]

Professor Ferdynand Zweig's recent book is in many ways built up on the same pattern as the *London Survey*. (See Ferdynand Zweig, *Labour, Life and Poverty*, 1948, pp. 22 sqq.). He distinguishes between the consumption of drink by casual drinkers, week-end drinkers, semi-regular drinkers, and the everyday or nearly everyday drinkers. The incidence of the drink bill on the domestic budget of the casual drinker may be quite small. The bill of week-end drinkers, of which Zweig says 'there is a lot', is not necessarily and not always lower than that of the regulars. The lowest drink bill would be about 5s. to 10s. a week, while that of a typical semi-regular is estimated at 15s. to 25s. a week. The drink bill of the regular is far heavier: it is, according to Professor Zweig's investigation, rarely below 30s. a week, and more frequently in the neighbourhood of £2. Professor Zweig then assumes that the net wage is in the neighbourhood of £5—and, as he says, it is very often below that—and thus comes to the conclusion that as far as the regular is concerned, 'the drink bill absorbs about 40 per cent of his earnings'.

As a general guide, the assumption about the net wage may be questioned. In particular, in times of almost full employment there are others who contribute to the household, for instance, the housewife or daughters, who are in general not regular or heavy drinkers. Viewed from the present family income the percentage of the domestic budget spent on drink may be much smaller than

[1] See also a partial reprint, Basil Nicholson, *Drink, a London Survey*, a pamphlet issued by the London Diocesan Church of England Temperance Society, n.d., pp. 5–7.

[2] See Elster, op. cit., p. 219; the author rightly draws attention to the fact that in non-drinker families the compilation of figures relating to domestic expenditure is more accurate than in others. It is to be regretted that Mark Abrams, op. cit., pp. 82 sqq., in his chapter on 'Working-class earnings and incomes', does not specify the expenditure on drink in the domestic budgets he quotes, though even such small items as licences for dogs and postage are mentioned separately!

40 per cent even in families where drinking is regular. And recent increases in net wages have reduced the proportion further. But despite these possible amendments to his calculations, Professor Zweig 'came across some cases of conspicuous poverty caused by the drinking habit'. (Ibid., p. 29).

DRINK VERSUS FOOD

The full significance of the drink bill for the domestic budget only emerges when we confront this expenditure on drink with the expenditure on items of necessary consumption. For persons with a higher income than working-class people, a sum of £1 10s. a week, or roughly £75 a year, may entail curtailing other, but probably optional, expenditure: it may mean less spending on a holiday or less on theatrical entertainment, or on books. But for the working-class family with an income of £5 to £10 a week the cuts to be made in other items of the budget may well affect the expenditure on necessary items, possibly including food.

In assessing the incidence, in the domestic budget, of the expenditure on drink on the expenditure on food, two problems should be distinguished. The one is to find out whether expenditure on drink infringes purchases of basic foods, the sorts of foods, in short, which are bought in much the same quantities despite different incomes. A study of 1,152 family budgets showed that the lowest income group as compared with the highest consumed per head per week:

Ounces	*Lowest Income Group*	*Highest Income Group*
Bread and flour	64·5	47·4
Beef and veal	9·5	9·5
Potatoes	51·2	39·4
Tea	2·2	2·1

(see Sir John Boyd Orr, *Food, Health and Income*, 1936, p. 65). The other is, what relation it bears to the more elastic and, to a larger extent, optional expenditure on food. The first problem is of importance mainly because it is concerned with the comparative significance of expenses: the expenditure on basic and fundamentally necessary foods is compared with the money spent on an item which is undoubtedly of far less importance. The second problem gains in importance over the first in so far as it applies much more widely: it involves the question of how far savings in alcoholic drink could be used in order to spend more on additional food, which would benefit the health of the working-class family. Both problems lead to very different issues. If, for instance, the cost of bread or potatoes or of both were to rise considerably in the working-class budget, the gap might have to be bridged by reducing the expenditure on drink. If, on the other hand more money became available, for instance, through higher money wages, it may be doubted whether the surplus would be primarily used to raise the consumption of more varied and wholesome food rather than on the consumption of drink. The doubt is supported by what has tended to happen in the case of milk.

The impact of the domestic drink bill on the total expenditure of food can only be estimated within wide limits. If we take as a basis the Board of Trade figures of 1940 relating to domestic budgets in 1937–8, it emerges that out of an income of 86s. 3d. a working-class family of 3·8 'adults' spend as much as 34s. 1d. on food (see *Ministry of Labour Gazette*, December 1940, p. 305). If, at the same time, we accept the figures of the *New Survey* that 10–12s. was spent by a London family on alcoholic drink—this figure is almost certainly too low for 1937–8—this would mean that an amount about equal to one-third of the expenditure on food went into drink. If we accept, for the immediate post-war years, Professor Zweig's statement that with regular drinkers the drink bill is rarely below 30s. a week and that the working-class family expenditure on food is about 50 per cent more than in normal pre-war days, this would mean that expenditure on drink would be equal to about 60 per cent of the sums spent on food. Where current weekly expenditure on food is below 40s., as for instance, in a family whose net household income is less than £5 a week,[1] the regular expenditure on alcoholic drink of 30s. would represent an altogether exorbitant proportion of the domestic budget available for food. The extravagant relation of some domestic drink bills to the static or little-flexible items of the working class food budget becomes probably most obvious when we take the expenditure on bread as a comparative measure. In

[1] See Mr. A. W. Burrows, Acting General Secretary of the Union of Shop, Distributive and Allied Workers, in *The New Dawn* of 9th September 1947, p. 303.

1930 Dr. Alfred Salter, M.P., reported that in 1925 the amount paid over the counter for drink in the Metropolitan Borough of Bermondsey totalled £1,335,000; he estimated that the consumption of bread in the borough in the same year was £230,000. Thus, even though only the expense on drink outside the home was considered, the drink bill was nearly six times as great as the bread bill (see Amulree Report, A. 26,041).

If only some of the money spent on drink were devoted to increasing the expenditure on foods additional to the staple foods or to increasing the amounts hitherto consumed of the less vital though still most desirable foods, a great change in the nutrition of the working classes would result. Sir John Boyd Orr took pains to estimate what increases in quantities would be required in the United Kingdom for families with an average income of 30s. per head per week, if consumption of the lower groups were to be brought up to the standards of the higher groups as regards such foods as milk, butter, eggs, etc. (see Boyd Orr, op. cit., p. 30). In the case of milk, for instance, all groups taken together would have to increase their consumption by 80 per cent to reach the level of the highest (see ibid., p. 67). It was estimated that the expenditure on fresh milk in the highest groups was 17·8d. per head per week as against an average of 9·8d. for all groups. A sum of 8d. per head per week would have been sufficient therefore to bring the average expenditure of all groups to the level of the expenditure in the highest. This may illustrate adequately what a few shillings per week more or less spent on drink may mean in terms of these flexible items of the domestic food budget.

War and post-war restrictions and regulations have further increased the complexity of the relationship of the expenditure on alcoholic drink to expenditure on food in the domestic budget of the ordinary working-class population. Had the purchases of such necessities as bread, flour, potatoes, meat, butter, margarine, sugar and bacon not been rationed and their prices subsidised, the margin left for the expenditure on drink would, even with increasing wages, probably have become rather narrow. In the event, because of the scarcity of supplies and financial necessity, it was thought necessary to ration purchases and to subsidise prices, so that neither prices nor wages could react to a runaway market. In 1945 the total annual cost of keeping the cost of living even at 102 per cent above the 1914 level was about £218,000,000; by the beginning of 1947 the officially quoted figure for food subsidies was £364,000,000; the estimated figure was £400,000,000 for 1948 (but this included some subsidies other than food).[1] Quite naturally, these financial burdens had their effects on the domestic budgets of the people as, together with the other enormously increased public expenditure, their cost had to be covered, to some extent at least, by indirect taxation. Thus a part of the subsidies by which the food item was kept down in the domestic budget had to be paid by the consumer of drink in the form of higher cost of drink. In this way the drinker had to pay to some extent for the benefit which the budget of the non-drinker derived from the artificially low prices of the most necessary foods.

Under these circumstances it is very difficult to draw conclusions about the interaction of drink and food, in particular optional foods, in domestic budgets during the war and in the first years of the post-war period. Scarcity must, of course, have changed many trends that would normally have been active. There is no doubt that the restricted consumption of food would normally have set free larger amounts to be spent on drink. But higher prices of many kinds of food which could still be freely obtained and the great increase in the cost of drink must have upset this tendency or at least reduced its force. In an address to the Royal Statistical Society, 1945,[2] Mr. Richard Stone expressed the necessary implications of these abnormal conditions as follows: 'Between 1938 and 1943 the price of beer rather more than doubled, while according to official estimates retail prices in general rose in the same period by a little more than 50 per cent. At the same time, the strength of the beer declined.' On the basis of Mr. Stone's analysis and conclusions, these changes should have led to a fall in beer consumption. But this was not the case. 'The reasons', he suggested, . . . 'are to be found in the fact that with rationing and restrictions of all kinds almost any commodity on which it is possible to spend money will be bought in abnormal quantities. It is not therefore surprising to observe an unusually high consumption of beer in war-time, but at the same time it is exceedingly difficult, and with the information at present available quite impossible, to allow for the effect on beer consumption of the fact that the public has been unable to buy as much as it would normally take in the circumstances of other commodities.' Mr. Stone also

[1] See *Statement on the Economic Considerations affecting relations between Employers and Workers*, January 1947, p. 6; *Economic Survey for 1948*, p. 45; *Economist*, January 1947, p. 111, 'Facts about Food'.

[2] *Journal of the Royal Statistical Society*, 1945, 'The Analysis of Market Demand'.

emphasised that his elaborate theoretical picture, based on mathematical principles, of the various factors normally influencing the consumption of drink could not be tested against normality before war-time restrictions were removed.

SECONDARY POVERTY

In the absence of further knowledge of the domestic budgets of various sections of the working class, we are left mainly with the broad distinctions between primary and secondary poverty which we owe to B. Seebohm Rowntree, the pioneer investigator of domestic budgets in this country (see especially B. Seebohm Rowntree, *The Human Needs of Labour*, 1937). As Professor Bowley observes, such terms are essentially 'descriptive rather than logical',[1] for 'poverty' generally means different things to different observers. Rowntree defines secondary poverty as 'a standard of life of families who are obviously living in poverty although their total earnings would be sufficient for the maintenance of merely physical efficiency were it not that some portion of them is absorbed by other expenditure, either useful or wasteful'. By calculating the cost of 'the maintenance of merely physical efficiency' he established his standards of minimum incomes for families of different sizes, i.e., a poverty line. On this basis, Rowntree found in 1937 that a family of five members—parents and children—required a sum of 53s. per week to be able to afford the absolute necessities of physical health. This income did not allow more than 3s. 4d. a week for 'all else'. Out of this 3s. 4d. had to be paid all recreation, all luxuries, such as beer and tobacco, all travelling except that of the breadwinner to and from work, and other extras; and there was no allowance for contingencies (see Rowntree, op. cit., pp. 117, 122, 123). About ten years earlier the minimum for a workman with wife and two young children of school age had been put at 39s. a week. It is clear, and most observers are explicit on the point, that such poverty lines allow virtually no surplus for beer, tobacco or amusement (see Bowley, op. cit., p. 61). From data given by Professor Bowley it appears that between 4 and 10 per cent of all families in the United Kingdom were living below the poverty line just before the Second World War.[2]

[1] See A. L. Bowley, *Wages and Income in the United Kingdom since 1860*, 1937, p. 61.

[2] Ibid., pp. 63, 66. Professor Bowley emphasises that the proportion of *people* living in poverty may be different: many poor families have numerous children below earning age; and at the other extreme are old people, many living alone, who have no adequate pension or assistance. Both proportions are significant to the study of poverty.

The problem changes decidedly when domestic budgets of the 'secondary poverty' level are considered; for here there is a margin for considerable expenditure on drink as an alternative to other optional expenses. Bowley wrote in 1937 (see op. cit., p. 66) that the average family income in London for weeks of full employment was 78s. per week; since the average cost of meeting the minimum needs was about 44s., 'necessities account for about 45 per cent of all income in a full week'. We do not know how much of this margin over the 'primary poverty line' is spent on drink instead of being devoted for instance to purchasing more food. But we do know that in many cases the proportion is very high, in fact that in numerous working-class families the margin in the first instance is devoted to buying alcoholic drink. For, as Professor Ferdynand Zweig recently confirmed (see op. cit., p. 22) the real sources of secondary poverty are 'drinking, betting and smoking'; as he says, 'very often the worker wastes a large part of his time and energy between the smoke of the factory and that of a pub'.

Secondary poverty then is a much more complicated concept than primary poverty. Primary poverty means having a smaller income than will pay for the minimum necessities of life; once the necessities are agreed the poverty line will change only with changing prices: it entails the possibility, at any time, of utter destitution. The income that goes with secondary poverty is undefined, except that it is more than adequate to pay for all prime necessities: what matters is that the extra expenditure may be, in Rowntree's terms, 'useful or wasteful'. Different observers will have different views on the 'correct' apportionment of expenditure, for instance, varying with the structure and social condition of families. It may certainly be viewed very differently by the people concerned. As one man put it to Professor Zweig 'bluntly and convincingly' (see p. 22, op. cit.), going to the pictures for 1s. meant to him saving money because in the same three hours he would have spent 'at least six shillings' in a public house. Yet the man who does not incline to drink might use the few shillings saved per week by not going to the pictures on spending some Sundays by the sea or in regularly buying extra milk for the children. For some workers recreation and entertainment may be distractions necessary for a healthy mental attitude towards life and work; for others abstention from such enjoyments and saving, though on a small scale, may provide the same satisfaction: 'Frugality means enjoying what we do not get', as the witty German poet Wilhelm Busch put it.[1]

But despite the many possibilities and complications in trying to agree what is and what is not 'useful' expenditure, wasteful expenditure in general contrasts markedly with useful expenditure; and one can agree with Professor Zweig when he emphasises that 'secondary poverty conceived as deficiency in necessities is only exceptionally caused by useful expenditure', and that there is no 'disproportionate expenditure on food, rent or clothes' (see op. cit., p. 20). On the contrary, as we have seen in connection with food and the domestic budget, the 'disproportion' lies in the fact that too little is spent on it; and the same applies to rent. The much deplored housing conditions of many working-class families are perhaps not entirely due to the lack of better accommodation but also to the dislike of many inhabitants to devote more money out of their budget to rent. It may be taken as of some significance that in a sample survey made in 1943 by the London Diocesan Church of England Temperance Society, it was said of the district that though most homes had a 'reasonably high income', the housing conditions were deplorable (see *Our Street*, London 1943, pamphlet). Sometimes accommodation is underlet to increase earnings. If the increase in income is devoted to more expenditure on wasteful things, such as immoderate drink, the change is certainly not one for the better.

It is particularly with secondary poverty that there is the danger of that reciprocal action to which the Amulree Report called attention: the withholding of sums from domestic improvements and their application to drink may allow deteriorating conditions at home to deteriorate further. As the Report observed: '. . . the dangers of a vicious circle need to be reckoned with. By seeking refuge in the public house, a man or woman may become tolerant of bad conditions at home, and *pari passu* the means to remedy those conditions may be seriously prejudiced by the amounts spent on intoxicants. We were impressed by the evidence put before us in this regard by a number of witnesses from their own experience and observations of social conditions in the poorer districts of large cities' (see Amulree Report, para. 101).

The conclusion then is fairly clear: secondary poverty, that is the unhealthy allocation of an income itself adequate to meet the prime necessities of life, is the main problem for the reformer.

[1] 'Enthaltsamkeit ist das Vergnügen an Dingen, welche wir nicht kriegen.'

And very often it is drink which is the main agent, direct and indirect, of maldistribution.

B. EFFICIENCY, SAFETY AND CRIME

The effects of drink on industrial efficiency, in terms for instance of output, of absenteeism, and of accidents, have been recognised for many years, and directly prompted the restrictive legislation dating from the First World War. Early this century W. H. Rivers stated that in one of his subjects 'a subjective feeling of lassitude and disinclination for activity of body and mind' came on within half an hour of the taking of 40 c.c. of alcohol, and a fellow worker could always recognise the days when alcohol was taken 'partly from his lassitude and partly from his very obvious inability'.[1] Data of this kind multiplied remarkably quickly and all pointed the same way. By February 1916, as a prelude to official action, Mr. Lloyd George could say in a speech at Bangor: 'Drink is doing us more damage in the war than all the German submarines put together.'[2] His language soon became even more drastic than in this example; to the Shipbuilding Employers' Federation he said in April 1916: 'We are fighting Germany, Austria and Drink, and, as far as I can see, the greatest of these three deadly foes is Drink.' And drink was one of the earliest subjects studied by the Industrial Fatigue (now Health) Research Board of the Medical Council which took over from the Health of Munition Workers' Committee towards the end of the war.[3]

The Report of 1931 on 'The Social and Economic Aspects of Alcohol' provided a great deal of interesting case material showing the adverse effects of alcohol on industrial efficiency. It stated that 'there is a free admission that heavy drinking, apart from arduous work performed by exceptionally strong men, leads to a loss in general efficiency;' 'it is admitted that for work demanding concentration, special skill, quick decisions, and the exercise of judgment, the best results are obtained from workers who indulge least in alcoholic refreshments'. (See p. 77.) An investigation undertaken by economists and submitted to the Royal Commission contained a statement of an assistant general manager to an

[1] W. H. Rivers, *The Influence of Alcohol and other Drugs on Fatigue*, 1908, p. 132.

[2] See H. Cecil Heath, 'The Drink Problem in Wartime', *Alliance Yearbook*, 1940, pp. 58 sqq.

[3] See W. McDougall and May Smith, *The Effects of Alcohol and some other Drugs during Normal and Fatigued Conditions*, 1920.

iron and steel company employing 17,000 men to the effect that foremen could not, as a rule, drink during the day, even at lunch-time, and 'keep up a high standard of efficiency and clear thinking in the afternoon'. (See *Evidence* by W. Hamilton Whyte and H. R. Burrows, A.11,584.) The Industrial Health Research Board failed to mention alcohol in their Report, published in 1942, on Industrial Health in War—an unfortunate omission, particularly considering their own previous work on the subject; but they did state that 'apart from the diminished accuracy and speed consequent upon a fatigued state, as experienced by feelings of weariness and disinclination to make an effort, there are well-known fatigue symptoms, e.g., inco-ordinated movements, organic disturbances, irritability, listlessness'. When it was recently suggested that workers should be encouraged to go for food to the public house and have 'a' drink with their meal, a worker wrote in a letter to *The Times* that 'The one drink will become two, and instead of alertness and preparedness governing all that he (the worker) has to do, there will be, until the effect wears off, a sluggishness that will be the enemy of his maximum production,' and that most works managers would be appalled to read that midday drinking should be propagated among workers.[1] Similar evidence has been collected in other countries. For instance, in the United States at the time of prohibition, Feldmann sent out a questionnaire to a number of employers: out of 175 employers who answered the questions relating to the productivity of the individual worker, 101 attributed an increase of productivity to prohibition; out of 223 firms answering on industrial accidents, 74 claimed a reduction due to prohibition; concerning application to work on Monday and the day after pay, out of the 287 firms replying, 184 noticed an improvement attributable to prohibition and only 9 reported to the contrary (see D. W. McConnell in *Encyclopædia Britannica*, vol. xiv, p. 568, 14th edition). In Germany sample tests have shown the same results; 'the reduction of efficiency due to alcoholic drink', writes Elster, summarising these results, 'which is sometimes quite considerable, has been overwhelmingly proved by graphical and statistical examples' (see op. cit., p. 217).

The seriousness of the effect of drink on industrial efficiency varies of course with many factors, including obviously the physical predisposition of the individual worker and the kind and quantity

[1] See *The Times* of 9th November 1948, letter by A. J. Donaldson of Culwell Works, Wolverhampton.

of drink. It relates also to the nature of the work: when the work requires only physical strength it is less serious than with work requiring a high degree of concentration, hard thinking or quick control. With engineers on fine work or typesetters, and also, for instance, with the blockers and stiffeners in the hat trade who work on delicate and sometimes expensive materials, alcoholic drink may immediately reduce the output of work (see Amulree Report, A. 11,576–8); in that respect it should be taken into account that there are different kinds of 'fatigue'; local sensations of fatigue, especially in the muscles, which may even amount to pain, may be distinguished from a feeling of general tiredness and incapacity for effort, and both these may again be distinguished from the sensation we call sleepiness (see *Action*, p. 96). An official of a printers' union in Leeds reported that 'the old handsetting of type did not call for so much concentration . . . four times the matter had now to be read and set up in the same time. This called for greater concentration, and the beer drinker was not equal to the strain' (see *Social and Economic Aspects*, pp. 71–2). It was perhaps due to this factor in particular that some evidence seemed contradictory: for instance, while a manager of an ironstone mine stated that 'best workers seem to be those who can take a glass of beer and avoid excess' (see p. 80), and another manager, that 'best workers are those who are moderate drinkers'; another was convinced that 'drink was still undermining efficiency' (see 1931 Report, p. 84).

Sir H. M. Vernon emphasised before the Royal Commission that the time of drinking was also important: drinking by workers in the middle of the day affected efficiency differently from drinking put off till the end of the day's work; and week-end drinking affected the efficiency of the worker at the beginning of the next week, while possibly the spreading of drink 'evenly over the whole week' harmed his efficiency less (see Royal Commission, A.32,558–9). It was the influence of these and other factors, and the general extent of the influence of drink on industrial efficiency that the Amulree Commission was referring to when it stressed the 'extreme difficulty' of the subject and the need for further research (*Report*, p. 20); for of the general nature of the effect of drink on efficiency there could be no doubt.

Absenteeism is similarly the result of many factors. But, as Sir H. M. Vernon told the Royal Commission, alcoholic excess at the week-end 'creates a desire to escape work. Men do not feel like starting on the grind, especially if they have been drinking rather freely on Saturday and Sunday' (ibid., A.32,416). At the time of the Commission it was possible to contend (*Report*, para. 51) that, largely owing to the depression, 'absenteeism . . . which formerly was a feature in many industries and which was attributed in a large degree to excessive drinking, particularly at week-ends, has in large measure disappeared'. But in the next fifteen years there was a very different development. Recently, voluntary absenteeism (i.e. excluding sickness absence) in the coal industry, for instance, was said to entail a loss of output of 13,000,000 tons per annum.[1] It is significant in this respect that on Sundays and Mondays voluntary absenteeism was 8·46 per cent as against an average of 6·26 per cent for the normal week. From being a problem of minor importance in the days of the depression, absenteeism has come to the forefront of discussion during the period of full employment. The Royal Commission took pains to emphasise that 'one effect of widespread unemployment may be . . . to render the individual, be he manager or manual worker, more careful not to risk the loss of it by intemperance, should he be inclined in that way' and that the 'economic depression is undoubtedly in a measure responsible for the present standard of sobriety', (see op. cit., p. 12). It may also well be, as Lord Stamp said, that 'if there were no alcohol at all, the man might be absent on Monday because he wanted to go off to a football match or to a cinema' (see A. 10,534). But this does not invalidate the influence which at any time alcoholic drink may exert on a worker to stay away from work.

The same applies in the case of industrial accidents. Sometimes drunkenness is a direct cause of an accident. Sir H. M. Vernon mentioned a number of cases in his published studies (*The Alcohol Problem*, 1928, and *Accidents and their Prevention*, 1936), and believed, in his evidence to the Royal Commission, to 'have given specific proof that alcohol caused an increase in the accidents at munition factories' (*Evidence*, A.32,460). But normally, he agreed that 'you cannot get evidence except under very exceptional conditions' (A.32,449). Usually drink is at most a contributory cause; and often an accident might never have happened, even though the worker was affected by drink, had there not been defects in conditions of work. Did the taking of a drink cause the drowsiness which

[1] See for details *Coal, Facts about an Unknown Industry*, by a Colliery Manager, 1945, p. 34 sq.

led to carelessness or negligence on the part of the worker? This has been the crucial question in many cases arising under the Workmen's Compensation Acts: it had to be decided whether an accident was to be considered as due to the influence of drink or to the technical circumstances which would have anyhow resulted in danger, and whether the accident thus happened 'in the course and out of the employment' of the worker who suffered the injury; and it is for this reason that 'drunkenness' is regularly dealt with in the commentaries to the Workmen's Compensation Acts.[1] We have to content ourselves with the fact that drunkenness can and does lead to accidents. Also that persons given to alcohol recover with more difficulty, if at all, from accidents, as a body and a nervous system continually under the influence of alcohol do not stand up well to the shock of injury. Many an industrial injury of moderate severity to a normal worker may therefore mean permanent disablement to the alcoholic.

DANGER TO OTHER PEOPLE

A person under the influence of drink is an immediate danger not merely to himself but also to other people. This is most tragically clear in the case of the motorist. As the Amulree Report put it, 'the intoxicated motorist offers a special problem' (pp. 149–50). A special committee of the British Medical Association examined this in 1935 at the request of the Ministry of Transport, and in 1938 a Select Committee was set up by the House of Lords 'to consider what steps should be undertaken to reduce the number of casualties on the roads'. Medically, it is particularly relevant that alcoholic drink, containing a narcotic, leads in its earliest effect on the nervous system 'to an impairment of the faculties of judgment, concentration, self-criticism, and the power of estimating risk' (see Wilson, op. cit., p. 265). The motorist, for instance, is liable to take risks and to make rapid decisions less judiciously than he normally would do. The House of Lords pointed out that 'the effect of even moderate quantities of alcohol on drivers is not generally realised'. The public generally did not know that 'under the influence of drink' did not necessarily mean intoxicated in the ordinary sense; nor that driving skill is affected long before a man is consciously under the influence of alcohol.[2]

[1] See, for a more recent case, Bulmer v. 'Baluchistan' (1934) 50 LL.L.Rep. 39; 27 B.W.C.C. 399, where a seaman was under the influence of drink but there was evidence and a finding of inherent difficulty in negotiating the ladder.

[2] See Report of the 'Select Committee to consider what steps should be taken to reduce the number of casualties on the Roads', House of Lords, 1940, para. 39.

As in the case of industrial accidents, it is often a nice question to what extent the negligent driver is responsible for an accident, and to what extent his negligence was the result of drink. Lord Brocket said before the House of Lords Committee that in 1931 there were 1,900 convictions for driving under the influence of alcohol out of a total of 331,000 convictions, that is, a ratio of 1 in 173. The comparative but not the absolute figures in 1936 showed a slight improvement, a ratio of 1 in 200. These figures are serious enough, but they do not indicate the severity of these offences, which in this case may be particularly heavy. For the driving of a motor car under the influence of drink entails dangers to life and limb which the great majority of minor offences connected with motoring do not involve. It would be just as misleading to belittle the significance of serious accidents in industry by a comparison with the great majority of light injuries. It is far more the total number of offences due to the alcoholic factor which remains of importance. As Mr. Heath put it to the Committee: 'It depends really on the number of minor offences and so on, and that would tend to lower the percentage of the other offences', and that 'the fact remains that the total is increasing' (see also *Alliance Yearbook*, 1940, p. 48). The Report of the Special Committee of the British Medical Association concluded that 'to what extent . . . action of small amounts of alcohol may in the aggregate be responsible for motor accidents there is no means of estimating. It is, however, a serious objection to the consumption of alcohol, even in small amounts, by anyone who is to drive a car.' In some countries, for instance in Norway, a person is not allowed to have any alcoholic drink within several hours of driving (House of Lords Report, p. 14), and in Britain also it is the practice of a large majority of motor transport undertakings, municipal and public, and also private, to require of their drivers total abstinence from intoxicants while on duty (see ibid., para. 704).

The relation of crime to drink has been much confused by disputes about its frequency. We have already had occasion to mention the private report on the Social and Economic Aspects of Alcohol. It prefaces the section devoted to the relationship between drink and crime (see op. cit., pp. 129 sqq.) with the warning that 'extreme statements are often made as to this. Some say that most crime is due to drink, and others that drink is only a cause of crime to an insignificant extent.' Both views are certainly incorrect. As in the case of motor accidents, and indeed of all the social effects of alcohol we have been discussing, 'there is no means of estimating' the general incidence of alcohol on crime. And as in connection with the other aspects of the problem, the danger is to lose sight of the fact that the relationship between crime and drink as such has never been seriously disputed. This can be stated as a general experience with people suffering from dipsomania. But quite apart from their special case, scientists have reached the definite conclusion that a considerable percentage of offences generally is due to what Germans have called 'Deliktsantrieb', an urge to commit an offence, which is largely fostered by alcoholic drink.[1]

Van der Woorde, a Dutch investigator, has made an attempt to classify crimes and indictable offences according to their relation to economic, sexual and aggressive motives, and again, their frequency as regards 'chronic alcoholism' and 'chronic and occasional alcoholism'. As a percentage of convictions, the aggressive crimes due to drink were the highest; 72·9 per cent of assaults on officials were connected with 'chronic and occasional' alcoholism. The importance of drink in offences primarily due to economic motives was much lower. Yet chronic and occasional drink was responsible for 34·3 per cent of the sentences for begging and vagrancy and for about 20 per cent of the sentences for simple larceny, embezzlement, fraud and false pretences.[2] The Buckmaster Report, whose very cautious attitude we just mentioned, came to the conclusion that as a 'moderate estimate', about 40 per cent of common offences covered by the committee's investigators were attributable directly or indirectly to drink (see op. cit., p. 148). The effect of drink, it was further stated, as a cause of crime is seen most frequently in offences associated with passion, such as assault, wilful damage, and the serious cases of crimes of violence apart from murder: the proportion of cases of assault and wilful damage due directly to drink can be taken as very nearly 50 per cent (see ibid., p. 149).

It is not the same with burglary and robbery with violence, in which there is usually an element of premeditation and preparation, and which require coolness of nerve, alertness, and readiness to meet sudden emergencies. It can be easily understood why criminals indulging in these offences abstain from drink. 'The

[1] See for this, Elster, op. cit., p. 216 where a number of German scientific publications on drink and crime are quoted.

[2] See Henry T. F. Rhodes, of the Institute of Criminology of the University of Lyons, *The Criminal in Society*, 1939, pp. 161–2.

men', says the Report, 'who make this type of crime a profession have a strong inducement to be extremely abstemious'—a sound confirmation of the effects of alcoholic drink and an intriguing suggestion as to the possible reasons for abstinence.

CHAPTER IV

COMPLEXITY AND SEVERITY: SOME CASE EVIDENCE

THE possible ramifications of the problem of drink are legion, and the effects of drink can be severe—so far the general statement; how wide and how severe can be learnt only from examining single cases. It is important to do so not merely because we do not want to go back to the times when tragic conditions and happenings were not regarded as worthy of attention because they were rare or even exceptional. Great mining disasters, though limited to a comparatively small number of miners; severe railway disasters, though only happening once to twice a year; epidemics, even if they appeared to be due to casual, perhaps accidental circumstances, all have sometimes been more effective in creating a desire for more knowledge and improvement of conditions than minor tragedies of greater frequency.[1] C. F. G. Masterman, commenting on the single cases of industrial accidents recorded in the Annual Reports of H.M. Inspectors of Factories, observed that in many instances 'the result of occasional complaints, of sporadic surprise visits, appears as the letting down of dredges into the depth and the bringing to light of the things which exist far below the surface' (see C. F. G. Masterman, *The Condition of England*, ed. 1910, p. 134). In the problem of drink, too, every single case may reveal something of the things below the surface; the complex inter-connections also in terms of importance of some aspect, say the medical, with a great many other problems, and the total effect.

What is 'secondary poverty' and an excessive expenditure on drink in the family with one, two, three, or more children? How differently may it exhibit itself under conditions of very bad

[1] A case in point is the effect which the disaster at the Darnley Main Colliery on 24th January 1849 had on the factory legislation, despite the fact that the type of explosion which caused it was considered to be quite rare; see Sir Arnold Wilson and Professor Hermann Levy, *Workmen's Compensation*, vol. I, 1939, p. 21.

housing? What happens when the health of the whole family, or of one or several of its members, is already affected by disease? What are the conditions in which money which might be spent on necessities is all or mostly spent on drink, or else on distractions? What kind of accidents tend to be due to drink, solely or only as a contributory cause? What were the first indications of matrimonial difficulty, and consequent tragedy: was it primarily due to drink or merely aggravated by it? And by way of this sort of detailed question: how far in this or that case would a change in certain environmental conditions, for instance, better housing or a greater choice of healthy distractions, have led to a reduction and restored the matrimonial balance through creating generally a better atmosphere at home? It is this sort of differentiation which is the foundation of the social study of drink.

This fact, that real knowledge is founded on familiarity with single cases, and builds up from there in a way that we shall attempt to discuss in the next chapter, has tended to get lost in the modern quest for statistics and in what Tom Harrisson has called the 'obsession for the typical'. What this obsession can lead to was well illustrated by certain passages in the Buckmaster Report. This, for instance, is what it had to say about the effect of alcohol on industrial efficiency (see p. 158): 'The evidence as a whole certainly appears to suggest that, at the present time and under prevailing conditions (namely of depression), drink is not, noticeably and directly at least, impairing industrial efficiency.' There was no indication, for instance, of what was meant by 'seriously'—one might just as well say that motor accidents do not 'seriously' affect traffic. The Committee could not apparently get away from the fact that drinking in factories in general had diminished, even though, incidentally, it might have been only a temporary reduction. The Amulree Commission similarly paid very little attention to the great mass of case data which was given to it as evidence. In this deficiency the students of the problem of drink have been merely in line with the majority of contemporary students of society.

It is only in the last decade or so that the significance of case work is again becoming recognised. Institutions like the National Council of Social Service or the Charity Organisation Society (now the Family Welfare Society) have realised that it is only on the basis of a great mass of what at first may appear to be 'single cases' that homogeneous happenings and experiences can be sifted out and all the cases gain some typical significance. And so 'case work' has been resurrected, in the words of U. McCormack, as 'the youngest of the professions'.[1] Similarly the Charity Organisation Society also wrote in 1940 that 'the social worker, whether voluntary or official, should be a case worker—that is to say, he should deal with each successive case on its own separate merits, he should ascertain and consider all the facts of each case'.[2] And when we are convinced to-day that alcoholic drink is one of the causes of secondary poverty (see Zweig, op. cit., p. 22), when investigators even rank it as the first of 'the real sources of secondary poverty', it should be well to remember that the Society with its great experience in the matter points out also that 'the problem of poverty is not one single problem. There are as many problems of poverty as there are persons in distress.' Any classification of problems is man-made, as also is the grouping of features into 'a problem'—added grounds for remembering that every family whose secondary poverty is due primarily to excessive expenditure on alcoholic drink may well exhibit social effects different from any other.

The case evidence that follows is subject to the qualification, mentioned by the *Report on the Social and Economic Aspects* of 1931, that it varies 'in qualitative value and in degree of authority which attaches to individual statements' (see *Report*, p. 55). In that it does not differ from most case evidence. But in the question of drink, closely bound up as it is with moral and ethical considerations, there is perhaps a particular danger of bias in the selection of facts and conditions, even though collected primarily for description and regarded as quite objective. And this difficulty is not necessarily met by the statement in the 1931 Report that the investigators were chosen solely on the ground that they possessed the necessary qualifications and experience for the work, and that, while no attempt was made to ascertain whether or not they were abstainers, they were given to understand that they should exhibit full impartiality (see *Social and Economic Aspects*, pp. 9–10). But in many cases this danger is slight. And the case evidence will

[1] See, for an able description and analysis of case work and its 'individualising' significance, U. McCormack, 'Developments in Case-Work', in A. F. C. Bourdillon, *Voluntary Social Services*, 1945, pp. 86 sqq.; see also the study by Hilda Jennings on 'Voluntary Case-Work Societies' in *Voluntary Social Services since 1918*, 1948, p. 55: 'Case work is usually understood to be concerned with the welfare of the individual.'

[2] See *How to help cases of Distress*, June 1940, pp. 225 sqq., also p. 1: 'Every case of distress differs from every other case and should be considered independently on its own merits and demerits.'

certainly serve to indicate what does happen in certain circumstances, and what may happen again, however unusually complicated and severe the incidence of alcoholic drink.

CASE 1

'One steel-worker found his whole body out of gear; another, an office clerk, said to me: "When I don't go to the pub, the first night I take an aspirin in order to get sleep, the next night I take two aspirins and they do not help me, and the third night I must go back" (Professor F. Zweig, *Labour, Life and Poverty*, 1948, p.27).

CASE 2

'I can say without hesitation that five out of the six ablest men I have worked with on the same staff were alcoholics. And three of them died of drink. Naturally, I am giving no names; but the first and finest of them, who came into journalism after a career of great distinction at the university and in the public service—a kindly, charming man without an ill-thought for anybody—died in hospital after unavailing efforts by the doctors with a stomach pump. Another dropped dead from a stroke. This was largely due to his drinking whisky into the small hours, then rising early to put all his remarkable energy into an exacting, highly responsible job. . . . The third, one of the most popular men in Fleet Street, also died before his time' (J. R. V., Managing Director of Wren Books, Ltd., in preface to *I am an Alcoholic*, by an anonymous newspaper man, 1948, p. 10.)

CASE 3

'We have also received quite recently a baby, aged six months. The father, who is a labourer, is a drink victim, and the mother is suffering from consumption and is too ill to do anything for the seven children, all of whom are living at home. It is a most pitiable case. I may add that we receive scores of similar cases throughout a year in the home.' (Mrs. Randolph Clarkson, evidence to the Amulree Commission on behalf of the National British Women's Total Abstinence Union, A. 25,331, quotation from a memorandum submitted by the principal of the National Children's Home and Orphanage on 'The close connection between drinking and child destitution.')

CASE 4

'M. B., ship's fireman . . . of Newcastle, who was said to have struck his three-year-old daughter when she asked him for something to eat, was sentenced at Newcastle to six months' imprisonment. Mr. W. E., prosecuting for the N.S.P.C.C., said B. kept his wife short of money and came into the house with a piece of steak which he fried himself and sat down to eat. His three-year-old daughter, who was hungry, asked him for something to eat, and B., who had been drinking, replied that he would rather give it to the dog . . . He pushed her away with his foot, and, when she cried, hit her with a belt, and threw a shoe at her, hitting her head. B. denied that he struck his daughter with the belt, but agreed that he threw a rubber shoe at her and a cup, which he said was intended for his mother-in-law.' (*Evening News*, 31st August 1948.)

CASE 5

'Q. With regard to the cases of cruelty to which you refer, are they attributable to drink?

A. Yes, very often, I think; not in the sense that the man was a constant drunkard, but that on the particular occasion when he got drunk he assaulted his wife, and that had happened more than once. That is sufficient grounds for "habitual cruelty".'

(Amulree Commission, A. 5,819, evidence of Mr. J. H. Brodrick, Metropolitan Magistrate at the South Western Police Court.)

CASE 6

'Lord Chief Justice Goddard passed a nominal sentence of five days' imprisonment on J.R.C., aged 41, a greengrocer, at Stafford Assizes, who was found guilty of manslaughter of his wife by strangling her. He was released immediately. He described the prisoner as a decent, sober, respectable man, who had the misfortune to marry a drunken virago. C. said that his wife was dangerous and showed the jury scars she had made on his forehead in two previous attacks with bottles of beer. On this occasion she came home with a carving knife in one hand and a poker in the other. There was a desperate struggle and he must have put his hands to her throat, though he could not remember it. Lord Goddard said it was a righteous verdict.' (Quoted from *Alliance News Summary* of 12th July 1948.)

CASE 7

'Strong drink has been the ruin of this home—both parents drink to excess, although neither of them will admit it. Mother has £5 per week, but seems always in financial difficulties.' (Hermann Mannheim, Reader in Criminology in the London School of Economics, *Delinquency in an English Middletown*, 1948, p. 23.)

CASE 8

'A corroboration of the friend's remark that his wife would have a Guinness whenever he ordered a pint is furnished by a story told us by a barman; its hero is a local policeman who drinks at this pub, and is known as Thirsty. He is famous for cadging drinks and general mean behaviour. He goes into the tap-room, and sends his wife into the parlour, paying the waiter on her drinks. This, the general custom, sometimes results in the husband finding that he has to pay for a big round for his wife's friends, which causes trouble. Thirsty, although far better off than most pub-goers, only pays for mild for his wife, and the cheapest mild at that. She, however, has an arrangement with the waiter-on, so that when her husband orders and pays for her gill, she has a Guinness fetched for her and pays the extra from housekeeping money. The habit is widespread.' (Mass Observation, *The Pub and the People*, 1943, p. 149.)

CASE 9

'In my inquiry I came across some cases of conspicuous poverty caused by the drinking habit. One labourer of 34, who has two children, and who earns £4 a week, drinks heavily, giving his wife only £1 for housekeeping money, and has paid no rent for the last two months. Another man aged 40, with eight children, who earns £6, spends £2 on drink alone. Another man of 42, single, spends 70 per cent of his earnings on drink.' (F. Zweig, *Labour, Life and Poverty*, 1948, p. 29.)

CASE 10

'Allegations that the wife of a solicitor in twenty-three months spent £2,900 in drink were mentioned by the prosecution at the Old Bailey when eleven charges—"only token items"—were made against Mrs. M. S. B. She was charged with falsification of accounts in respect of sums of £1,079 and £971; of stealing £459, and with falsification of accounts by mutilating a client's accounts ledger . . . Discovery came after Mr. B. had been dismissed for everlastingly being drunk.' (*Evening News* of 14th July 1948.)

CASE 11

'Questioned about occasions when he visited Mr. Stanley's flat without Mr. Belcher, Mr. Cross said the first occasion was when Mr. Belcher was in hospital last May. He thought Mr. Stanley might be able to help him when Mr. Belcher came out of hospital.

The Attorney General: In what way?

The circumstances under which Mr. Belcher went to hospital I felt to have been that he was drinking too much, and I thought probably one of the reasons was that Stanley was providing him with too lavish hospitality.

Was it a fact that Mr. Stanley was providing very lavish hospitality to Mr. Belcher?

Not when I was there. Of course we had drinks there. It seemed to me that Mr. Belcher was drinking too much, and one of the places at which he was drinking too much was Mr. Stanley's.' (*The Times*, 24th November 1948.)

CASE 12

'A workman employed by the railway company had stopped at a public house and left the van and was mounting it when the horse moved on. He was killed. One of the company's rules was that employees must not consume intoxicating liquor while on duty. The accident was held not to have arisen out of the employment and accordingly compensation was denied.' (F. N. Ball, *Statute Law relating to Employment*, 1946, p. 49, 'Knowles v. Southern Railway Co.' (1936), 2 All E.R. 682.)

CASE 13

'. . . 44, motor car dealer, of Highfield Road, South Shore, Blackpool, was sentenced to three months' imprisonment, and had his licence suspended for two years at Preston Quarter Sessions, when found guilty of driving a motor car while under the influence of drink. He was alleged to have driven at speeds up to ninety miles an hour on the Preston-Blackpool road. It was stated that there had been previous disqualifications, including one imposed for life in 1934, but later removed.' (*Manchester Guardian* of 14th October 1948.)

CASE 14

'. . . a private car containing four members of the Royal Wiltshire Yeomanry mounted the grass verge and turned somersault at night on a bend on Chapel Hill, Whelnetham, near Bury St. Edmunds. . . . S.Q.M.S. A. E. Brown had been thrown out presumably through the window, lying on the road, gravely injured. Less than two hours later he died in Bury St. Edmunds Hospital. . . . At the inquest, S.Q.M.S. R. Coleman said that Sergt. Lawrence borrowed Major Bibb's car, and also in the car were Trooper Vennell and the deceased. Leaving Livermore Camp about 6.30 p.m. Sergt. Lawrence drove them to Bury St. Edmunds, where they each had a pint of beer, to Long Melford where they had two pints of beer each, and to Lavenham where they each had another two pints. . . . Police Constable Ward said that the car travelled on the grass verge for 128 feet. Returning the verdict of "death by misadventure" the Deputy Coroner said that he "could not help feeling" that the accident need not have happened.' (*Alliance News*, January-March 1946, p. 7.)

CASE 15

'The driver of the car had four or five half-pints of beer at Loughborough between 12.30 and 2, and then went to Kempstone at 3.15 p.m. Evidence was given that his speed was "terrific"; he collided with a furniture van whose driver was exonerated from blame; the driver of the car was killed instantly and his three passengers severely injured.' (*Alliance News*, January-March 1946.)

CASE 16

'Sentence of four years' penal servitude and a life driving ban were imposed upon the driver of a lorry who, while under the influence of drink, ran down and killed a woman on a road without a footwalk. The accused had twice been convicted of being drunk in charge of a motor vehicle and had been fined on both occasions. Mr. Justice Oliver described the case as one of the worst he had ever heard.' (*Sussex Express*, 19th March 1948; see also *The Pedestrians' Association Quarterly News Letter*, April 1948.)

CASE 17

'On 13th September 1948, a jockey was at Bow Street fined £50, disqualified from driving a motor car for five years and ordered to pay £5 costs for being under the influence of drink while in charge of a car in the West End of London. He pleaded guilty. It was said that his car mounted a footpath, went into Cork Street, then back into Clifford Street, and back into Burlington Gardens, where it stopped. The magistrate described the driving record of the accused as appalling, with six convictions in ten years for driving to the danger of the public. In defence of the jockey it was said that he had two rides that afternoon but nothing to eat except a sandwich, and, normally, when getting down his weight he never took anything to drink, but unfortunately he went to a club to see a man about riding a horse and had two drinks to fill in the time.' (*Evening News*, 13th September 1948.)

CASE 18

'A man was pushed under a train at the Angel Underground Station and was killed. The person charged with "unlawfully killing and slaying" was found to be under the influence of drink.' (*Evening News*, 6th May 1948.)

CASE 19

'The man who climbed the statue of Eros last Monday and, after traffic had jammed in Piccadilly Circus, was brought down by fire escape, was jailed for three months at Bow Street to-day . . . he was fined £2—or fourteen days in default—on a second charge of being drunk and disorderly. . . . The magistrate, Mr. J. F. Eastwood, K.C., told him: ". . . Drink is no possible excuse for hooliganism. It may have seemed funny to you at the time, but there is nothing funny about it."' (*Evening News*, 10th January 1949.)

PART TWO

THE EXTENT OF THE PROBLEM

CHAPTER V

SCOPE AND METHOD OF STATISTICAL ENQUIRY

OUR concern so far has been with gaining an impression of the various aspects of the drink problem and to see, through descriptions of single cases, just how complex was the relationship between them and how severe the results. Each case indicated what had happened in one instance, and what could in similar circumstances happen again. We have paid only the most cursory attention to the typicality of the cases; that is, we have merely excluded from consideration instances that came about through coincidences so strange that they were highly unlikely to happen again; and we have assumed a certain typicality in our more general discussion. In this part we propose to see how those general impressions are built up and to what degree they can be extended into increasingly exact indications of frequency.

It is perhaps characteristic of our age of standardisation that, partly through confusing their function, an exaggerated value is placed on statistics in this connection. Statistics presuppose some generality; they do not prove it. They do not precede but follow observation; that is, observation must show that units are sufficiently similar to be measurable. If the uniformity is merely assumed, this must be taken into account when it comes to interpreting the figures.

The statistics collected about the drink trade are manifold and as we shall see, in many respects useful. For instance, figures of the total consumption of beer are of obvious use to economists, the trade and the Exchequer. But they are misleading as indications, say, of consequential drunkenness, accident or poverty. Lord Stamp, for instance, explained before the Royal Commission (see A. 10,536) that 'if you took a period of years and tried to correlate the number of accidents with the alcoholic consumption you would get a correlation which was totally false or impure because of other factors'. The same applies to drink and crime: for instance, it is jumping to conclusions to infer that 'if the number of crimes due to drink becomes less the total crime will necessarily be less', as was confirmed by figures relating to the past four decades in Sweden (A. 10,577). There is hardly any statistical table which does not require some unknown adjustment as a prerequisite to satisfactory interpretation. Britain's leading statistician, Professor A. L. Bowley, was a member of the private committee which reported in 1931 on the social and economic aspects of the problem of drink. The report reminded its readers that it was 'admittedly difficult, if not impossible, to answer' the more important questions related to the problem of drink 'fully or with statistical precision' because, 'in fact, it would not be easy to find a subject of inquiry more complicated, or one which raises so many perplexing human and social issues'; and its summary conclusions again made it clear that 'the drink problem is many-sided, and so complicated in its reactions and interrelations as to require the utmost caution in exposition and inference.' (See pp. 11, 155). More adequate interpretation awaits the collection and collation of more evidence.

The pyramid of knowledge on the drink problem has been built up by many methods, and here even more than in the description of cases there are wide variations 'in qualitative value and in degree of authority which attaches to individual statements' (1931 Report, p. 155). Some of the knowledge applies only to one street or one factory, a small area or a particular industry, or to the nation generally. And at each level, there has been a certain amount of observation by people with varying opportunities to come into contact with cases, and with varying facilities for analysing them and interpreting them in terms of frequency. They note similarities and recurrences in successions of cases, and more or less general conclusions are then drawn as to this or that aspect of the problem.

MONOGRAPHS: LOCALITIES

Early writings on the drink problem relied frequently on quite isolated observations. Samuel Smiles, for instance, concluded from his travels that there was an intimate connection between slums and drunkenness: 'It is perhaps not saying too much to aver that one-half the money expended by benefit societies in large towns may be set down as pecuniary loss arising from bad and unhealthy homes. But there is a worse consequence still. The low tone o physical health thereby produced is one of the chief causes of drunkenness' (op. cit.). It is in more recent times that the first attempts have been made to relate such observations and experiences to a more integrated field.

The monographical approach to social research did something to achieve this: a limited field could be covered more intensively. Lady Bell was one of the pioneers in this field and her *At the Works* has become an English classic. As the wife of one of the leading industrialists of the time, she lived for many years in a North Yorkshire town and acquired an intimate knowledge of the workers. The collection of working-class budgets brought her into immediate contact with expenditure on drink, and she devoted a good part of a long chapter to the subject.[1] She writes for instance: 'That a man should drink occasionally does not prevent him from being a capable workman, and he is not permanently discharged because he has been seen intoxicated at the works; but it would be too great a risk to keep him there in that condition, and he is fined and sent home until he is sober. It is hardly necessary to dwell upon or describe the effect of drink on the households, unhappily too numerous, in which it prevails; such descriptions are multiplied everywhere, and are familiar to those who have the opportunity of witnessing for themselves the terrible results of this tendency.' Lady Bell then enumerates a number of what she considered typical cases. They relate to destitution as the result of too much money going into drink; the effect on the children; deplorable drink customs in the factories; the evil of touts employed by publicans, who are given drink for nothing if they bring in a customer, and who stand on the pavement and ply the workmen with offers to drink; the darkness of the small streets which gives women the opportunity to 'slip out in the darkness to the nearest public-house and stumble back again home'. Cases are given by way of illustration and without much attempt to arrive at their frequency.

DIRECTIONS OF ENQUIRY

The *New London Survey* is typically monographical. It is limited in place, time and direction of enquiry. In contrast to Lady Bell's study, it does not present case evidence; the case work is there, but remains in the background. It sets out to attempt 'on the basis of the facts observed to throw some light on three main

[1] See 'The General Problem of Drink', Lady Bell, *At the Works*, 1911, ch. x.

points—who drink, what and how they drink, and what is the effect and the extent of the effect that drinking has on their lives'. How they drink in London has been described also by other students. Here is a J.P.'s evidence before the Royal Commission: 'In the early years of my life in Lambeth I almost invariably found that the children were not able to go to bed because the key of the rooms was in the possession of the father or mother who was stopping at the public-house till the closing hour.' (Mr. Frank Briant, J.P., before Royal Commission, A. 30,575). Mass Observation, concentrating on juvenile drinking, found that in Stepney and Fulham children are often left to wait outside the pubs for their parents. While it is more usual for them to be seen on the pavement or near the doorway, they quite frequently come inside the passage-ways, getting a glimpse of their parents and the inside of the pub when the bar door is opened. In the evenings this practice is probably encouraged by the hanging black-out curtains between bar door and passage door. 'I drink sometimes inside the house. My mother gives it to me, but I haven't had it for a long time. Sometimes I have it with lemonade too.' 'We went to the pub near our house, and I stood outside, and my mummy came and let me have a sip. I don't like it.' (Mass Observation *Report on Juvenile Drinking*, n.d. [1944], p. 15). And a Metropolitan magistrate: 'The normal stimulus to drink in London is added to by disagreeing authorities. The inner county of London is divided into eighteen districts, each with its own licensing authority, while the suburban extra-county areas have further authorities of their own. The result is that the legal hour at which pubs must close varies in many parts of London. Thus many miles of London streets see a tipsy pilgrimage every night: at 10 o'clock the drinkers in the borderline areas leave their pubs for others which are still open; at 10.30 there is another flight into the 11 o'clock area. Each departure from a pub, each arrival at another, means another ceremonial round . . .' (Robert Sinclair, *Metropolitan Man*, 1937, p. 124).

On drinking at home, the *New London Survey* found that 'it has shown to be probable that drinking at home is becoming more important, and that this may account for a part of the decrease in women frequenting public houses; but it is certain that drinking at home in the case of the working-classes, is still much less important than that which takes place in public houses and clubs'. Enquiry could be yet more intensive. Stimulated by that excellent publication in 1934 on *Our Towns*, the London Diocesan Church of England Temperance Society made a survey into conditions of a single street which remained anonymous.[1] This survey contains some summarised conclusions about the incidence of drink in the street under review and confirms that 'drinking at home is becoming more popular'.

FOCAL POINTS OF STUDY

But public houses are still the focal outlet for the consumption of drink among the working classes, and an enquiry into their conditions, atmosphere and daily experiences had necessarily to provide clues to many social and sociological aspects of the entire question. Many of the effects of drink in the social sphere could be checked by what could be heard in the public houses from people who would never be witnesses at any Committee or Commission. It is here that Mass Observation's *The Pub and the People* filled a gap. (Mass Observation, *The Pub and the People*, 1943.) It was a frankly monographical study of Worktown, a town in the Midlands. The authors emphasised that the complex of locally integrated Worktown pubs which they studied was not necessarily typical, but contended that it could not help but contain traits and facts characteristic of conditions elsewhere, just as a study of the drink problem selecting one particular focus—in this case the public house—had to touch on the wider conditions, for instance, the influence of family life, or the effects of occupational conditions on the consumption of alcoholic drink, which could not be revealed by mere statistical enquiry. On this basis they systematically built up their study. The stages of investigation were: public-house reconnaissance and description, taking three months; penetration by observers into all parts of pub life, taking two months; observation without being observed, taking ten months; work conducted more openly, active operation with all sorts of people in all spheres of life, study of individuals, letters, diaries, documents, taking three months; data from important people, taking two months; and studies of statistics as far as available, organisations and published sources, taking three months. Studies of this intensity lift the monograph to a higher level.

Professor F. Zweig's study was less intensive (op. cit., 1948); but he found it helpful and possible to categorise the people who

[1] See *Our Street*, published by the British Association of Residential Settlements and the London Diocesan Church of England Temperance Society, n.d.

drank in public houses into regular, week-end, and moderate drinkers, and to throw some light on the question of how much they drank. 'Week-end drinkers start on Friday and end on Sunday, but the peak time is Saturday. . . . If they drink more heavily on Friday, it is not merely because it is pay-day, but because Saturday is only half-day's work, and if all have their biggest booze on Saturday it is because they can have a long sleep on Sunday. Even regulars drink an extra pint or two on Saturdays and have a good booze. There is very little drunkenness in London on week-days, but still a lot at week-ends. The bill of a week-end drinker is not always lower than that of a regular, but on an average it is lower. . . . A lot of treating of friends goes on which beings up the total of drink, and also means that more spirits are drunk. Further, there are now more women in the pubs who drink mostly short and expensive drinks. . . . A regular pub-goer drinks at least four to six pints a night, and very often ten pints or more. A regular would never drink half-pints—even if he bought half-pints he would pour them into pint glasses. He spends the whole evening at the pub, and in an evening he cannot do with less than four or five pints. . . . He treats or is treated, which makes no difference in the distribution of the bill, but makes the total expenditure of everybody higher. If he plays darts he loses or gains in pints, and this brings the drink bill up. The idea of the regular pub-goer is to have company, but he has formed such a strong habit of drinking, and his organism is already used to drink to such a degree, that breaking this habit is dangerous, and often impossible. . . . Many regulars told me that they had tried to break with the habit, but had to go back to the pub . . .' (pp. 26–7).

He also indicated important differences between communities and threw light on the social background of the drinking habit. 'The most frequent sentence one hears is that what a man spends does not depend so much on the man himself, as on his friends—on the company with which he mixes. If a man finds a new company, he changes. The same is true of his workmates, who are not his friends but with whom he spends most of his time. This is especially true in the case of teams of workers who determine the way of living of their members, because a man is then under heavy pressure of opinion and he is being afraid of being classed as queer or strange. . . . Some workers, such as seamen, bricklayers, painters, steel-workers, coal miners, have a tradition of heavy drinking, and it is impossible to break away.' (p. 30.)

STUDIES OF SPECIAL GROUPS

There are other vantage points from which aspects of the drink problem can be observed and recorded, though almost invariably only in relation to special groups of people. In hospitals and surgeries, knowledge has been built up particularly on the relation of alcohol and health, on the basis of experience with people who became patients. *Safety News*, the Journal of the Royal Society for the Prevention of Accidents, wrote in 1943: 'Of male pedestrian victims of last winter's blackout—one in ten were stated to be to some extent affected by alcohol', and 'round about ten o'clock at night', or more colloquially, 'closing time', was a specially dangerous period.

Relief cases are a similarly restricted group that can be well investigated intensively. 'From 25 per cent to 30 per cent of the whole of the poverty in a typical working-class district is caused wholly or partly by drink. Having regard to the careful selection of outdoor relief cases in Edinburgh, the proportion of the cases in that city attributable primarily to drink may be taken as a general minimum, namely 13·2 per cent. The inquiries into the cases of indoor relief suggest that the minimum proportion of this extreme class of poverty due primarily to drink is not likely to be less than 15 per cent on the average. Drink is a predominant cause of "secondary" poverty [for term see above, page 37]. The proportion may be as high as 85 per cent; 10 or 11 per cent of the primary poverty in urban working-class districts may be attributed to drink.' (Buckmaster Report, 1931, p. 127.)

Voluntary societies see the drink problem through their various clienteles. Here are two examples from London:

'I have a report which has been received from a social worker doing work for the Central South London Free Church Council. She has been a social worker for forty years, and for the last twenty-six years on the street in Waterloo Road, the Strand, Leicester Square, Piccadilly and the streets around the Elephant and Castle. . . . Only four girls in all her experience of twenty-six years have not placed drink as their first reason for leading such a life . . . no girl could lead this life without drink. There is hope for her if she will give up drink.' (Amulree Commission, A. 25,343.) A report from another South London worker says: 'I have gone over one hundred cases up to the end of the last year and the following list—that is at least thirty out of the hundred—is of girls who were under the influence of drink, either after amusement or at supper parties or at night clubs and dances.' (Ibid., A. 25,344.)

There are studies dealing more or less intensively with problems from the point of view of different industries and sections within them. Some point to the connection between work and drink. Here are four examples:

Shipbuilding: 'In the Clyde shipyards the evidence was that the "helpers" and labourers were, and still remain, the heaviest drinkers. It was explained that the helpers are employed by squads, and not by the employers direct, that their work is exceptionally precarious, and that they are therefore drawn from an inferior class. Formerly the boilermakers were heavy drinkers, and the work of the riveters was strenuous and wearying. There was also evidence that the workers in the machine shops drink less than those on the building berths. Six officials on one of the most important shipyards suggested that occupational drinking might be atributed to the work of riveters, on account of its arduous nature; to that of the redleaders, by reason of the fumes inhaled; and to that of the casuals, because of the irregularity of work . . .' (Buckmaster Report, 1931, p. 66.)

Coventry Works: ' . . . the casual workers, and the lower-paid workers generally, probably drink more heavily than the more secure and the more highly-paid workers.' (Ibid., p. 67.)

Journalism: 'Nearly all the alcoholics I have known in Fleet Street have been highly strung, imaginative men who "used themselves up" at their jobs to an extent that has few parallels in other professions. . . . Not all of this class, nor the brightest of them are drunks or near to it. There are probably as many teetotallers or very moderate drinkers among them as the reverse. . . . Among the more average pressmen, I could give many instances of lives cut short or careers ruined through drink. . . . There are scores of public houses in and immediately behind the Street which at night are almost exclusively used by newspaper workers. In addition there are one or two clubs whose membership is confined to the Press . . . the staffs . . . form an almost self-centred community. All the drinkers congregate, and the impression is gained that everybody in Fleet Street must drink. The street is certainly a drunken place in one sense. . . .'[1]

Public House Work: 'So far as the retailers of liquor are concerned, even when full allowance is made for long hours of sale, insanitary condition of many licensed houses, for the unhealthy atmosphere, and for absence of opportunities for adequate exercise, the difference between their mortality rate and that of other shopkeepers, e.g. grocers, is so remarkable that it is clear that some other factor —not common to both—is present to cause the discrepancy. That factor, in the case of both manufacturer and retailer, is . . . the special quality of the article manufactured and sold.'[2]

Other experience points to the significance of the time factor in the consumption of drink with special reference to workers on night-shift. Thus Mr. R. F. Smith, General Secretary of the National Society of Woolcombers and Kindred Trades, told the Amulree Commission:

'We consider that the proper time for a man to consume alcoholic liquor is not immediately prior to starting work, as this has a tendency to cause them to absent themselves from work, or makes them incapable of giving of their best, in addition to which they become more liable to accidents. . . . I believe this fact is peculiar to night workers . . . there are more accidents occuring between eight and twelve of an evening than there are between twelve and seven the next morning. With regard to the day turn, the reverse is the position; the majority of accidents occur in the afternoon, that is, late in the shift. . . .

Q. What conclusion do you draw from that?

A. That in a number of cases the man has probably had more drink than is usually good for him. I might add this, that the day which is worst for accidents from our point of view is Monday, the day upon which the man has had all day to play. He does not work on Sunday night. He starts on Monday night for the first night of the week. The result is that he is up at dinner time and he has all the afternoon in which to have a drink or two before he goes to work at night. I have seen men come into our club rooms on a

[1] Managing Director of Wren Books Ltd., in preface to *I am an Alcoholic*, by an anonymous journalist.

[2] See Wilson, op. cit., Part B of ch. xix, pp. 207 sq., also p. 218 for the very interesting observations on inn and hotel keepers' wives whose duration of life is affected adversely through the 'selection, environment, opportunity or example, or through actual participation in the husband's occupation'.

Monday, which is our busy day, pretty far gone by the time the bars have closed at 2 o'clock or 2.30. They have hardly been fit to go to work in the evening owing to the fact that they have been drinking instead of being in bed. Accidents have occurred mainly on Mondays and usually the majority happen before 12 o'clock midnight. . . . It is all very well to say that there are regulations to the effect that men must not clean the machinery free while it is in motion. They have to keep the wool free. If they go a little too far they get their fingers in the machinery with nasty accidents in some cases. If a man has had more than he ought to have the probability is that he will reach slightly too far and get caught in the machines.' (A. 33,361–4.)

This links up with the general observation, frequently confirmed, that accidents tend to be particularly high during the night shift (see Wilson and Levy, *Workmen's Compensation*, vol. II, 1941, pp. 25–6). Eric Farmer also found that the accident rate during night was highest in the first hours of the shift, and fell to a minimum in the last hours.[1] He suggested that this was due to the habit of night workers to get up some hours before they started work and to spend the time in amusement and having substantial meals.

Sanitary Inspectors have special opportunities to gain insight into the connection of drinking habits and domestic conditions. A Sanitary Inspector from Liverpool wrote to the Royal Commission: 'My experience was that the homes of teetotallers were more comfortable, the children healthier, happier, better fed and better clothed than where the parents indulge in alcoholic drink. . . . I have found such contrasts in conditions where men are earning the same money—comfort in one house; and next-door, confusion, broken furniture, children unhealthy, crippled and ill-fed; the mother miserable and despondent and dreading the return of the husband at night.' (See also A. 25,340.)

Courts of Law also come into close contact with numerous aspects of the drink problem but almost wholly through cases brought before them and examined in court. A number of law officers gave evidence to the Royal Commission on experience in their various areas. The following examples are from Magistrates and Chief Constables:

'I dare say in two-thirds of cases which come before me there

[1] See *The Cause of Accidents*, 1931, p. 19; see also H. M. Vernon, *Accidents and their Prevention*, 1936, pp. 29 sqq.

is history of drink, at any rate allegations of drink, and I should say in most instances probably well founded.' (Metropolitan Magistrate, A. 5822.) 'One of the things that surprised me, when I became a magistrate, was the enormous quantity of these matrimonial disputes—people married in the first week of January coming before me for a separation order in the third week of January; and so also with others who have stuck it out year after year and at last the strain has become too great. The woman tells you: "Yes, he is a good-for-nothing drunken fellow; he would rather stay in bed and then just go round to the club." Well, no doubt it is so; but whether it is the unhappy home that has driven him to drink and club, or the club that has made the unhappy home, I should be afraid to say.' (Stipendiary Magistrate for Hull, A. 7,434.) 'A high percentage of all assaults on women and children are still committed when under the influence of drink. Cases of incest, indecent assault or carnal knowledge of lodgers committed or attempted in the home (and not outdoors) are generally done when the assaulter is in a semi-drunken condition. Fortunately such crimes, especially incest, are much rarer than they were.' (Stipendiary Magistrate of Pontypridd and Rhondda (Glamorgan), A. 6,994.) 'Whilst drunkenness may be responsible for a good deal of domestic unhappiness and cruelty to or neglect of children, it is not the principal causation of these troubles. In my opinion the causes of domestic unhappiness and cruelty to or neglect of children are as follows, and are given in their relative sequence of importance, viz.: 1, Incompatibility of temperament; 2, Infidelity; 3, Drink; 4, Gambling; and 5, Unemployment. With regard to cruelty to children, I think the causes are: 1, Laziness and indifference; 2, Gambling; 3, Unemployment; and 4, Drink.' (Chief Constable of Bristol, A. 8,550.)

Q. 6,583: Have you Probation officers attached to your court?

A. Yes, I have a special one as well as the general one for the district; and also the county police court missioner. I have had reports sent me from throughout the county, and although they vary on particular points, the general principles of their reports are the same, although varying on particular points, one report laying, for example, more stress on drinking by women, or even gambling by women. . . .

A. 6,584: The strongest report I have is one which I received from the police court missioner of longest experience, and is as follows: 'I may safely say that 75 per cent of married women cases are caused or contributed to by drink.' . . . The Report goes on: 'The younger children are put to bed; those older are left to themselves, and the mother joins the husband at the club, too often gambling and betting as well as drinking.'

Q. 6,773: Is it the custom of the police officer, when he sees children unattended for a long time outside a public-house, to draw the attention of the parent or licensee to it?

A. As it happens, on Thursday last week one of the inspectors of police said that he had mentioned this very matter to one or two of the licensees. Of course, the police are in a certain amount of difficulty in this matter. They have no control over the pavement except as regards the selling of liquor for consumption outside the house on the pavement. The licensee can speak to the wife, and say: 'Is it not time for you to go, they tell me that your child is outside?' But he cannot go outside and see if there are any children on the pavement.' (Stipendary Magistrate for the District of North Staffordshire.)

Annual Reports of Chief Constables to the Licensing Justices, for instance, are another source of knowledge. Here is a paragraph from a wartime report: 'In my last report I drew attention to the number of these cases (driving under the influence of drink), and it is with regret that an increase has to be recorded, in spite of the fact that very few private cars were being driven in the evenings of February and March, owing to inclement weather, and in December, when private motoring was officially severely curtailed. Ten men were prosecuted for driving, or being in charge of, motor vehicles whilst under the influence of drink, and convictions were recorded in nine instances. . . . Drivers should beware of their "friends", and, unless sober reflection leaves no doubt of their own competence, should resist the proffered 'one for the road'.

SPECIAL STATISTICAL ENQUIRIES

In most of these statements, impressions as to the frequency of certain combinations of facts are rough and general, and even where figures are given, they are used, as it were, incidentally. But some of the relationships indicated by these data have been subject to special statistical enquiries, at the national as well as the local level. For instance, the Buckmaster Committee engaged, on the recommendation of police officials, the services of an ex-police sergeant who was about to undertake a private enquiry upon completing his service with the Force. He was asked to enquire over a period of some months into all cases within the following categories: assaults, cruelty to animals, prostitution, indecent exposure, and malicious damage to property. His classification of 198 cases covered by the enquiry included the following results: of 98 cases of assault, 38 were directly due to drink, 9 were indirectly due to drink and 51 were unconnected with drink; and of 15 cases of wilful damage to property, 11 were directly due to drink, 1 was indirectly due to drink and 3 were unconnected with drink. Altogether, out of a total of 198 cases, 33 per cent were due directly to drink, 10 per cent were due indirectly to drink, and 57 per cent were unconnected with drink. (Buckmaster Report, 1931, pp. 132 sqq.)

Before the Royal Commission, Mr. George Bailey Wilson referred to a summary of cases which he had carefully compiled from information contained in approximately fifty of the weekly newspapers in Lancashire and some of the big dailies in which were recorded happenings concerned with drinking and drunkenness, public houses, publicans and clubs. The study thus consisted only of cases of sufficient public interest to warrant reporting in this particular section of the press. It was also confined to cases where drink and the agents and agencies for distributing drink were especially mentioned.[1] The 1,600 cases recorded there referred to six months and were classified under the following headings: Murders and Manslaughter, Suicides, Inquest Cases, Assaults, Woundings, etc., Thefts, Matrimonial, Drinking Motorists, Drinking Scenes and Drunkenness, Miscellaneous Occurrences, Clubs, and Cases affecting Licences. Where a great variety of effects was obviously to be expected, Mr. Wilson noted what he called 'typical cases'; for matrimonial cases, for instance, he noted 193 typical cases.

Similarly, an examination of the records of 867 cases of cruelty to children, dealt with by a branch of the Society for the Prevention of Cruelty to Children, yielded valuable information concerning the proportion of cases in which it could be said that drink was a primary or a contributory cause of ill-treatment. There have also been valuable contributions on a local plane, chiefly drawn from the reports of the Chief Constables, relating to such matters as the effect of closing hours, Sunday drinking, local distribution of drunkenness, municipal health, motor accidents and so on

[1] See Amulree Commission, Appendix 'B' of Mr. Wilson's evidence, 19th June 1930.

which, taken together, give an impressive statistical picture in this respect.[1] The files of probation officers have been specifically used to provide material for an enquiry to ascertain the extent to which juvenile crime could be attributed immediately to the effect of parental intemperance (see Buckmaster Report, pp. 12–13). In some respects, records such as these are sufficiently standardised to provide reliable national figures.

SAMPLE SURVEYS

Intensive sample surveys on the local or national plane have built up knowledge of the frequency of cases outside the orbit of courts, hospitals, and voluntary societies. For instance, the long section devoted by the *New London Survey* to the problem of drink is largely based on sample investigations; they included visits to 620 public houses, that is approximately one in ten of all public houses in the London Survey Area (see *The New Survey of London Life and Labour*, vol. IX). The Buckmaster Committee tried by similar methods to gain insight into certain aspects of the drink problem not merely in one locality, but for the whole working-class population of the nation, and was therefore concerned to have its local surveys carried out in areas which they considered typical for the whole country. The problems they selected for particular attention were the relationships between drink and industrial efficiency, drink and poverty, and drink and crime. The Committee emphasised that 'in mapping out the various investigations, great care was taken to ensure that they were representative.' Thus, in selecting the areas for an investigation into the effect of drink on industrial efficiency, the Committee found it essential that it should cover districts so diverse occupationally as to represent, as it were, a cross-section right through industry (see *Social and Economic Aspects*, as cited above, p. 10). To investigate the relationship between drink and poverty, five trained investigators visited one in each of 7,381 households in the poorer working-class districts of a 'representative' industrial city. More recently, typical family budgets for different income levels have begun to be regularly collected, by official as well as private institutions.

From these sources, and combined with trade figures published by the drink industry, there is therefore a great and increasing array of statistical information on such questions as drink and

[1] See, for instance, 'Drink' in the 'Social Statistics for the City of Glasgow' as compiled by *The Alliance Yearbook for 1947*, pp. 133–8, by Hassal Hanmer.

population, drink and disease, drink and crime, drink and insurance, drink and industrial efficiency, drink and accidents, just to mention the more important fields (see for interesting examples C. C. Weeks, op. cit., chapters XII–XIII). *The New London Survey* stressed the importance to its study of the statistical information contained in the reports of the Royal Commission on Licensing, the data submitted to the Licensing Magistrates, the Census of Production, the 'hypotheses' of the Committee on National Debt and Taxation (Colwyn Report), and the calculations as to sales trends in the hands of private firms.

IMPORTANT GENERAL LIMITATATIONS

Many of these data are of great value, and we shall use them more in the chapters that follow: no modern study of the drink problem could do without them. But it is necessary to emphasise their important limitations. In part they are due to the questionable methods sometimes used in collecting the data—problems of research techniques, which it is possible to overcome. But the basic limitation springs from the complexity of social problems such as the drink problem. The figures relating to averages hide the important fact that the maximum effect is a long way from the minimum. If they include, as they often do, data relating to the many people who will have nothing or very little to do with drink, the average will be especially misleading for many purposes. The official surveys of family incomes and expenditures are among them. As they necessarily deal with families where little or no drink is consumed, simultaneously with others with a normal or high consumption, the average figure must necessarily be low and cannot give an indication of the incidence of drink on the domestic budget. Expenditure on, say bread, margarine and other food as well as that for rent may be almost the same with all families of a certain income class; but to make any useful comparison with expenditure on drink, families would have to be selected in which drink is normally consumed. As it is done at present, the result may be just as misleading as if the incidence of children's diseases per family were to be calculated by taking the figures of families who have children and adding the figures of those who have none. (It may be useful to remember this when consulting the figures given by the Board of Trade in 1940; here the expenditure on drink was only 9¼d. with budgets averaging 86s. 3d. a week (see *Ministry of Labour Gazette*, December 1940, p. 305).

But most important is another fact, which only partly arises out of the previous point: namely, that prior to great advances in our knowledge not merely of the intricacies of the drink problem, but of many other social problems, the value of figures for purposes of interpretation is small, and in some cases virtually absent. To take one example: the investigations of the 1931 Committee were regarded as 'representative'; but there is little indication that the 'cross-section of industry', as it is used normally, is really as significant as might appear. The Committee found, for instance, that lower-paid workers, whose task required mainly physical strength, tended to drink more heavily than more highly paid workers, especially if their work required constant and detailed attention (Report, p. 67.) To be truly 'representative' for the drink problem in industry, the cross-section might well therefore have to be a different one.

Again, the causal relationship between the different facts is, as we have seen, by no means simple or clear: Does low-paid heavy manual work lead to drink, or does drink lead to low-paid manual work? It probably works both ways, and almost certainly only as one factor among many. The same difficulty arose in connection with Professor Pearl's study of the effect of drink on mortality. As he himself pointed out, in two groups of soldiers, suffering from 'disordered action of heart' and 'shell-shock', a 'large proportion were teetotallers', and he rightly assumed that 'probably they were weaklings from their birth up, deficient in vigour of body and mind, and refraining from the use of alcohol by an instinct of self-protection'. (See *Action*, pp. 157–8.) Clearly their mortality could shed little light on the advantages and disadvantages of being teetotallers. Conversely, Dr. Masters has said that the alcoholic indulgence of American business people is largely due to the 'tremendous activity and competition in the ordinary work of life, the intensity of living, the constant excitement and challenges calling out every energy, putting them to a constant strain, followed by lack of sufficient rest, neglect of body functions, etc.' (See Dr. Masters, op. cit., p. 56); such people might therefore be predisposed to shorter life, whether they drank or not.

Enough has been said to show how generalisations on drink are built up and to prevent an incautious interpretation of statistics on drink. Specific difficulties will be mentioned in connection with the figures that follow. Their use is clearly limited, often to the purposes for which primarily they were collected. Statistics of accidents on the road and in workplaces are of use in planning preventative measures as well as the activities of hospitals and police courts, and figures of consumption help the Chancellor of the Exchequer to shape his budget. But the Buckmaster Report pointed out after studying the 'available documentary and statistical evidence, . . . if reliable answers were to be given (to the most important questions) it would be necessary to institute a number of special investigations.' (Op. cit., p. 9.) For all that, statistics play a valuable part in the study of drink—no more and no less. As Mass Observation pointed out in their study, 'the issues cannot be fully viewed by statistical interviewing, the formal questionnaire, and the compilation of data on the library level. . . . There is room for every sort of sociology in this country, because there is so little of any sort.' (See Mass Observation, op. cit., p. 10.)

CHAPTER VI

STATISTICAL ANALYSIS

THERE are few trades in the United Kingdom that are so well served with statistics as the drink trade. A particularly impressive array of them is published year by year by the United Kingdom Alliance in their Year Book, and the annual drink bill which this body has estimated since 1885 (until 1937 for Great Britain only) has become famous not only for this country but also among foreign students of the drink problem. The Royal Statistical Society recognised their value with the award, in 1910, of the Howard Medal of the Society to George Bailey Wilson, the political and literary secretary of the United Kingdom Alliance, for his study of 'the variations in the consumption of intoxicating drinks and in offences connected with intoxication'.

In this chapter we shall examine successively the trends of consumption of drink, its effects in terms of drunkenness, and its direct implications for the national economy, with a view to deriving some indications as to their general importance.

A. CONSUMPTION TRENDS

The main figures of consumption relate to home-produced and imported spirits and of beer. Four kinds of spirits are mainly consumed; two are of British make, gin and whisky; and two are imported, rum from British countries and brandy from France. In Scotland and Ireland whisky has been almost exclusively consumed by spirit drinkers, though in the early part of the last century brandy was a favourite spirit among the wealthier classes (see Wilson, op. cit., p. 15). The consumption of wine is insignificant in comparison, and may here be ignored.

The most striking fact is the remarkable decline over the past fifty years in the consumption of spirits and beer, particularly of spirits. Even the great increase in the consumption of imported spirits since the end of the war has not been adequate to offset the decline in the consumption of home-produced spirits.

CONSUMPTION OF HOME-PRODUCED SPIRITS
(*Proof Gallons*)

	Total		*Per Capita*	
Year ending Dec. 31st	*England and Wales*	*Scotland*	*England and Wales*	*Scotland*
1895	26,954,382	7,228,603	0·88	1·71
1935	7,854,000	1,710,000	0·193	0·344
1945	6,567,598	1,574,834	*	*
1949	3,908,229	895,086	0·092	0·173

CONSUMPTION OF IMPORTED SPIRITS
(*Proof Gallons*)

Year ending March 31st	*Rum*	*Brandy*	*Geneva*
1914	3,428,550	1,554,153	401,493
1939*	582,524	410,895	57,547
1945	1,344,157	56,778	3,369
1949	2,783,257	568,438	665,212

* Figures relate to Great Britain only.

These figures show the decline in the consumption of spirits in terms of alcohol: the decline in the volume of spirits consumed is somewhat less. The difference is due to changes in the alcoholic 'strength' of spirits. For purposes of commercial transaction and assessment of duty the strength is referred to a standard known as 'proof'. Where a spirituous liquor has a higher percentage of alcohol in it than 57·10 it is said to be 'over-proof'; where it has a lower percentage, it is said to 'under-proof'. If 100 gallons of spirits is 100 o.p., it contains as much alcohol as 110 gallons of absolute alcohol. If, on the other hand, it is 10 per cent u.p., 100 gallons contain only as much alcohol as ninety gallons of proof. Spirits are not, of course, sold at 'proof' strength (57 per cent of alcohol volume) but at much lower strengths, and, since the heavy taxation in 1918 and subsequently, whisky, for instance, has been sold at a much lower strength than formerly. But the general margin of difference cannot be precisely stated.

With beer the position is reversed: the figures relate to bulk or liquid barrels. Owing to the decline in the alcohol content—

U.K. PRODUCTION OF BEER
(after 6 per cent deduction for waste)
(Bulk or liquid barrels)

	Number	*Average Specific Gravity*
1905	35,415,523	1023·47
1915	34,765,780	1052·35
1925	28,826,665	1042·75
1935	20,864,658	1041·02
1939	24,674,992	1040·93
1940	25,366,782	1040·62
1941	26,203,803	1038·51
1942	29,860,796	1035·53
1943	29,296,672	1034·34
1944	30,478,289	1034·63
1945	31,332,852	1034·54
1946	32,650,200	1034·72
1947	29,261,398	1032·59
1948	30,408,634	1032·66
1949	29,990,144	1033·43

the 'specific gravity'—the decline of consumption in terms of alcohol is greater than is shown by the figures. For taxation purposes, bulk barrels are converted into 'standard' barrels, i.e., of a certain gravity—1055. The beer, however, actually brewed to-day is of a considerable lower average gravity—in 1946, 1034·72—which means that the number of barrels of beer actually produced is considerably larger than the number of standard barrels. As taxation increases the gravity of beer tends to fall, and, accordingly, the proportion of 'bulk' to 'standard' barrels tends to rise.[1]

The figures relate to the home production of beer which, owing to the insignificance of imports and exports, is virtually the same as home consumption. Exports in 1949 were 226,342 standard barrels as against 652,000 barrels in 1914; imports, almost wholly from Eire, were 690,000 standard barrels in 1949 against 74,000 barrels in 1914.

At the time of the *New Survey of London Life and Labour*, the best estimate of the *per capita* consumption of beer in London over nearly forty years was that it had declined from about forty-six 'standard' gallons in 1891 to twenty-three 'standard' gallons in 1928. In the meantime the strength of London-brewed beer had diminished, so that in 'bulk' gallons, consumption per head had fallen by about two-fifths. Thus it 'would appear that for every ten glasses of beer consumed in 1891 by the average Londoner, he drank in 1928 about six glasses of lighter beer, with a total alcoholic content of not more than half that of the ten glasses consumed in the earlier year. For this reduced quantity of lighter beer rather more than half as much again was paid in money.'[2]

One factor which clearly influences consumption trends is the state of trade and employment. When the Amulree Commission reported in 1931, the impression gained from the figures of beer production had to be quite obviously that the consumption of beer had been 'remarkably' reduced during the last thirty years. But the report added cautiously (see p. 11): 'It is not possible, in reviewing the changes which have come about during recent years in habits of sobriety, to leave out of the reckoning the industrial and general depression which has characterised the greater part of the post-war period. It stands to reason that over a period of general prosperity larger amounts are likely to be spent on alcoholic liquor, as on other luxuries, than in times when spending power is low.' In 1931 the consumption in bulk barrels was 23,905,707. Two years later consumption had shrunk to 17,957,533 barrels. But after 1933 the figure began to rise, and the trend was consistently upwards after 1939. By the end of the war, consumption in terms of volume, though not in terms of alcohol, reached the

[1] See Amulree Report, p. 7. For a comparison, cf. Wilson, op. cit., pp. 58–9.

[2] See *New Survey*, op. cit.; the London Diocesan Church of England Temperance Society, *Drink*, as cited above, p. 4.

highest level since 1915. The consumption of beverages, largely alcoholic beverages, thus increased while the consumption of some foods declined.

CONSUMPTION OF FOOD AND DRINK IN GREAT BRITAIN

(lb. per head)

	Pre-war Annual Average	*1947*
Dairy Products		
(milk solids)	38·3	48·9
Meat	109·6	82·2
Fish, game, poultry		
(edible weight)	32·8	36·1
Oils and Fats		
(fat content)	45·0	33·9
Tomatoes and Fruit ..	141·5	126·6
Vegetables	107·4	117·9
Beverages	14·7	15·2

Since the end of the second World War, the number of unemployed in Great Britain has never exceeded 400,000 or 2½ per cent of the insured population, and outside the Development areas it has not, in general, exceeded 1½ per cent (see *Economic Survey for 1947*, February 1947, p. 9), whereas at the end of 1930, 2,500,000 or 19·9 per cent of the insured work-people had been unemployed (see *Statistical Abstract of the United Kingdom*, 1938, pp. 132–3). The Amulree Report had therefore been wise to emphasise that changed trends in trade and employment might drastically influence the figures of production and consumption of alcoholic drink.

THE DECREASING NUMBER OF CONSUMERS

These figures do not indicate how many people were really consuming the drink: reduced consumption of drink could wholly or partly be due to a decline in the number of consumers. In this connection, and particularly for comparisons over long periods, changes in the age distribution of the population may be significant. Between 1911 and 1938 the population increased by 13 per cent and the following changes in the age groups took place:

Age-group	*Per cent Increase*	*Per cent Decrease*
0– 4	–	27
5–14	–	16
15–24	–	–
25–34	14	–
35–44	23	–
45–64	58	–
65 and over	86	–

(See Abrams, op. cit., p. 28.) From these figures it becomes clear, as Mr. Mark Abrams has pointed out, that the two populations of 1911 and 1938 must be regarded as two very different groups of consumers. Consumers under fifteen years of age declined by 20 per cent while consumers of sixty-five and over almost doubled. These divergencies have to be taken into account when the 30,900,000 'consumer units' of 1911 are compared with the 37,139,000 in 1946. (For the calculation of 'consumer units' Mr. Abrams has used a special scale of equivalents: one male between the ages of 15 and 65 represents 1·00 unit, and a female in the same age-group 0·60; an infant of 0–4 years is counted as equivalent to 0·33 consumer unit; (see op. cit., pp. 28–9, 31).

Changes in the age distribution of the population affect the consumption of some commodities differently from others, according to the dependence of the demand for certain goods on particular age-groups. The consumption of bread and meat, for instance, may be influenced only slightly by an increase in the proportion of the higher age groups. But with drink the position is different. Since the members of low age-groups do not consume any alcoholic drink at all, it is only from fifteen to eighteen years of age that they may become consumers. The 'older' the population grows as a whole the greater the potential increase in the consumption of drink. If, therefore, the consumption of spirits has decreased in the last decade, and if the consumption of beer has remained stationary or has only slightly increased in 1946–7 compared with earlier years, this means that the potential increase due to the ageing population has not come about.

In his evidence before the Royal Commission (see A. 25,641 and Appendix XVI), Mr. George Bailey Wilson compared the consumption of drink in 1928 and 1901, and took the changes in the age structure of the population into account. On that basis the consumption of spirits declined by about three-quarters; the decline for the adult population alone was even heavier.

CONSUMPTION OF SPIRITS IN ENGLAND AND WALES, 1901 AND 1928

(*per head*)

	Total Population	*Adult Population (20 and upwards)*
1901 (proof gallons) ..	0·98	1·71
1928 (proof gallons) ..	0·25	0·38
Percentage decrease ..	74·5	77·8

But in order to assess the consumption of drink by real consumers it is also necessary to take some account of the total number of abstainers and moderate drinkers. As Mr. Bailey Wilson took pains to point out to the Commission, there had undoubtedly been an increase in the total number of abstainers between 1901 and 1928 and a much greater increase in the number of extremely moderate drinkers: he assessed the increase in the number of total abstainers at seven million. (Cf. Amulree Commission, A. 25,641–2.) This meant that the decrease in the consumption of drink by consumers of drink was probably very considerably less than the decrease of 77·8 per cent registered by the total adult population. (The evidence given by Messrs. W. Hamilton Whyte and H. R. Burrows before the Royal Commission was illuminating as to this point (see A. 11,646 sqq.). From their enquiry, which related mainly to the industrial population and included interviews with over 150 employers, it seemed to emerge that there was a 'change taking place in the personnel of the drinking community; that is to say, you may have, first of all, an increasing number of moderate drinkers offsetting a diminution of excessive drinkers'.)

The question marks at this stage are already numerous and

important and make it difficult to interpret the figures of consumption trends. In particular, while as a general trend the statistics seem to reveal that on the whole beer drinking has not materially increased and that the nation as a whole has possibly become more sober, it cannot be enough emphasised that they give no indication of the generality of heavy consumption of drink. When Sidney Webb made his famous report to the Labour Party in 1923, he emphasised strongly that 'it is not clear to what extent the aggregate decline has been due to an increase in the proportion of total abstainers and to a diminution in the daily consumption of moderate drinkers. The decline is, in fact, statistically not inconsistent with an actual increase in the number of drinkers to excess and their consumption.' Seventeen years later Mr. Wilson expressed a similar opinion: in view of the very much larger number of abstainers—the persons who do not like beer or cannot afford it (an unknown number)—'the beer that is drunk to-day is consumed by a very much smaller number of persons than is commonly supposed, and the same applies even with greater force to spirits' (see Wilson, loc. cit., p. 11).

The two points, then, the total quantity consumed and the quantities consumed by moderate and heavy drinkers, need to be carefully distinguished. A statistical enquiry on the latter point might throw significant light on the sociological implications of the problem; and there seems to be no reason why it should not be possible. It is an important task for the future to ascertain whether there has been an increase in that part of the population which may be classified as 'heavy', or, at any rate, as more than 'moderate', drinkers, and to what extent and how evenly the consumption of drink in that class is increasing or diminishing. For instance, are there within the group of 'heavy' drinkers great variations between maximum and minimum consumption, and are there any changes in this? In short, it should be taken into account that the crucial factor for evaluating the national drink consumption is not just what total amount is consumed but what amount by whom? It is significant that investigators like Professor Zweig came immediately up against this point in their study of drink consumption. But the usefulness, for instance, of Professor Zweig's distinction between 'week-end drinker' and 'semi-regular' and 'regular' pub-goers is limited. It throws only an indirect light on the consumption of alcoholic drink, for consumption is not necessarily accurately reflected by the frequency of visits to public houses. As Professor Zweig observes himself (see Zweig, loc. cit., p. 27): 'The bill of a week-end drinker is not always lower than that of a regular, but on an average it is lower.' Such observations show again the difficulties of reaching definite conclusions on the basis of available data. In the background there is the very obvious truth that little can be deduced from general figures of consumption without paying due consideration to the greater or lesser volume of consumption by particular groups of consumers.

B. DRUNKENNESS

To arrive at some assessment of the severity incidence of drink consumption, attention fastens naturally to the most obvious manifestation of excessive drinking: drunkenness. Drunkenness constitutes the maximum degree of severity which the drinking habit may exhibit and the habitual drunkard is certainly the person whose own health and safety is in greatest danger and who is of greatest danger to the welfare of others. Through the statistics of conviction for drunkenness we know at least something of the matter. They are a very inadequate basis, as we shall see, for reaching general conclusions as to the incidence of drunkenness. But the reduction in the number of convictions has been so striking over some decades that it is safe to conclude from them that drunkenness has substantially diminished.

In 1899, according to criminal statistics, there were 189,633 convictions in England and Wales; and in 1903 the figures were 209,385. For the year 1905 and subsequently, more comprehensive figures, specially collected for the purpose, appear in the Annual Volume of Licensing Statistics issued by the Home Office. In 1905, the convictions for drunkenness were still 207,171, but they decreased till 1910 when they numbered 161,992, and then increased again till, in 1913, they numbered 188,877 out of 213,188 proceedings. But after 1913 convictions decreased rapidly. In 1929 they numbered 51,080 out of 61,455 proceedings. The later development is reflected in the following figures (taken from the *Alliance Yearbook for 1950*).

There, has been, therefore, a great decrease in convictions and this can be regarded as evidence for less drunkenness. But the development has not been quite consistent. The sharp drop after 1930 reflects the effects of the severe depression in trade. The fact is particularly interesting because a witness before the Royal Commission on behalf of the Whisky Association contended that the 'idea that people drink more when trade is good' was mistaken (see evidence by Mr. Charles Hay Marshall, A. 37,716). In fact, the depression after 1930 revealed that there must have been a close interrelation between the condition of the trade and the incidence of drunkenness; and the rise after 1934 when trade recovered again points to the same effects in reverse.

DRUNKENNESS:

PROCEEDINGS AND CONVICTIONS IN ENGLAND AND WALES

<table>
<tr><th>Year</th><th>Proceedings</th><th>Convictions</th></tr>
<tr><td>1929</td><td>60,728</td><td>51,966</td></tr>
<tr><td>1930</td><td>61,455</td><td>53,080</td></tr>
<tr><td>1931</td><td>49,029</td><td>42,343</td></tr>
<tr><td>1932</td><td>35,407</td><td>30,146</td></tr>
<tr><td>1933</td><td>42,492</td><td>36,285</td></tr>
<tr><td>1934</td><td>46,293</td><td>39,748</td></tr>
<tr><td>1935</td><td>50,032</td><td>42,159</td></tr>
<tr><td>1936</td><td>52,988</td><td>44,525</td></tr>
<tr><td>1937</td><td>55,304</td><td>46,757</td></tr>
<tr><td>1938</td><td>55,688</td><td>46,603</td></tr>
<tr><td>1939</td><td>54,301</td><td>52,929</td></tr>
<tr><td>1940</td><td>48,299</td><td>46,998</td></tr>
<tr><td>1941</td><td>42,072</td><td>40,964</td></tr>
<tr><td>1942</td><td>28,336</td><td>27,435</td></tr>
<tr><td>1943</td><td>28,189</td><td>27,363</td></tr>
<tr><td>1944</td><td>23,405</td><td>22,628</td></tr>
<tr><td>1945</td><td colspan="2">20,617</td></tr>
<tr><td>1946*</td><td colspan="2">20,545</td></tr>
<tr><td>1947*</td><td colspan="2">25,170</td></tr>
<tr><td>1948*</td><td colspan="2">32,871</td></tr>
</table>

* Charges proved.

The reduction in convictions during the war does not fit this interpretation: probably the times were too unusual in too many ways. It seems characteristic enough that when the war was over and more normal conditions returned together with almost full employment, there was a general increase in convictions. In some communities reputed for heavy drinking the increase was particularly pronounced. After a sharp downward movement in the years of war, the number of arrests for drunkenness in the Metropolitan Police Area, for instance, again increased.

Number of Arrests for Drunkenness in Metropolitan Police Area

1938	19,705	1947	11,562
1940	14,145	1948	14,289
1945	8,483	1949	14,408
1946	9,118		

This increase was not offset by the increase in the estimated population since 1945. The proportion per population was 1·228 in 1945 and 1·398 in 1947.[1] It is significant that there was an increase also, for instance, in Southampton. But there were decreases also, for instance, in Birmingham and Liverpool (see *Alliance News*, July–August 1947, p. 40).

SHORT-TERM AND LONG-TERM TRENDS

The connection between prosperity and drunkenness should not be interpreted to mean that a general improvement in the social conditions of the people leads automatically to more drunkenness: by and large the opposite is true. It is necessary to distinguish the short-term from the long-term trends. Sharp fluctuations in trade, bringing along in few years large fluctuations of prosperity and distress, may certainly have a direct influence on the extent of drunkenness: workers spend more money on drink when they enjoy prosperity and when their means allow them to do so; and dismissal for being drunk is not so much feared when immediately another job is waiting for the dismissed. But these tendencies finding expression in trade cycles of four to six years have to be carefully distinguished from the general trend observable over decades with unfailing regularity: this is that drunkenness is in general on the decline. The Amulree Commission concluded that 'It was a matter of general agreement amongst the witnesses who appeared before us that the present century has seen a distinct advance in

[1] See Report of the Commissioner of Police of the Metropolis for the year 1947, May 1948, Cmd. 7406, pp. 66–7 and 73; the arrests exclude cases in which proceedings were taken under Section 15 of the Road Traffic Act, 1930, against persons deemed under the influence of drink and cases where persons were charged with drunkenness and at the same time with more serious offences; these cases together numbered 857 in 1947.

sobriety'. With material progress a greater recognition of the evils of excessive or heavy drinking is certainly developing; and this factor must be regarded as being active whatever the special ups and downs of the short-term trends may be. As the Amulree Report stated (see para. 40): 'A marked change in general social standards has come about, and this has been reflected in a very appreciable alteration in the public attitude towards drunkenness. Drunkenness has gone out of fashion, and a drunken person is not tolerated as he used to be. The vital importance of this change hardly needs emphasis.' The Report further observed that 'the magnitude of the change in former habits has been apparent in industry' as much as in social life (see para. 50), and that 'by almost universal consent, excessive drinking in this country has been greatly, even spectacularly, diminished'. The private Report of a year later similarly regarded 'the changes in drinking habits' as a fundamental explanation for the 'increasing tendencies towards sobriety' (see *Social and Economic Aspects*, p. 42 and *passim*). And the figures up to our time of proceedings and convictions for drunkenness testify to this even further.

SOME STATISTICAL LIMITATIONS

The dominant limitation of figures of legal action against drunkenness is that they can give no indication of the real incidence of drunkenness in the country. The Amulree Report emphasised on several occasions that it should be 'clear that the figures of convictions cannot be taken as an accurate measure either of the total amount of insobriety at any given time, or . . . of comparative conditions in different localities'.[1]

The figures do not tell us, for instance, about drunkenness and excessive drinking that happens in the home of the drinker, though it may be assumed, at any rate, that this concerns mostly the wealthier classes, since working-class drink consumers take their drink mostly outside the home, and, when at home, only in small quantities and usually at meals.[2] More important than this de-

[1] See Amulree Report, p. 9, para. 37; see also p. 83, para. 399: 'We have indicated our general distrust of argument based on statistics of drunkenness, particularly where it is sought to compare conditions in different localities, or even in the same locality in changing circumstances.'

[2] See Sir William Crawford and H. Broadley, *The People's Food*, 1938, an interesting study for which the field work and tabulation of information collected were handled by Sales Research Services in co-operation with the research department of W. S. Crawford Ltd.; page 74: 'Whatever may be the share of the working-class in the "national drink bill" it is certainly not in respect of alcoholic drink consumed at home, or paid for out of the weekly housekeeping allowance.'

ficiency is the fact that heavy drinking is not synonymous with drunkenness, though, of course, drunkenness is always due to too much drinking. A man may in the course of the day drink twenty or more glasses of spirits without being visibly affected by them;[1] therefore, excessive though this consumption may appear from the social and economic point of view, it may not entail the supreme physical manifestation of excess. Continued heavy drink leads often to an increased ability 'to take it', and the habitual drunkard, without becoming intoxicated, may consume quantities of alcoholic beverages which would cause well-marked signs of drunkenness, or even prove fatal, to the person not accustomed to it (see *Action*, loc. cit., p. 186). It is not without humour to note that persons who have been arrested for drunkenness often choose, as a not altogether unplausible defence before the magistrates, that they had 'only a glass or two', because the possibility of intoxication by even small amounts cannot be excluded: drinking on an empty stomach, for instance, has an important bearing on the degree of inebriation. There are also great individual variations to susceptibility: some people, it is said, become intoxicated at the very 'smell of the cork', while others are capable of consuming large doses without showing any signs of inebriation, and this apart altogether from 'acquired tolerance'. (See for this *Effects*, pp. 54–5 and 57–8.) As things are it is clear that heavy drinking need not lead to drunkenness; and drunkenness cannot itself lead to conclusions as to the amounts of drink consumed. Drunkenness as a manifestation of an excessive consumption of drink may therefore mean something very different when considered from the angle of the individual who has had 'too much' and when considered from that of statistics of convictions for drunkenness: there, some cases of drunkenness may be responsible for less consumption of alcoholic drink than may be entailed in heavy drinking without intoxication.

Further, there are particular complications concerning convictions for drunkenness. In the first place, a person convicted has to be first caught committing an offence. This applies on the road no less than elsewhere. The Committee on Road Safety which was set up by the Government in December 1943, and published its Final Report in 1948, came to the conclusion that 'the number of persons who, though not actually drunk, were not able to take care of themselves must have been very much greater' than the 2,864

[1] See Wilson, pp. 286–7, who quotes for this evidence before various committees.

motor drivers who had been convicted for being 'under the in-ence of drink'. Again, the legal interpretation of drunkenness is different from the medical interpretation, yet it is the latter which is more significant because more comprehensive. A special committee of the British Medical Association gave the following definition of 'drunk' (see *Effects*, p. 50). 'The word "drunk" should always be taken to mean that the person concerned was so much under the influence of alcohol as to have lost control of his faculties to such an extent as to render him unable to execute safely the occupation on which he was engaged at the material time.' But 'there is unfortunately no legal definition of the word "drunk" ', as was emphasised again recently by H. Cecil Heath (see H. Cecil Heath, *The Control of a Dangerous Trade*, 1947, p. 20).

Usually persons have to be 'drunk and incapable' before they are likely to find themselves in the hands of the police. And even then practice differs widely as to what is done with them. Being drunk is, itself, not a crime; as L. Page has put it (*Crime and the Community*, 1937, pp. 356–7), it is 'less a crime than a folly' in the eyes of the law. Mr. Frank Briant, J.P. was asked by the Royal Commission, (Q. 30,593) whether 'statistical drunkenness is only a fraction of the actual intemperance.' He answered: 'Certainly. I should not think that anybody thought otherwise. The police are an excellent body in many ways. The most experienced policeman is the policeman who induces the man to get home without being arrested.' There is a much stricter standard of the term in regard to persons driving motor cars, as in their case an offence is committed if the driver is 'under the influence of drink'; but even here there is no legal definition which can be accepted as infallible. Mr. W. J. H. Brodrick, the well-known Metropolitan magistrate, told the Commission (see A. 5967): 'I take the view, and I think my colleagues take the same view, that where respectable persons are charged with being drunk and incapable and nothing is known against them, and there are no aggravating circumstances, it is very undesirable to register a conviction, and I invariably ask them whether they will promise not to do it again. If they say "Yes", then I say "Go away", and they go.'

Wilson refers to another element of uncertainty which reduces the value of the figures of convictions: the discrepancies between proceedings taken and convictions (see Wilson, loc. cit., p. 285). There is great diversity in this respect; the ratio between proceedings and actual convictions varies very widely in different districts.

In 1935 in Manchester, for example, 65 per cent of those proceeded against were convicted, whereas in the neighbouring Salford the percentage was 85; Portsmouth convicted 68 per cent, but Southampton only 29 per cent (see ibid.). Part of the differences may be accounted for by differences in the kind and degree of police activity. But further, it may also happen, and indeed, happens frequently, that those charged before the magistrates for being drunk and disorderly may at the same time be charged with other offences and convicted on account of these, so that the charge of drunkenness is not pressed to a conviction.

The law aims at the punishment only of public drunkenness; and then it discriminates between cases where drunkenness is accompanied by certain circumstances, such as incapability, disorderly conduct, etc., on the one hand, and what is sometimes called 'simple' drunkenness on the other. In the former class the police have powers of arrest; in the latter they can only take out a summons. As the Amulree Report emphasised, prosecutions in the latter class are not very frequent; the Report referred to an important police force whose policy has been to refrain from instituting proceedings in 'simple' cases, largely, it seemed, on the ground that, without evidence afforded by an early medical examination, it would be very difficult indeed to establish the fact of drunkenness in court.[1] Mr. Charles Thomas Barton, Clerk to the Licensing Justices for the City of Liverpool, confirmed (see A. 2739) that 'the proceedings for drunkenness may be undoubtedly affected by the attitude of the police authorities'. This still holds good to-day, though we may assume that in general the practice of the police has tended to greater uniformity since earlier times. Sir Edgar Sanders, past General Manager of the Carlisle and District State Management Area, stated in a Memorandum that, according to his experience, the test of drunkenness was getting 'stiffer every year and the man who would be arrested for being drunk and disorderly to-day would have been allowed to stagger home' in previous years.[2] On this ground the decline in convictions probably understates the real decline in drunkenness since the first World War.

[1] See Amulree Report, p. 149; there was a good deal of evidence on this point, see in particular the evidence of Sir Hugh Turnbull, K.B.E., Commissioner of Police for the City of London, A. 5552 sqq.; also under 'Drinking and Drunkenness, Convictions' in Subject Index, pp. 62–3.

[2] See A. 20,033, para. 8 of Memorandum; also A. 20,172: 'The idea a policeman has of what is drunkenness gets stiffer every year. I can remember thirty years ago when a man would stagger home, but to-day he would be arrested for drunkenness.'

Finally, figures of drunkenness give no indication of the incidence of drink on different groups of people. We do not know how they are related to habitual or casual drunkards: yet cases may relate to a large number of casual drinkers and may therefore be in some ways more harmless than if they related to a small number of heavy drinkers. The Amulree Report refers to the change between 1913 and 1929 in the proportion of convictions of men and women: in 1913, when the proportion of males to females in the population was 1,000 to 1,067, 81·06 per cent of the convictions related to men and 18·94 per cent to women; in 1929, when the proportion of men to women was as 1,000 to 1,088, 84 per cent of the convictions related to men and 16 per cent to women (see Amulree Report, pp. 8–9), but this again gives little indication of the relative incidence of drunkenness between the sexes. Lord Stamp's respect for statistical information was accompanied by equally strong criticism when he explained to the Royal Commission on Licensing that, as regards the interrelation of crime and alcohol, one must be far more careful than had been generally the case 'in eliminating particular classes of crime' in which drink played no part. He warned against jumping to the conclusion that 'if the number of crimes due to drink becomes less, the total crime will necessarily be less', and produced Swedish figures for four decades confirming the need for this caution (see Amulree Commission, A. 10,577).

Even fuller statistics do not eliminate the difficulties of interpretation, for so much of the problem cannot be subjected to measurement. For instance, (see A. 10,579) '. . . generally when you try to make something of statistics of crime in America, you find yourself almost in a quagmire'. Unwarranted or meaningless conclusions can be reached by ignoring the limitations of relatively simple figures. In this way the Committee on Road Safety set the 567 motor drivers under the influence of drink and primarily responsible for accidents in 1937 against the 206 pedal cyclists and the 534 pedestrians held similarly responsible, and then drew the conclusion that 'of the total casualties due primarily to alcohol or drugs the number of other users at fault was greater than the number of motor drivers' (see *Final Report of the Committee on Road Safety*, 1948, paras. 93–9). As the Pedestrians' Association rightly pointed out, there are, of course, a far greater number of pedestrians than drivers using the roads, and a clearer picture would have been given by stating the figures as a percentage of each type of road user; but even this correction by no means dealt with the major possibilities of misunderstanding.[1]

C. DRINK AND THE NATIONAL ECONOMY

The most striking fact about the National Drink Bill is its size. Here is the Bill, by decades, together with the estimated expenditure per head of the population.

U.K. ESTIMATED EXPENDITURE ON DRINK, 1885–1945

	Total £000	*Per Head* £ s. d.
1885	141,039	3 18 4
1895	163,134	4 3 5
1905	164,168	3 16 0
1915	181,959	3 18 11
1925*	315,000	7 4 0
1935*	237,732	5 1 0
1945	685,000	

* Figures relate to Great Britain only.

The population was not ascertained during the war and no comparable estimate is therefore available as to the average expenditure per head: on the assumption that about 45 million people lived in the U.K. at that time, the average expenditure per head in 1945 was over £15 4s. 0d.

The £685 million spent on drink compared with £1,650 million spent on food, and exceeded the £601 million spent on clothing and the £603 million spent on tobacco. Excluding betting, expenditure on drink was the largest single item in what is termed optional expenditure; it accounted for between 40 and 45 per cent of the total sum spent on smoking, reading matter, and entertainment (cf. *The Enjoyment of Life*, the Conservative Political Centre, 1947, p. 2).

[1] See Pedestrians' Association, *Commentary on the Final Report of the Committee on Road Safety*, January 1948, p. 9.

The size of the Drink Bill is perhaps even more striking when it is compared with other than personal expenditure. Samuel Smiles did this in an article in the *Quarterly Review* of 1875. He mentioned, for instance, (see Samuel Smiles, *Thrift*, 1905 ed., p. 114) that the annual expenditure of the working classes alone on drink and tobacco, which was at that time estimated at £60,000,000, was adequate to finance 500 new cotton mills, or the purchase of 500,000 acres of land. In the same manner, the Drink Bill of 1938, which amounted to nearly £300 million, exceeded, for instance, the total value of the agricultural and horticultural output of England and Wales which was approximately £223,000,000; or the value at the mines of mineral and metals produced in Great Britain which was £208,000,000. It was almost half the sum which all exports of the United Kingdom realised in 1937. It was, to add a comparison with an item of immediate social expenditure, between nine and ten times as large as the total sum spent on benefits under the National Health Scheme in England during that year, and exceeded in fact the total sum spent on such benefits over the whole period of 1912–28.[1]

The more recent figure of almost £700,000,000 spent on drink was only little less than our adverse balance of payments at the the time of the loan negotiations in Washington in 1946; it amounted to about half of the foreign exchange to be found in 1947 for imports, then approximately £1,450,000,000; and it exceeded by far the estimated total private saving (undistributed profits, changes in tax reserves and personal savings) in 1947 and 1948, respectively £605 and £575 million (see for figures *Economic Survey*, 1947 and *Economic Survey*, 1948). The total current expenditure in the Revenue Account of all Public Authorities in 1946 was, at £3,425 million, only five times that of the Drink Bill in 1945. And, last but not least, of the total estimated national income for 1946, £8,200 million, the Drink Bill alone represented about one-twelfth.

We have already seen that the rise in the national Drink Bill has not coincided with a rise in the consumption of drink: the reason for the disparity is the great increase in the price of drink. This is due only to a small extent to higher manufacturing costs passed on to the customer, but has been caused almost wholly by the increase in taxation.

[1] See for figures, *Statesman's Yearbook*, 1939 and Annual Report of the Ministry of Health, 1939, p. 274.

U.K. NET RECEIPTS OF CUSTOMS AND EXCISE FOR BEER, SPIRITS, WINES AND LIQUOR LICENCES 1915–1945

	Total £000	*Beer* £000	*Home Spirits* £000
1915	46,484	15,882	20,302
1925	141,451	81,987	40,825
1935	100,172	56,696	28,305
1945*	360,621	287,731	63,610

* The figure for spirits includes both home spirits and foreign and colonial spirits.

We are by now familiar with some of the limitations of figures. The figures for expenditure and taxation do not indicate what groups spent the money and paid the taxation, nor how well they could afford it, that is, without infringing 'essential' expenditure. They do not indicate what poverty is mainly caused by expenditure on drink, nor how the money would be spent if it were not spent on drink. The figures can only show the general significance of the total drink bill and the immediate boon to the Exchequer. The sort of conclusion that can be validly drawn from them is like that pointed out by the *New London Survey*: if the purpose of taxation 'be to promote economy, by reducing the amount or the proportion of income spent on drinking by the average family, the result has not been attained' (see *New Survey*, op. cit., pp. 263 and 265). Whereas the trends of consumption and conviction point downwards, expenditure on drink is unmistakably on the increase.

CHAPTER VII

THE SCOPE FOR REDUCTION

THE main impression to be gained from the statistics—and a warranted one—is that the consumption of drink and drunkenness have declined, and that it is only due to the efforts of the Exchequer that no decline has been registered in expenditure. But there are no grounds to conclude, as the trade would no doubt like us to conclude, 'that drunkenness has now been reduced to a point at which it is no longer a social evil': this was their main case before the Amulree Commission. And equally unwarranted are the statements of independent observers, of Professor Zweig among others, (see F. Zweig, op. cit., p. 30) that 'drinking is no longer a moral or health problem of great magnitude', and that 'the problem of drunkenness in this country has been more or less solved', except, perhaps, for some economic considerations. It is particularly unfortunate that in public debates, as for instance in the Second Reading of the Licensing Bill, 1948, statistics of conviction for drunkenness are quoted generally as a proof of the slight significance of the evil. As we have seen, they tell a very imperfect story (see H.C. Debates, 14th December 1948, col. 1051 and col. 1127).

We are not aware, in the first place, of any data on the absolute extent of drunkenness; and the indications concerning heavy drinking are even scantier. The trends shown in the statistics give no clue to these. But one thing is certain: it is that drunkenness and heavy drinking are still extensive. The Amulree Report observed that (see para. 105), despite the great general improvement, the drink problem, if no longer a 'gigantic evil', as it was described by our predecessors, was still serious, in that excessive drinking—with the evils it brings in train—still persisted in large measure (Paras. 57 and 86): 'What appears to be beyond question, and is shown even by the figures of conviction with all their limitations, is that a substantial amount of excessive drinking, over the country as a whole, still exists. So long as that continues to be the case it cannot, in our view, be maintained that there is no problem of drunkenness.' The Commission thought it appropriate to devote in the Index a special section to the 'Magnitude of Problem presented by Drunkenness and Drinking' (see ibid., p. 299).

Accidents on the road pose even by themselves an important and, moreover, a growing problem. To the Amulree Commission 'the intoxicated motorist offers a special problem'. (See Amulree Report, para. 703). He has undoubtedly added not only to the incidence of accidents due to drunkenness, but certainly to their severity rate too. We have no definite evidence as to the severity of accidents and the physical injury caused by motor cars driven under the influence of drink, but it can be assumed that careless driving tends to lead to more severe accidents than mere speeding when the attention of the driver is not impaired by the consumption of alcoholic drink. It is noteworthy that, as the Chief Constable of Leicester, Mr. O. J. B. Cole recently pointed out to members of the Industrial Transport Association, 'it was not the drunkard that caused accidents, but the man who had had a few drinks, thought himself a wonderful driver, and took unnecessary risks when his judgment had been impaired through alcohol'.[1] There are cases of great severity, where the driver of the car has to pay with his life for driving under the influence of drink; in those cases, incidentally, no conviction is added to the statistics. In other cases grave injury or death is caused by a drunken driver to a pedestrian.[2] Drunken bicyclists and pedestrians may be as much of a danger to themselves as drunken drivers, though probably not as great a danger to others. The Committee on Road Safety commented generally that 'preventive measures are clearly needed, not for drivers only, but for all road users'.

But there are two considerations of even greater importance and of general relevance to all aspects of the problem of drink: the first concerns the discussion of the incidence of the problem; the second refers again to severity. Even if the statistics of convictions for drunkenness were an adequate measure of the extent of the problem, this would surely not allow us to draw the conclusion

[1] See *Alliance News* of January–March, 1946, p. 6; cf. also the Committee on Road Safety, which cited the statement of the Alness Committee that '. . . a small quantity of alcohol is for many drivers most dangerous. The driver who has imbibed alcohol experiences a feeling of "euphoria", of careless well-being, and entertains a mistaken idea that he is driving better than usual'. See *Final Report of the Committee on Road Safety*, 1948, sections 94 sqq.

[2] Cf. *Sussex Express*, 19th March 1948; also *Quarterly News Letter* of the Pedestrian Association, April 1948, pp. 7–8.

that the problem was not serious. Murder is regarded as a serious problem: yet murder is of rare occurence. Moreover, there has in recent decades been an abatement of many evils: for instance, the nation has become more hygienic, and the grossest evils which existed in factory occupations, such as, for instance, industrial accidents, have been considerably reduced.[1] Yet none of these reductions has led to the conclusion that deficiencies no longer existed. On the contrary, with every improvement, we are apt and, indeed, justified, to consider even the reduced figures with greater anxiety; the argument that it was formerly 'much worse' is not one which leads to further progress.

In the same way, it is to the absolute incidence of the drink problem in our own days that we must look in order to pass judgment as to whether the evil still exists to a lamentable extent. And as to that we can join Robert Sinclair in stressing that even the figures for conviction for drunkenness, with the very limited indication they give of the total amount of drunkenness, give cause enough for 'disgust' (see Robert Sinclair, *Metropolitan Man*, 1937, pp. 120 sqq.). Sinclair emphasizes that the more sober aspects of the streets, for instance, should not detract our attention from the still existing evil. It is true that 'many Londoners living grooved lives must hardly ever have seen a drunken man and most certainly not an arrested man, as thousands of children living in the greatest ports in the world have never seen the sea'. Indeed, it is, as he says, 'an unfair generalization to associate arrests for drunkenness with a picture of a hatless gentleman clinging to a lamp post and singing. We all know that that picture is scarcer than it was, and what the policeman does not see the magistrate does not grieve over.' But, he suggests, 'an excellent testing instrument of communal witlessness is the motor car: to drive through public-house districts any evening, and particularly near the closing hour, and above all on a Saturday night, is to save many more lives than one is called upon to save in busier places in daytime'.

The second consideration arises from the fact that the figures give no indication of severity. Yet severity, as in the case of murder and fatal accident, is important. Average consumption and expenditure per head of population make it easy to minimize the effects of drink, just as it is easy to minimize the effect of industrial

[1] See, for the latter point, an interesting survey in the Annual Report of the Chief Inspector of Factories, for 1932, p. 8 and table XII.

accidents by showing that on the average the physical impairment of the injured worker is trifling and his disablement of very short duration: of some 400,000 industrial accident cases terminated in 1937 under the Workmen's Compensation Acts, more than 230,000 were of a duration of less than three weeks. 'Only' 7,000 cases had lasted more than twenty-six weeks. But surely the latter were, from the social point of view, the far more important ones and their prevention should claim by far the greatest attention.[1] Also, in the case of drink we have no reliable measure of the incidence of more severe cases, and to draw misleading conclusions is consequently even easier.

THE NEED TO INTERFERE

Assessing the importance of the problem in terms of the national economy immediately leads to controversial issues. For instance, should the annual drink bill of the country be considered as unduly high in relation to the total national income and expenditure? And if it could be agreed that it is too high, how far would it be desirable to curtail it by official measures aimed at reducing the consumption of alcohol? Does the drink bill, enormous though its annual incidence, not represent the wish of the consumer to spend this amount on what seems to him an outstanding pleasure of life? Is the State, particularly in a democratic and liberally minded country, entitled to interfere directly with the traditional habits by which its citizens like to dispose of their earnings and arrange their budget? This is, probably, the strongest rhetorical question put forward in defence of the high level of the drink bill.

Examples are not lacking of legislative interference with private expenditure which was regarded as unduly high and unjustifiable from an economic point of view. One is provided by Industrial Assurance. In 1933 an official committee drew attention to the large amount of money spent annually on industrial assurance and produced figures comparing the enormous annual premium income of this business—then £54,200,000—with other items of national expenditure. The advocates of the existing system of iife assurance had repeated for many decades that working-class people liked to spend that much money on funeral policies, and that the expenditure was indicative rather of their thrift. Despite these protestations, the anomalies of the system, mainly through agents pressing people to insure, were, after all, so manifest that its

[1] See Home Office: *Workmen's Compensation Statistics for 1937*, 1939, p. 22.

principal features were abolished by the incorporation of funeral benefit in the National Insurance Scheme.[1] In the same way, as the need generally to economise and to increase production became increasingly pressing, a business like the football pools employing 300,000 to 400,000 persons became the focus of much criticism for its apparent waste of man-power; and the Essential Works Order continued to interfere with it in peacetime.[2] It may also be noted that the same applied to employment in shops: throughout, the aim has been to draw workers into industry by reducing their numbers in the 'less essential' trades.

It is in 'hard times' that interference with the 'enjoyments of life' becomes perhaps clearly necessary. Taking this subject as a title of a pamphlet, the Conservative and Unionist Central Office pointed out in 1947 that no less than a quarter of all our private spending was on 'optional expenditure'. Of this, tobacco and alcohol accounted for over 80 per cent; and for every pound spent on food eight or nine shillings went on strong drink. Such statements made by politicians who are least prepared to concede interference with the individual's freedom to earn and spend can hardly be ignored.[3]

The necessity to interfere with the citizen's expenditure may also arise when new and costly programmes come up for discussion and the question is put: 'Can we afford it?' This question was repeatedly asked when first the Beveridge proposals, and later those of the Government relating to the new social security schemes, made their first appearance.[4] Expenditure of the Government scheme in benefits and cost of administration for 1948, covering retirement pensions, widows' benefits and guardians' allowances, unemployment benefit, sickness benefit, maternity benefits and death grant, was estimated by the White Paper published in 1946 at £452 million, and the 1944 White Paper on the National Health Service estimated the total cost of the new Health Scheme for Great Britain at £148 million.[5] It seems illogical that the question

[1] See for a full description of the system, its defects and abuses, Sir Arnold Wilson and Professor Hermann Levy, *Industrial Insurance*, 1937; also later: the Beveridge Report.

[2] See Hermann Levy, 'Wasteful Employment' in *Contemporary Review*, June 1947, pp. 354 sqq.

[3] See Conservative and Unionist Central Office, *The Enjoyment of Life*, also *The Times* 'Cost of Enjoying Life', 1st September 1947.

[4] See for a refutation of this question, e.g., Professor G. D. H. Cole, *Beveridge Explained*, 1942, p. 38: 'Can we afford it?'

[5] See Ministry of National Insurance, *National Insurance Bill*, 1946, p. 12, and *A National Health Service*, 1944, pp. 84–5.

'Can we afford it?' should have been asked in that connection when the sums required for these great social security and health services were lower by £100 million than the sum spent by the people annually on alcoholic drink.

It is from perspectives and by comparisons of this kind that the significance of the drink bill for the national economy should be analysed. How much of the expenditure on drink we cannot afford upon such considerations, everybody will answer according to inclination. But it will probably be agreed that it depends largely on an assessment of the expenditure on enjoyment which is liable to lead to excess. This observation can be related in particular to alcoholic drink. Here a distinction should immediately be drawn between two points of view. Firstly, exaggerated expenditure on drink may be viewed merely from the angle of national economic policy: the task of the State would then be to strike, as far as possible, an economic balance between expenditure on drink and expenditure on other items of consumption, in particular expenditure on goods of primary necessity. The other point of view takes in more comprehensively the undesirable effects of excessive drinking on the nation's welfare in general and not merely on the distribution of its income. It would include the effects of drink on health, safety, crime and efficiency, which all have of course some greater or lesser interconnections with purely economic problems.

Professor Alexander Elster made an attempt to estimate the 'excess' expenditure on drink in Germany before the first World War. He estimated that RM. 1,800 million were spent justifiably out of a national income of RM. 30,000–35,000 million on what he considered the normal consumption of drink in working-class families. But the total drink bill was RM. 3,500 million. From this he drew the conclusion that between RM. 1,500 million and RM. 2,000 million must have been what he called 'Unmässigkeitsausgabe', i.e. expenditure on immoderate or excessive drinking. We mention this rough estimate, not for its exact validity, but because it was published in the leading German economic Encyclopædia (see Elster, op. cit., p. 220), and indicated the desire on the part of an authoritative economist to arrive at an approximate figure of the excess consumption of alcoholic drink. It may not be possible to express in a simple formula of this kind the extent to which the nation's drink bill contains the element of excess: such terms as 'immoderate', 'unreasonable', and 'excessive' will always contain an element of subjectivity.

TWO FAULTY ECONOMIC ARGUMENTS

The Amulree Report mentioned the two economic arguments which are generally brought forward in opposition to any calculation of excess expenditure on drink and to suggested interference with it. The first contends that the money so saved would not necessarily be spent on more useful purposes. This argument is usually brought forward by private interests connected with optional expenditure. It used to be the stock argument in defence of the excessive expenditure on industrial assurance, even though much of it was just 'wasteful thrift' owing to the enormous number of lapses of policies.

The assumption that people's money diverted from expenditure which must be regarded as wasteful and uneconomic would simply find its way to other kinds of equally useless expenditure is hardly confirmed by experience. On that basis, the increasing wealth of nations would have found its outlet overwhelmingly in an increase of optional consumption and in an ever increasing preponderance of expenditure on tobacco, drink, betting or gambling over the more necessary expenses for food, housing or clothing. This is not what has actually happened. On the contrary, we find that, with increasing prosperity, the consumption of necessary commodities has become larger, more diversified and more refined. Comparing the years 1937–8 with the years 1913–14, Mark Abrams comes to the conclusion that family 'real' income was up 37 per cent, 'real' consumption of food per head was up 35 per cent, 'real' consumption of clothing per head was up 45 per cent and expenditure on the home 125 per cent (see Mark Abrams, *The Condition of the British People*, 1945, p. 86). There is no reason to suppose that there is not even more room for such expenditure—apart altogether from increased expenditure on cultural entertainment and learning—if extravagant drinking were reduced, that is, that the same trend would not continue. This conclusion is strengthened when it is taken into account that the current extravagance springs to a large extent not from a spontaneous desire of the consumer, but from a desire constantly fostered and stimulated by misleading advertisement and attractions of all sorts. We tend to agree with the Amulree Report when it stated: 'While it would be absurd to maintain that all of the money so diverted would be transferred to useful or productive ends, we believe that the greater proportion of it is likely to be better spent and at least a useful proportion saved or devoted to constructive purposes' (see Amulree Report, p. 22).

If the State has not yet approached the problem of a reduction in alcoholic drink consumption from that angle, the reason may rather be sought in some part in the fact that drink always was and still is one of the most favourite means of public finance. This is the second economic argument. Yet it is very doubtful whether the drawing of large amounts of revenue from sources which give rise to permanent stimuli to wasteful spending—which is not even much repressed by high taxation—can be regarded as a policy conforming to the fundamental principles of sound economics.

It is the increasing prosperity that expresses itself in higher income, larger investment, and greater savings, which the national economy should regard as the most appropriate object of increased taxation, not sums spent in pursuits which, far from increasing the accumulation of wealth, tend to burden its progress. This has an immediate and particular significance in times when there is a shortage of capital seeking investment. Sir Josiah (later Lord) Stamp said before the Amulree Commission (see A. 10,526): 'I take the view that at the present time we are suffering from capital hunger'—it was in 1930—'that our rate of progress economically could and would be much more rapid if capital were more abundant. Therefore, anything that was spared out of £100, otherwise spent in alcohol, that would go into the capital field would in the course of half a generation be very important and in the course of a whole generation very remarkable; that is a matter of arithmetic. It is not demonstrable how much out of £100 not spent in alcohol would be saved; we can only form our own guesswork upon that; but one cannot help feeling that with all the new attractions that exist for attracting savings from the individual worker, with that very material change in the average household budget, quite an appreciable proportion could be spared.'

This view should be acceptable even to those who subscribe to Lord Keynes' cautious views about the relative benefits of saving which may lie outside the savers' influence.[1]

It should also remain valid if the enormous yield of taxes on

[1] See John Maynard Keynes, *The General Theory of Employment, Interest and Money*, 1936, pp. 210 sq., and *passim*: an act of individual saving may, in his view, not always be a substitution of future demand for goods for present-day demand, because the will of the saver may not be directed towards the consumption of any specified thing at any specified date; on page 211, Keynes speaks with a view to this of 'the absurd idea, though almost universal, that an act of individual saving is just as good for effective demand as an act of individual consumption'.

drink is, from the point of view of public economy, interpreted as 'saving': At a time when the State has taken over so many activities, including production formerly undertaken by private enterprise, it may be argued that the public income derived from the consumption of drink may in the same way as post-office savings again be canalised into productive channels. But this interpretation can hardly invalidate the principles on which sound public finance should be built; and one of the most fundamental of these would appear to be that the State should not just rely on sources of taxation from which it can most easily get money, but link up the policy of public finance with that of economic and social welfare. Money wasted by the individual cannot be regarded as the proper source for public finance, even if it may be returned, to some extent, to the productive organism of the nation. How little regard is sometimes given to this point emerges from the rather cynical observation made once by a Chairman of the Board of Inland Revenue when he explained to brewers that it was not the brewer, distiller or wine merchant who paid the tax on drink, but the consumer. 'Through your agency I am enabled to extract from the pockets of the people a sum of money . . . and to do this without their knowing anything about it at all. What the people pay to me I think they generally charge to you, and that seems to me an extremely satisfactory result to both of us. . . . If the unfortunate taxpayer knows nothing about it, so much the better for him, so much the better for you, and so much the better for me. Where ignorance produces such bliss, do you think it wise to enlighten?' (See for the quotation George B. Wilson, op. cit., p. 197.) As long as this is the official attitude, little regard may be expected for the broader economic implications of the taxation of drink: if the public is to be kept in ignorance as to what it actually pays in taxes to the State for the enjoyment of drink, the desirable aim of linking the needs of public finance with those of the general economic and social welfare has, indeed, little chance to assert itself.

The practical implications for the Exchequer of a reduction in the consumption of drink are not, in any case, serious. As the Amulree Report emphasised (para. 104), 'the probable loss of revenue need not . . . be a matter of great alarm. A sudden withdrawal from the revenue of the total amount of the taxation on intoxicating liquor would certainly provide a formidable problem. This, however, is not in the picture. Reduction in expenditure on intoxicants, if it be to come about, must necessarily be gradual; and it is our belief that the benefits to be derived from the present excessive expenditure would progressively compensate for any loss of taxation yield from that source.' With this the Commission removed the only doubt as to its general conclusion: 'It is a difficult matter to question the discretion of the individual to spend his money in the way which seems to him best; but we are bound to record that the evidence which we have received has left upon us the definite impression that a substantial reduction of the present expenditure on intoxicants by all classes is desirable.' (See Amulree Report, pp. 21–2.) And the same applies to the consumption of alcoholic drink.

PART THREE

THE ABATEMENT OF DRINKING: ACTION AND COUNTERACTION

CHAPTER VIII

MODERATING INFLUENCES AND COUNTER-ATTRACTIONS

CONSIDERATIONS of the likely extent of excessive drinking and the indications of the severity of its effects go far to offset the satisfaction to be derived from the reduction in the evil over past decades: it is still a serious problem. To deal with it, attention naturally focuses on the developments and lines of action to which the reduction to date can be attributed.

Analysis cannot do justice to their complexity, which matches the complexity of the 'causes' of drink, and it is hardly possible to sort out the interconnections in order to apportion success among even the major developments and lines of action. The problem would certainly be less complicated if it related to heavy drinking only: just as in the case of motor driving, dangers might then be dealt with by the imposition of a speed limit. In this case, freedom to drink would at any time entail that the fine and the none too obvious border-line between moderate and immoderate drinking would cease to be effective. Yet it is the demarcation and fortification of that line at which a policy directed towards abatement of drink must aim. Weeks describes how the moderate drinker can become a confirmed alcoholic (see Weeks, op. cit., p. 309): 'First, under the influence of example, or suggestion, or it may be at the actual solicitation of a moderate drinker, the individual wills to embark on the sea of what is to be moderate drinking.' Secondly, there is 'the will which has gradually lost his guidance and power, until by almost imperceptible changes, the alcoholist, the would-be-moderate drinker, has succumbed to the deceptive power of the drug and becomes the alcoholic. This, of course, is the root of the whole business—through the example of the moderate drinker, and through the social forces of convention and custom, the tradition of alcoholic indulgence is maintained.'

The Amulree Commission examined numerous factors as causes

of the decrease in insobriety. Many were mainly of a general social nature, covering a wide field, with particular emphasis on the marked growth of counter-attractions to drinking, such as cinemas, the wireless, allotments and gardens on new estates, playing fields, and travelling facilities. Among the efforts aimed straight at the abatement of drinking those of the temperance movement and the advance in real knowledge about the effects of drink were of much indirect as well as direct importance, mostly by way of general dissuasion from the consumption of drink. And finally there was clear and direct repression by means of legislation, which expressed itself, for instance, in restrictions of time and place for drinking. We may similarly distinguish, in this and the following chapters, between the general social developments that have entailed a reduction in the consumption of drink, and the two powerful agencies which have been directly active in the abatement of drinking, and of heavy drinking in particular.

CHANGING SOCIAL STANDARDS

We have already mentioned that excessive drinking has tended to become less with the progress in material welfare and education. Just as we see fewer children in dirty and worn-out clothes even in slum districts, just as there is more cleanliness to be observed in towns, and people have become more conscious of the care and hygiene of their bodies, so the most flagrant abuses of drink have declined. The Amulree Commission did not overlook this factor, though there was the possibility that its perspective might have been blurred by the fact that its investigation took place at a time when trade depression affected the consumption of drink. 'A marked change in social standards' was rightly mentioned by the Report as a powerful factor in altering 'the public attitude towards drunkenness'. 'The general progressive tendencies of the age' were enumerated as a factor promoting sobriety, without prejudice to the effects of direct and positive legislative interference, and without denying the necessity of the latter (see Amulree Report, paras. 40 and 107). Heavy drinking, and drunkenness in particular, have passed from being something of a fashion to a more or less deprecated exhibition on the part of individuals. The Right Rev. Bishop of Kingston stated this about drunkenness before the Amulree Commission (A. 26,705): 'I should say that there has been a change of fashion rather than a change of moral conviction about it. Undoubtedly in the old days there was a fashion to overdrink a good deal and people did not think anything wrong about it. Now, the fashion has changed and people think it is bad form, stupid, and that kind of thing.' Basil Nicholson in the *London Survey* in the thirties similarly reported (see op. cit., p. 7, of reprint), 'where once frequent drunkenness was half admired as a sign of virility, it is now regarded as, on the whole, rather squalid and ridiculous'. The change may be even more marked in the better-class districts than in the very poor areas (see Amulree Commission, A. 26,707, Bishop of Kingston), although it is, of course, possible that this difference might be due to the varied manners and habits which go with different social standards. Another general factor, applying mainly to industry, is the increasing tendency to mechanisation which calls for enhanced qualities of concentration on the part of workers and also, for instance, of pedestrians (see Amulree Report, para. 52).[1] The general tendency would perhaps be yet more pronounced were it not that some drunkenness remains connected with certain social events in almost unbreakable, traditional cycles. As Mass Observation point out that 'the ordinary, week night, quiet evening at the local pub represents social relaxation, "week-end drinking"—in its extended sense—is playing the same sort of social role as the Cup Tie, the Coronation, religious and political revivalism'.[2]

The Amulree Commission did not attempt to analyse the social conditions which it had enumerated as having conduced to the reduction in heavy drinking. In particular, it did not distinguish clearly between two sets of conditions which seem to have very different significance. One consists mainly of factors important to the domestic life of the worker: a happy and satisfied domestic life may immediately exert a moderating influence on the consumption of drink; instead of being regarded as a definite 'counter-attraction' to drink, a satisfactory home life should be regarded as a desirable normal condition which, as such, reduces the temptation to spend more on drink than would be economically permissible and which relegates drink to some altogether casual role in

[1] These general factors are not mentioned by George B. Wilson who, on pages 233–4 op. cit., gives a list of the factors which in his opinion have affected and still affect liquor consumption. He mentions under C 'Educational and Moral Causes', *sub* 1, 'The factor of general education and the achievements of the temperance movement', but does not deal with the wider sociological factors which have contributed to the change as well, such as that of fashion, progress of decency, etc.

[2] See op. cit., *The Pub*, 1943, p. 338. In Bavaria the custom still prevails of very great amounts of beer being reserved over the few weeks before the Catholic feast of Corpus Christi—Fronleichnam—for consumption on that day.

people's social life. 'Counter-attractions' ought to be distinguished from this sort of influence: they are factors which definitely compete with the drinking habit in terms of money, leisure time and other resources, and are in these respects on the same level as drink, though in many others, of course, very different. Though such general conditions as a happy home life and specific counter-attractions such as the cinema both operate towards the abatement of drink, it seems sound to distinguish between the former which 'moderate' the drinking habit and the latter which 'divert'from it.

IMPROVEMENTS IN HOUSING

We have seen that bad housing conditions are frequently associated with heavy drinking and drunkenness. The improvements in housing, past, present and future, therefore deserve to be mentioned as an important factor in moderating the drink habit. The contrast between what exists by way of housing conditions and what is envisaged can be well gathered by a study of the excellent Report of the Design of Dwellings Sub-Committee of the Central Housing Advisory Committee appointed by the Minister of Health and of the Report of a Study Group of the Ministry of Town and Country Planning on Layout in Relation to Housing, which deals, *inter alia*, with such points as space requirements, storage facilities, and, most important for the housewife, equipment and fittings, including heating, kitchen equipment, and laundering facilities (see *Design for Dwellings*, 1944). Another report, a private publication by Mr. Gilbert McAllister, also gives a vivid analysis, supported by illustrations, of homely houses contrasted with the grim streets of the slum. It is also of interest that 'a welcoming meal after work' is one of the attributes of the real home to which the author draws special attention (see G. McAllister, *Houses that are Homes*, n.d., p. 25).

Better household equipment is stressed sometimes as the matter next in importance to 'housing accommodation'.[1] Up-to-date equipment makes for better homes for the housewife. But the feeling of having a genuinely attractive home demands also aesthetic improvements, and it is with satisfaction that one observes modern plans laying stress on the importance of aesthetic considerations in the building of new homes (see for instance, *Design of Dwellings*, pp. 22–3).

[1] Cf. e.g. Memorandum presented to the Royal Commission on Population by Innes H. Pearse, November 1944, printed privately as *Observations on the Population Question*, p. 9.

Town planning and the development of new communities on a more suburban and rural pattern is related to the improvement of the house. It is to be regretted that the Amulree Report did not pay more attention to the matter, even though it had been forcefully taken up by Mr. Ernest (now Lord) Winterton, M.P., who described the transfer of several hundred families from Hulme, an over-licensed area of Manchester, to the Wilbraham Road Estate. The new housing estate, he said, has been made to 'blossom like the rose' by 'tenants who, in their former surroundings, could do little more than put a plant pot in the window'. (See Amulree Commission, A. 33,753.) In all these respects, the new garden cities, and schemes like the Reilly plan with their strong emphasis on green surroundings and the revival of what used to be the 'village green', are of great importance and, happily, increasingly appreciated.[1] If recently Mr. Anthony Eden claimed that 'man should be master of his environment, and not its slave', this is precisely what matters in this case (see *The Times*, 4th October 1946): the drinking habit, so extensive among the slaves of America, was no less fostered by the drabness and hopelessness of environment than is that of the worker living in slums.

The field of counter-attractions, of which the special amenities and social improvements connected with new housing and with experiments in social co-operation such as the Peckham Health Centre are only a sector, is so large that its analysis has led to some exaggerations in so far as everything and anything which may divert from drink has by some writers been classified as 'counter-attraction'. Thus Wilson ranges even the 'chain-store' within the factors which affect the consumption of liquor, since its enormous development since the first World War 'points to another interest which is playing its part in competition with alcoholic beverages' (see Wilson, op. cit., p. 252, *sub* f.). This sort of deduction, however, must lead straight back to confusion as to what counter-attractions really are and mean. An improvement of general social standards, an increase in national wealth, and a better distribution of the social product among the working classes inevitably widen the range of wants and provide a greater differentiation of goods and pleasures available to the majority. But nothing definite can be said about their influence on the drinking habit before any

[1] See the interesting book by Lawrence Wolfe, *The Reilly Plan*, 1945, *passim*; see also E. A. Gutkind, *The Revolution of Environment*, 1946, in particular, what he has to say about a 'park city', pp. 94–5.

effect in this direction is actually proved. It may well be that with increasing wealth and a greater differentiation of wants there remains enough money over—perhaps more money than used to be enough—that can be spent on alcoholic drink. This relates, for instance, even to a counter-attraction as important as the cinema: Professor Zweig, for instance, emphasises that the worker frequenting the local cinema does not spend on it so much as to justify the assumption that his budget is 'affected to any appreciable extent' (see Zweig, loc. cit., p. 22); there remains enough for drink, and though in many cases the evening in the cinema may prevent the worker or his family from spending larger sums in public houses, it cannot be assumed for certain that he will not do so on other evenings if he is given to drinking. It may all depend on whether his budget allows him to enjoy many pleasures or only a few. The exact effect of the counter-attraction is therefore difficult to assess.

The crucial point is whether or not the expenditure on more and differentiated wants will reduce absolutely the consumption of drink: that all sorts of conditions will reduce it relatively, that is, that the consumption would be higher if these conditions did not exist, is not open to doubt. We may here refer again to the contrast between moderating influences and counter-attractions. We have seen that a better house may immediately lead to abatement of drinking outside the home, and in promoting better housing conditions, we agree with Mr. G. B. Wilson's stress on the importance of services rendered by building societies (see Wilson, pp. 244–5): they certainly have indirectly had a moderating effect. But they are significant in connection with counter-attractions only when they provide possibilities, for instance, of occupation which are chosen as alternative to going to the pub. A clear example of such substitution is work in and care of the garden which goes with the new house: this occupation has only very limited possibilities for dwellers in flats and blocks of tenements in congested areas. The same may be said of 'thrift' and saving. The latter has enormously increased in the last decades, and the official savings movement may be said to have had the beneficial effect of reducing uneconomic spending, among which expenditure on drink figures so prominently. (The growth of building societies is of course to some extent a function of the increase in savings.) But in how many cases is saving the outcome of a decision on the part of the saver to put into reserve what he would have otherwise spent on drink? In how many cases is it not more likely that he can save without even curtailing his passion for alcohol or pub-going? Again, it may be said that more would be spent on drink were it not for more saving. But the figures of beer consumption hardly justify the assumption that all such attractions have led to an absolute decrease in the consumption of alcoholic liquor. This applies also to gambling and betting or smoking. If they did not exist, or if they did not exist to the extent they do, more might be spent on drink. But this does not mean that gambling, for instance, has been an active force towards the reduction of the absolutely high figure of drink consumption or the prevention of further rises in the annual drink bill, that is, in the total expenditure of those who drink. The criterion according to which we judge a factor as a counter-attraction to drink is whether or not it is immediately competitive with the drinking habit: it must be an obvious positive alternative to the consumption of alcoholic liquor.

THE GARDEN AND THE RADIO

Some counter-attractions are directly connected with the home life. Two appear to be of paramount importance: the garden and the wireless. Work in the garden, it is generally agreed, represents one of the most valuable counter-attractions to drink: it constitutes an enjoyable occupation and provides valuable relaxation which is definitely in the interest of health, for instance, since it takes place in the open air; and it does not reduce the owner's income, but rather tends to increase it through yielding home-grown vegetables and fruit, and sometimes eggs and poultry. The British predilection for small houses and gardens instead of blocks of tenement flats and communal parks has always aroused the envy of housing reformers on the Continent. Flat houses have recently been subjected to severe criticism by housing reformers. In his study on *How Should We Rebuild London?* Mr. Purdom, for instance, emphasises that 'Flats are unpopular with the majority . . . the flat policy . . . must be given up as socially unsound . . . those who live in these great masses of buildings, surrounded by hundreds of other people eating, sleeping, quarrelling, making love, drunken, sick, and dying, have no privacy, and life becomes unbearable'.[1] The mention of drunkenness clearly shows that no objective investigator ignores its connection with gardenless housing. Mr. Purdom strongly recommends private gardens. The Metropolitan Borough Councils in their reports on the County of London Plan have done

[1] See C. B. Purdom, *How Should We Rebuild London?*, 1945, pp. 28–9, 33 and 223.

the same (see ibid., p. 267). The point is stressed that the private garden, even when small, is of more value to the family than mere large communal gardens: while the latter may contribute to the greater homeliness of the dwellings from an aesthetic point of view, as also to relaxation, the private garden alone offers the occupational counter-attraction which may induce people to renounce distractions outside the house, for instance the visiting of public houses and clubs for consuming alcoholic drink.

The difference has been clearly observed in new housing estates providing private gardens. The Chief Constable of Bristol told the Amulree Commission (see A. 8,546): 'There appears to be a marked interest in home life by people, especially by those living on the new housing estates. These people show a greater interest in their gardens and hobbies, and the owner-occupier finds entertainment in the upkeep and improvement of his dwelling. I would like to say that particularly during the last two years I have noticed personally the very great attention and the very great interest the people on these new housing estates take in their little gardens and in their own premises. It is very marked. Many of these people a few years ago, instead of being employed in that very proper and innocent pleasure, would very likely have been spending their time in public houses.' And, as it was further stated, these were people who had previously had no opportunity of 'doing a little gardening'.

Allotments may be considered as belonging to this domestic sphere, though they are separated from the home, frequently by a deplorably long distance. Many represent a substitute for a garden, sometimes on a much bigger scale; but sociologically they may be regarded as being an adjunct to the home rather than an occupation outside it. The development of allotments has not been altogether continuous: a peak was reached in 1920 when over one and a half million persons were cultivating allotments, but the figure shrank to less than a million before the Second World War.[1] During the war years there was a new impetus to extension. The number of allotments in 'urban areas' rose from 600,000 in the years before the war to about 1,400,000 during the war and receded again after its end. They were recently estimated to number something over 1,250,000 by the Secretary of the National Allotments and Gardens Society, who kindly supplied the author with this figure as an estimate of current conditions.

[1] See *National Allotments Society Yearbook 1937–1938*, p. 13, also p. 39.

It is not within the scope of this study to enter into the nature and analysis of the various factors, some administrative (see ibid., p. 11–13), which have retarded the progress of urban allotments. But it can be safely stated that the shortcomings have not been due to any lack of enthusiasm on the part of town dwellers. Tenement dwellers have shown great anxiety to secure allotments to make up for the absence of gardens. A few years ago the Manchester University Settlement published a detailed survey of a new housing estate; there it was stated that tenants had no individual gardens, that there was a big demand for them, and that most of them wanted allotments and would be prepared to share them with a neighbour. 'The large majority of the flat dwellers want allotments'; only 5 per cent did not want a garden.[1]

The people interested in the sale of liquor are well aware of the significance of the allotment to town dwellers, and this is a fair indication of their importance to the abatement of drink. Mr. William J. Coates, for instance, speaking as a trustee and district representative of the Licensed Victuallers' Defence League of England and Wales, told the Amulree Commission (see Amulree Commission, A. 13,412) that the 'life of the working man after his working hours has undergone a revolution compared with the old days', on the grounds, particularly, of the 'advent of the allotment system' during and immediately after the first World War. 'There are thousands of men round our district to-day who, after they get home at night, after their day, work an hour or two in the allotments or the gardens.' The witness made this observation not to stress the social significance of this new leisure occupation, but to make it an argument for an extension of permitted hours, a point which he also related to the increasing habit of visiting cinemas and of bowling; he pleaded for 'half an hour extra'. Acceptance of such a recommendation was plainly designed to counteract the effect which work on allotments had on the consumption of alcoholic drink.

The wireless is another important counter-attraction in the home to pub going. The Amulree Report mentioned it as second in importance to the cinema in the general growth of counter-attractions (see Amulree Report, p. 9): it is, indeed, a novel and absorbing entertainment, and undoubtedly induces people to stay at home. The increase in wireless entertainment is to some extent

[1] See Manchester University Settlement, *A Survey of Housing and Social Amenities on Belle Vue, Gorton, New Housing Estate*, 1942–3, p. 17.

reflected in the sales of wireless sets. *PEP* suggests that the replacement demand alone for wireless sets is about 2,000,000 per year.[1] In 1946 there were as many as 10,500,000 listeners (see *Enjoyment of Life*, op. cit., p. 6). But this figure relates only to people who own or rent the sets and pay the licence: it does not show—and this matters to our subject—how many people may actually prefer the wireless entertainment at home to that of visiting public houses or clubs. If this could be shown the figure would be far greater. Public-house proprietors are realising the strength of the wireless as competitor for customers and have long since begun to provide wireless sets in their establishments (see Wilson, op. cit., p. 250).

COUNTER-ATTRACTIONS OUTSIDE THE HOME

Outside the home, the cinema is the latest and possibly the most important counter-attraction to drink. Its significance in that respect was emphasised by several witnesses before the Amulree Commission (see Amulree Commission, pp. 430, 440, 1441, 1742, 2027 and 2031). In 1934 it was estimated that the total number of cinema admissions amounted to 963,000,000 per annum (see *Enjoyment of Life*, p. 6). Wilson draws special attention to the fact that the cinemas, with their three-hour programmes which do not conclude until the public houses are mostly closed, constitute a competitive factor to public houses of the first order (see Wilson, op. cit., p. 250). 'The development of the habit of regular attendance at picture halls must also be viewed as an important aid to sobriety.'[2] Publicans are well aware of this danger to their trade.

It is, in this case again, not the expenditure on going to the films that matters primarily, though this conclusion is frequently drawn.[3] The money spent on cinemas is not a formidable item of the working-class budget, but that spent on drink is. Professor Zweig came to the conclusion that the sums spent on the cinema cannot be ranged among the factors responsible for secondary poverty (see Zweig, op. cit., p. 22), in contrast to expenditure on drinking, betting and smoking. The vast majority of just those who are likely

[1] See *PEP* 'Report on the Marketing of Household Appliances', 1945, p. 14.

[2] The Chief Constable of Newcastle-on-Tyne in a Memorandum to Amulree Commission, A. 8,220.

[3] See, e.g., Sir Arthur (later Lord) Balfour before the Amulree Commission, A. 35,645: 'I think people are spending more money on that type of amusement and less money on drink.'

to indulge in excessive drinking use the cheap tickets in the cinema; and probably nearly 50 per cent of the tickets sold are for cheap seats (see *Enjoyment*, p. 7). It is certainly not the case that money spent on the cinema reduces materially the money to be spent in public houses by those who want drink as well. What is important is that the visit to the cinema removes the person, possibly even man and wife, from the opportunities of drink at least for one or two days in the week, that it gives them the satisfaction of an enjoyment outside the home to interrupt its daily monotony, and, through this, makes enjoyment in the public houses less tempting. There may be many families to whom spending one or two evenings on enjoyment away from home would seem normal; if the cinema absorbs these evenings there is a smaller chance that they will want to spend another evening or two in the pub. Of course, the cinema absorbs more money than the wireless which, if one disregards initial outlay or rent charges, requires only a negligible sum per annum; and without this expenditure the national drink bill might be still higher. But most important is this removal of people, at least in a limited way, from the opportunity for purchasing drink. In other words, it is the time factor rather than the money factor which may here lead to an abatement of the consumption of alcoholic liquor. This is of particular significance for young people: they may not have yet acquired the drinking habit, and drink may be to them merely an alternative enjoyment to the cinema.

Sports, games and communal entertainments of various kinds also do not reduce by much the financial means available for drink, but similarly limit the time to be spent in drinking. Sports and games are also to a large extent incompatible with the drinking habit. The Amulree Commission heard a great deal of evidence on this point. Mr. Henry Riches, the Chief Constable of Middlesbrough emphasised this in his Memorandum to the Royal Commission (A. 7,751): 'Counter-attractions to the public house or club in the shape of healthy forms of recreation and amusement might bring about a reaction. Although a remedy is very difficult to suggest, I may mention that when large numbers of men are attracted to a football match on a Saturday afternoon, and remain in the open air for a couple of hours or longer enjoying the sport provided, the reduction in the number of charges—especially of drunkenness—on the following Monday reflects the advantages gained for the public welfare by the attention of large numbers of the male population of the town to this healthy form of recreation.'[1]

The counter-attraction is of course stronger still with people who wish not merely to attend sporting events and games, but to take direct part in them themselves. The very witness, Mr. William J. Coates, who emphasised so clearly the effect of allotments on the abatement of drink and thus on the trade of public houses, also complained that bowling was another factor which, particularly in the North, kept working-class men from visiting the pub (see A. 13,412). It is the same with many games and sporting activities. When the social club, consisting of 800 employees of a firm in Leeds, organised a special sports section, it found immediately that its bar lost custom heavily (cf. Amulree Commission, A. 11,609). Playing fields, of which an increasing number have been laid out on the outskirts of towns, have helped to attract young people and to divert them from becoming regular patrons of public houses (see evidence of Mr. Charles Thomas Barton, Clerk to the Licensing Justices of Liverpool, A. 2,596; also that of Sir Chartres Biron, Chief Metropolitan Magistrate, A. 5,653: 'I think perhaps younger people amuse themselves in other and better directions . . . I think the public house has ceased to have the attraction it did have'; and of Mr. William W. Love, A. 38,154: 'Wholesome and healthy enjoyment of the younger generation in various forms of sport . . . proved a great counter-attraction to the public house'), particularly where sport and games are the activities of youth clubs (see evidence of the Chief Constable of Bristol, A. 8,546).

Public houses have acknowledged the significance of this development to their trade by themselves supplying at least some opportunities for playing games—combined of course with drink. These are mainly small games, darts and raffles. Mass Observation speaks of the 'highly organised brewers' darts league and clubs' (see *The Pub*, p. 299). There are legal restrictions to prevent games in pubs providing opportunities for gambling, but darts matches for prizes are not illegal, provided that the prizes are not presented by the brewers or the licensee who owns the premises (see Heath, op. cit., p. 21). A fully licensed house is also entitled to provide a billiard table without taking out an additional billiard licence, so long as the game is played during certain hours. All this may

[1] See also the evidence of Mr. Frank Briant, J.P., A. 30,575: 'the general improvement is due to several causes . . .' and then, *sub* (d): 'the attendance at such sport as cricket and football'.

serve to enhance the social atmosphere of the pub or club and be a particular attraction to those who do not come mainly for drink: as Mass Observation puts it, 'no pub can simply be regarded as a drinking shop'. (See op. cit., p. 311.) But games are not viewed altogether with favour by publicans because of the immediate danger that police regulations might be violated by the players and the licensee lose his licence on that score.[1]

Independent opinion differs as to the effect, on balance, of the provision of facilities for games in pubs on the consumption of drink. The Amulree Commission believed that games in public houses have a 'definite value as distractions from the mere business of drinking' (para. 239). But in general, the combination of games with drinking opportunities has been regarded by the law and by many authorities as a direct encouragement to drink.[2] In 1939 for instance the licensing bench in Glasgow decided that 'dominoes, darts and games of any kind' must no longer be played in any of the city's 1,100 pubs; the reason given was, significantly, that 'games encourage drinking'. (See Mass Observation, op. cit., p. 307.) Whichever way the balance lies, for our present purpose it may suffice that, by providing such facilities, public-house managers have clearly shown that games and sports, and similar activities and entertainments outside the drinking places, are a considerable counter-attraction which it is worth while to counteract.

SOCIAL GROUPS

While one may agree with Mass Observation's shrewd statement that 'pools, radio, press, motor culture, cinema' do not compete with the public houses and clubs in so far as they do not create 'a social group of people sharing consciously the same experience' (see *The Pub and the People*, p. 78), associations formed for the purpose of sport and games are not subject to this deficiency. They immediately create social affinities and therefore compete with the 'community' atmosphere which may develop in the working-men's public house. This factor may make them stronger competitors even than the cinema or the wireless, or even allotments and gardens.

It is precisely for the development of community feeling that all

[1] The local police have sometimes exercised functions which, as the Amulree Report stated, were not implied in statutory authority, but even then the publicans have been eager to comply with official orders; see Amulree Report, p. 55.

[2] See for an early statement: Dyson v. Mason, 1889, 22 Q.B.D., p. 356: 'If games, whether of chance or skill, are allowed to be played for money, the tendency is to encourage spending of money in drink.'

interested in new housing schemes and modern community activities, particularly attend to the provision of communal facilities. Football clubs and clubs for other types of sport, and even such specialised societies as rabbit clubs, may emerge with growing community spirit and help it to grow further.[1] New housing schemes that provide equipment for play and sport deserve extra praise. In Becontree, for instance, where the London County Council has created the biggest housing estate in the world—on 2,770 acres no fewer than 25,000 houses have been built to provide accommodation for 100,000 people—over five hundred acres are reserved as open spaces and playing fields; the central park covers 118 acres, of which 86 acres are simply broad tracts of grass in which families can picnic and play games; and there are a cricket ground, a swimming pool and a pavilion for the players. If one adds that there are not more than nine public houses in the community the potential value as a counter-attraction of these amenities and facilities becomes particularly significant. The same applies to such ventures as Welwyn Garden City in Hertfordshire (see for this and other details McAllister, op. cit., pp. 18–23). 'Space for play' has, in Mr. McAllister's words, become next important to space for family life, space for work and space for study; this has been officially recognised and as far as possible put into practice. The future may much depend on whether there will be an extension rather of Garden Cities than of Garden Suburbs; the former probably possessing greater facilities for communal activities, such as sports, which require much open space.[2]

Community centres, and health centres of the Peckham type, are clearly designed for community activity. While community centres generally provide entertainment of an aesthetic and educational nature—concerts, discussions and lectures, dances, cinema shows, etc.—health centres tend to concentrate on more games and sport as complementary to the pursuit of health, gymnastics, boxing, badminton, swimming; on the 'Home Farm' attached to the Peckham Health Centre a playing field also is available to groups of members for cricket and football (see Pearse and Crocker, op. cit., pp. 295, 395 and *passim*).

These counter-attractions manifest their effects in various ways. They may result in people, young people in particular, being

[1] See, for instance, *PEP*, op. cit., on Watling, 1947, p. 67; see also Manchester University Settlement, op. cit., pp. 8–9.

[2] See for the distinction: A. Trystan Edwards, *A Hundred New Towns?*, 1944, pp. 8–9.

definitely drawn away from drinking in favour of other enjoyment. 'It is astonishing', the Chief Constable of Cambridgeshire told the Royal Commission, 'the amount of recreation that there is in Cambridgeshire. Young fellows now instead of spending their time in public houses go in for cricket and football . . . that is a great factor contributing towards the lessening of drunkenness.' (See Amulree Commission, A. 8,821.) To say this is not to detract from other developments tending in the same direction: indeed, they are often very closely related. For instance, the interest in sport and games may well have been fostered by the official limitation of drinking hours: it seems likely, for instance, that the midday break in the opening hours of public houses has released large numbers of men, especially on Saturdays, for taking part as spectators of open-air sports who otherwise, as Wilson suggests, would have been 'soaking' for hours after leaving work (see Wilson, op. cit., p. 247).

UNDESIRABLE COUNTER-ATTRACTIONS

There are counter-attractions of more doubtful general value. It has been frequently suggested that the enormous sums spent nowadays on gambling must act as a check on drinking and thus be a definite counter-attraction. A pre-war estimate put the turnover connected with horse-racing at £250–350 million. After the beginning of the war, totalisator receipts at horse races increased from £9 million a year in 1938 to about £14 million in 1946. If, as the Conservative Political Centre suggests, bets through bookmakers increased in the same proportion, they may be tentatively estimated to have increased to between £390 and £460 million (see the Conservative Political Centre, *Enjoyment of Life*, 1948, pp. 4–5). The same group estimated that in 1946–7 receipts of football pools, at £50 million, were back to the 1938–9 figure; in 1933–4 they had been only £9 million (see ibid., p. 6). The total gambling bill in 1946 represented therefore a turnover of between £700 and £900 million. Expenditure on smoking is similarly considered as a social change which must have affected the consumption of alcoholic drink. The monthly production of cigarettes in Great Britain has increased from 3,000 million per month in 1924 to 8,100 million in 1946, despite the considerable increase in prices. Expenditure on these items has been on the increase now for many years and the trend towards greater consumption shows as yet little sign of changing.

Sums of this magnitude may well detract from the expenditure on drink. 'It is obvious', observes Wilson, 'that when allowance is made for the expenditure in gambling by non-drinkers, the large sums spent in this way must seriously compete with alcoholic liquors for a share in the very small margins in the budgets of large numbers of families of limited means.' (Op. cit., p. 354.) But perhaps this is not quite so obvious as is here assumed. For we do not know how far the money saved in the absence of gambling would actually be devoted to drink rather than to the many other 'attractions' which life offers. If we accept, as the Amulree Report suggested, that money diverted from drink is not necessarily spent on other useless purposes, but might be 'transferred to useful and productive ends' and that 'at least a useful proportion' would be 'saved or devoted to constructive purposes' (see Amulree Report, para. 103), there is no reason to conclude that the same might not happen with money diverted from gambling and betting: it need not necessarily be drink which would 'profit' from it. From a moral angle it would certainly be undesirable to regard gambling or betting or heavy smoking as a counter-attraction to the drinking habit which ought to be looked upon with favour. As was rightly observed by Sir Arthur K. Yapp in his Memorandum to the Royal Commission, even from a temperance point of view, the harm to be done 'through encouraging gambling' would far outweigh the benefit as a possible counter-attraction to drink (for a sharp criticism of 'dog racing', see Zweig, op. cit., p. 37).

While neither gambling nor smoking can be considered counter-attractions to drink worthy of encouragement just because they limit the means of expenditure on drink available to working-class people—an effect which cannot even be regarded as certain—counter-attractions which limit the time potentially devoted to drinking are a different proposition. Here the counter-attractive effect is definite: when the cinema, sport, or open-air games are 'on' time is diverted from potential drinking and visits to public houses. In times of commercial prosperity it must appear particularly doubtful to lay stress on the possible effects of the monetary factor on drink consumption and to assume that other forms of spending are bound to affect drinking. The great increase in the consumption of drink despite the rocketing in price over recent years may be taken as some confirmation of the ineffectiveness of price changes in times of prosperity: the general picture of expenditure on drink since 1939 is one of heavily increased spending, despite successive heavy increases in price.[1]

Any sort of counter-attraction which by regularly absorbing leisure time removes at least for that time the potential consumer of drink from the public house or club is likely to be far more effective. It is here that the significance of counter-attractions to the abatement of drink mainly lies. If the time factor can be so mobilised that people are led to forgo the pleasure and indulgence of drink in favour of a less obnoxious entertainment, something is clearly gained. When Lord Beveridge urges that we should not be 'complacent about our use of leisure to-day' and that 'it is no ground for complacency that the commercial cinema and the football pools reckon their "regulars" by the million, while evening classes struggle for hundreds of thousands and youth organisations compete for thousands' (see Lord Beveridge, *Voluntary Action*, 1948, p. 272), this merely emphasises the wastefulness of the drinking habit and the need for better opportunities to use leisure released by less drink for purposes other than the cinema and gambling. Some counter-attractions, such as gardening and sport, do contribute directly also to general social welfare and are particularly desirable: in contrast to such counter-attractions as gambling, betting, or smoking, they can combine the abatement of drinking with the equally desirable improvement in the general physical and productive standards of the people.

[1] See *Enjoyment of Life*, p. 3; this very point in reverse is overlooked by Wilson, p. 235, when he writes: 'A striking case of the increase in consumption due to the reduction of price is seen in the movements of beer consumption during the years 1931–2 to 1935–6. In 1930–1 the duty was 103s. per standard barrel, less rebate of 20s. per bulk barrel, with a net consumption of 25,048,000 bulk barrels; but on the increase of duty to 134s. per standard barrel with rebate, the consumption fell to 22,217,000 bulk barrels, and the next year to 18,907,000. In the Budget of 1933, the basis of taxation was changed, operating in effect as a reduction of 1d. a pint, and by the end of the financial year 1933–4 the consumption had risen to 20,945,000 bulk barrels, and 22,013,000 barrels in 1934–5.' But in 1931 trade was so depressed that there were 2,776,000 unemployed, while in 1935 trade had recovered somewhat and the unemployment figure was down to 1,858,000. Surely this development significantly influenced the consumption of drink quite apart from any reduction in price.

CHAPTER IX

THE TEMPERANCE MOVEMENT

THE abatement of drinking has not usually been the primary object of the moderating influences and counter-attractions discussed in the previous chapter; often it has been merely a by-product of the pursuit of other social aims, and occasionally an unintentional result. This does not detract from their value, and movements concerned more directly with combating the evil have not failed to encourage trends that have indirectly had this desired effect. But their main efforts are concentrated on furthering knowledge about the problem of drink, on persuading people wholly to abstain, and on promoting legislation to restrict the consumption of drink.

The temperance movement tries to achieve voluntarily, by mere moral suasion, what legislation would attempt by means of prohibition: once a person abstains from the consumption of drink of his own will the immediate effect is much the same as if prohibition had rendered alcohol unavailable. The temperance movement or any movement which leads to abstention through moral suasion is therefore more comprehensive in its scope and more complete in its effect on the individual than any legislation based on partial restriction only. Legislation restricts the individual's freedom to drink and affects the whole population in this limited way: the only criterion for success in moral suasion is the abatement of drinking as a step towards the ultimate goal of total and general abstention.

The distinction between voluntary abstention and legal restriction has never been very strictly recognised by historians of the temperance movements. No doubt the temperance movements have always had this double function in mind: to influence the individual by suasion and education on the one hand, and to support legislation restricting the consumption of drink on the other. The latter function became more distinct as the movements grew in numerical strength and public recognition, and began to make sustained attempts to influence international opinion and, through this, react on national legislation. But this connection does not alter the fact that the temperance movement is in the first instance based on persuading the individual to keep voluntarily away from drink. One can hardly agree therefore with those who range early anti-drink legislation within the scope of the temperance movements. This has been done, for instance, in the otherwise excellent article by D. W. McConnell in the American *Encyclopædia of the Social Sciences* (see vol. XIV, 1935). Though we will follow him and fellow historians a little in their analysis, we shall try to bear in mind the distinction between the trends towards voluntary abstention and legislative restriction.

McConnell points out that 'temperance movements are almost as old in the history of humanity as the use of intoxicating drinks . . . the Chinese assert that as early as the eleventh century B.C., one of their emperors ordered all the vines in the kingdom to be uprooted'. Earlier, the laws of Hammurabi, whose reign in Babylon is estimated to have been around 2000 B.C., contain very drastic regulations as to wine drinkers; one of them lays down that 'if a priestess who has not remained in the sacred building shall open a wine shop, or enter a wine shop for drink, that woman shall be burned'.[1] This seems therefore to indicate that legislators considered wine shops as something more or less immoral, or, at any rate, not compatible with the life of the religious orders, merely one indication of the close interrelation early in history of the drink problem with religious and moral ideals which has been described in great detail and with much care by E. C. Urwin.[2] The impulse to agitate for the restriction of drink emanated from strong philosophical and ethical forces and these always tried to influence legislation in their favour. The early Greek conception of 'temperance' sprang largely from such broader principles as the conquest of passion and desire by reason and will. The Hebrew conception was that sobriety was ordered by Divine Law (see Urwin, pp. 11 and 22–3). The word 'temperance' does not occur in its modern meaning anywhere in the Old Testament.

The temperance movement of our days should not be considered as a mere continuation of movements which existed as far back as our knowledge of history goes. But in its case the close religious con-

[1] See Chilperic Edwards, *The Oldest Laws in the World*, 1906, p. 19 and *passim*.

[2] See E. C. Urwin, *The Teaching of Temperance and Self-Control*, 1938; see in particular ch. i, 'The Background of Greek Morality'.

nection persists. In this it must be distinguished from legislative action which also sprang in earlier periods mainly from philosophical and moral grounds, but is prompted in our days by immediate practical social and economic considerations. To say this is not to ignore that temperance has many motives in common with compulsory measures, but to stress their basic difference of approach. It is not of the essence of the temperance movements, for instance, that there was some temporary agitation at their earliest beginnings in America, which had compulsory as well as voluntary features, or that the advocates of drink reform stressed the compulsory aspects by seeking to pass laws prohibiting the manufacture and the sale of alcoholic beverages (see McConnell, op. cit., p. 569). The one aim did not in principle exclude the other then; and it does not exclude it to-day. But it would place the movement in the wrong perspective to consider both as of the same significance. As the prospects of prohibition have faded, and as, on the other hand, it has become evident that non-prohibitionist legal action could only partly solve the problem of excessive drink, the voluntary character of the movements operating with dissuasion has become ever more pronounced. In his preface to Sir. H. M. Vernon's book, the late Lord D'Abernon emphasised that 'for 300 years statesmen and reformers devised remedies for the abuse of alcoholic liquor', but that most of these remedies were declined by public opinion; that 'those that were adopted proved ineffective'; and that 'nothing short of abolition' then seemed to provide the remedy (see H. M. Vernon, op. cit., pp. v–vi, preface). Since abolition must be ruled out for all immediate practical purposes, as we shall see in more detail later, the conclusion should be drawn that moral suasion with the aim of effecting abstention by voluntary action has not only not lost significance, through the growth of legal action, but must have been enhanced in importance by the limited effect of compulsory measures.

THE RELIGIOUS CONNECTIONS OF TEMPERANCE

The strong connection between the temperance movement and religious bodies is a little confused by dating the beginning of the temperance movement to the year 1785 when Benjamin Rush published in Philadelphia his essay on 'An Enquiry into the Effects of Ardent Spirits upon the Human Body and Mind' (see Elster, op. cit., p. 230). The 'movements' began much later and from a largely religious background: they started in the first half of the nineteenth century, first in America, Ireland, and England, and then spread in the thirties as a great movement over Continental Europe. The Independent Order of Good Templars, founded in Utica, New York, in 1851, soon expanded to Canada and England, and then to the Scandinavian countries (see McConnell, op. cit.). In 1852 the International Order of Good Templars was founded; it began its work in Germany in 1883. The international character of the movement found its first comprehensive expression in the World Prohibition Conference in London in 1909. When in 1895 in the United States the Anti-Saloon League was founded, fully 3,000 churches co-operated. McConnell emphasises that, in some respects, it is the 'alliance with the Churches which made the temperance movement most effective'.

One of the earliest movements in England, pioneered by the famous pledge of the Seven Men of Preston and the foundation of the Preston Temperance Society, became very distinguished in 1847 when the Band of Hope Movement was started through the inspiration of Mrs. Carlisle, a devoted social worker among children in Dublin, and the Rev. Jabez Tunnicliffe, an ardent champion of temperance. Within a generation, the movement of Preston had caught the imagination of the Churches, and between 1860 and 1880 Denominational Committees, Baptist and Methodist, made their appearance, and the Church of England Temperance Society began its career under the leadership of Bishop Temple (see Urwin, pp. 61–2). Cardinal Manning became a champion of temperance in Roman Catholicism, following on the early lead of Ireland in the growth of temperance in the British Isles (see McConnell, op. cit.). The Church of England Temperance Society, founded in 1862, was reconstituted in 1873. It based its activities in connection with alcoholic temperance on the fundamental principle of total abstinence, and set itself, as it still does, the special tasks generally furthering the following objects: the promotion of habits of temperance, the reformation of the intemperate, and the removal of the causes which lead to intemperance. Its policy 'is a Christian spirit to reform drinking habits and customs' (see *Official Yearbook of the Church of England*, 1948).

Other movements promoting temperance in Britain have sprung from the side of friendly societies as a specific counteraction to the drinking customs that had developed at the regular meetings of clubs and benefit societies on licensed premises, where a sum was spent on drink 'for the good of the house' in lieu of rent. Temperance benefit societies offering benefits in case of sickness, accident and at death were formed to enrol abstainers. But they also had religious counteractions. The Independent Order of the Rechabites founded in 1835[1] is an outstanding example, and its relation to religious conceptions was immediately clear from the name alone.[2]

The chief political fighting organisation in the temperance movement in Britain, the United Kingdom Alliance, was founded as early as 1852. It has as its object the general prohibition of the drink trade, but has adopted the policy of local prohibition by means of option, to which we shall devote some comment in a later chapter. In contrast to the purely religious organisations, the Alliance is mainly concerned with the political issues as far as they relate to the abatement of drink. It has always proclaimed that its methods are the 'education of the people as to the nature of alcohol, and as to the moral, social, economic and political effects of its sale, distribution and consumption as a beverage': in the declaration of its principles, the attack on alcoholic drink as a 'traffic or system that tends to increase crime, to waste the national resources, to corrupt social habits, and to destroy the health and lives of the people' is exclusively stressed (see *Alliance Yearbook for 1947*, p. 9). But the moral and religious aspect is always in the background and, conversely, the Churches have not failed to acknowledge the services which the Alliance rendered to their own aims. 'To the action and the power of the Alliance', said Cardinal Manning, 'is to be ascribed the fact that the public conscience of England has been aroused, its intellect has been convinced, and its heart has been made half-ashamed of itself, and its will is already in motion' (see ibid., p. 8).

The close alliance of the temperance movement with the Churches finds its most prominent structural expression to-day in the Temperance Council of the Christian Churches, which is a federation of the Temperance Executives of all the Churches—the Church of England, the Roman Catholic Church, and all sections of the Free Churches, that is to say, all the major sections, including the Society of Friends, and the Salvation Army (see Amulree Commission, A. 27,875 and 27,876 for more details).

[1] See for this and for many interesting details of the historical development of the temperance movement, Henry Carter, *The English Temperance Movement*, 1933, p. 73 and *passim*.

[2] See Urwin, op. cit., p. 25: the Rechabites 'in the fear of God' had accepted the restrictions to abstain from wine, and to have no vineyard, see Jer. xxxv, 1–10.

There is also a Parliamentary Temperance Committee linked up with the national temperance organisations (see ibid., A. 25,128).

It is particularly important to recall the religious background of activity towards temperance in the English-speaking countries to avoid the apparently obvious interpetations of the fact that temperance movements have been strongest in the countries where also the use and abuse of alcoholic liquor has been notoriously prominent. It may, indeed, be that the strong temperance movement in America and Britain was due to the obvious prevalence of excessive drinking. But it must be remembered—this is particularly important in trying to make a proper assessment of moral suasion—that the religious convictions of these countries were anyhow favourable to a crusade against insobriety. It is true that the movement has also been strong in Ireland. But Protestantism, and in particular Calvinism and Neo-Calvinism, were by their very religious characteristics better prepared to fight alcoholism on moral grounds than Catholicism. The doctrines and also the practices of the latter have not been as strongly opposed as Puritanism to the enjoyment of the people. It may be recalled that Archbishop Laud, whose moral ideals were certainly nearer to the Catholic tradition than to the Nonconformist reformation, recognised the 'Book of Sports' in answer to the Puritan attacks on local pleasures, especially in Lancashire. The Puritan view that pleasure-seeking was unlawful and work the 'true' and 'godly' pleasure was widely accepted in the eighteenth century. In a typical eighteenth-century pamphlet admonishing craftsmen of their religious duties one reads: 'In some popish countries there is what they call a carnival; that is, a number of days or weeks in which they give themselves all loose to all kinds of sorts of riot and excess, and which they, with amazing ignorance and superstition, consider as a sort of compensation for a season of extraordinary mortification, which they are soon to enter upon.' The very idea of such festivity was abhorrent to Protestantism, yet the carnival, and even the 'Corpus Christi' day (Fronleichnam) tradition, with its extraordinary consumption of beer and wine, still persists unabated in the Catholic parts of Germany, in particular Bavaria and the Rhineland.[1] It should be realised that Catholicism did

[1] See for more details of the influence of Puritanism on enjoyment, Hermann Levy, *Economic Liberalism*, 1913, pp. 66–7. The pamphlet quoted is *The Religious Weaver*, 1773, p. 87. Lately the point has been successfully tackled by Dr. Klara Vontobel in her fascinating study, *Das Arbeitsethos des Deutschen Protestantismus* (*The Ethics of Work in German Protestantism*), Berlin, 1946. Dr. Vontobel tries to show that Catholicism took

not, of course, encourage drinking, and was not uninterested in its general abatement; and later periods showed it, as Cardinal Manning's statement proves, in full accord with temperance. But Protestantism, and Puritanism in particular, showed the way. The zealot Puritan Philip Stubbes may be taken as typical: in his famous *Anatomie of Abuses* of 1583, he deprecated strongly the manners of the countryside including 'church-ales' and general drunken jollifications on Sundays.[1]

The strong emphasis on methodical moral discipline and behaviour in Protestantism provided a fertile ground for all preaching of temperance. One may agree with E. C. Urwin's fine observation that mediaeval and post-mediaeval Catholicism often forgot its early ideals, which had also embraced the rules of Christian self-control and found their best expression in monastic poverty, chastity and obedience, and that 'Puritanic discipline was a Protestant counterpart of Catholic monasticism, and the regulated life to which Quaker and Methodist submitted themselves exhibited the attractive power of this virtue of temperance' (see Urwin, op. cit., p. 35).

The driving force was religious in an all-embracing sense. For instance, Protestantism had developed a conception of the 'ethics of work' into which temperance and abstention from bodily excesses fitted well. In contrast to Catholicism, it included honest profit in its concept of the truly religious man; its 'spirit of rational regular discipline in work', as Troeltsch has called it (see Levy, *Economic Liberalism*, op. cit., p. 57) opposed everything which might undermine labour and efficiency. Religion was thus used in support of economic development.[2] As Professor Tawney observes in a chapter devoted to the interrelation of Puritanism and trade, 'the good Christian was not wholly dissimilar from the economic man'. Once it was agreed that it was within the teaching of Christian religion to promote thrift and the accumulation of honestly acquired wealth for the benefit of the individual and the state, it became the duty of the preachers to assail everything that

---

little interest in what people were doing in their leisure time, whereas Protestantism tried to devise methodical ways by which both work and leisure could be morally influenced (see Vontobel, pp. 84–6). Thus Protestantism was from the beginning anxious to exclude drinking from the enjoyment of leisure.

[1] See Philip Stubbes, *Anatomie of Abuses*, 1583, republished by the Shakespeare Society, p. 140; see also for an interesting description of 'Puritanism and Amusement' Joseph Corough, *Puritanism and Art*, 1910, ch. x and *passim*.

[2] See R. H. Tawney, *Religion and the Rise of Capitalism*, Pelican edition, 1938, whole chapter iv (iii), 'The Puritan Movement', 'The Triumph of Economic Virtues'.

could detract people from this overriding object. Clearly one of these evil influences was drinking; and preachers and religious teachers generally felt called upon to further its abatement. Lay writers propagating the economic gospel of 'thrift' gladly accepted this help from the religious side. Samuel Smiles, in *Thrift*, quotes approvingly a chaplain who, after characterising drunkenness as the 'Great Sin', declared: 'It still rises in savage hostility against everything allied to order and religion; it still barricades every avenue by which truth and peace seek to enter the poor man's home and heart. . . . Whatever may be the predominant cause of crime, it is very clear that ignorance, religious ignorance, is the chief ingredient in the character of the criminal. This combines with the passion for liquor, and offences numberless are engendered by the union' (see Smiles, *Thrift* as cited above, pp. 68–9; see also Tawney, op. cit., p. 227: 'It was not that religion was expelled from practical life, but that religion itself gave it a foundation of granite. In that keen atmosphere of economic enterprise, the ethics of the Puritan bore some resemblance to those associated later with the name of Smiles').

The close alliance between religious ideals and the rational aims of improving the social life and the economic development of the nation, thus emerges clearly from any analysis of the temperance movement. The great chronicler of the temperance movement, Henry Carter, has come to no other conclusion that that 'the true objective of the Temperance reformer is moral' (see op. cit., p. 248). In the same spirit E. C. Urwin emphasises (see Urwin, op. cit., p. 92) that the 'virtue of sobriety' represents one of the ideals of 'the rounded and complete idea of a life of self-control over appetite and desire, carrying with it reverence for the body as the instrument of the spirit, and brought under the conception of utter devotion to the service of God and man'.

With religion as the sincere and undoubtedly the most profound source from which the temperance movement has sprung, it will be understood all the better that religious reformers of alcoholism have regarded the function of legislation as contributory only and as an imperfect means to the genuine end. In their opinion moral suasion is and remains the fundamental starting-point of any move towards the abatement of drinking: 'As the basis of personal conviction broadens, as the sense of social responsibility deepens, so progress in the legislative realm becomes practicable', Henry Carter urges, and adds that 'it is a fundamental error' to reverse this order of factors (see Carter, op. cit., p. 248). The campaign of moral suasion, initiated originally by Joseph Livesey (see Carter, p. 44) remains linked up, just as far as the temperance movements are linked up, with religious or semi-religious bodies.

THE CONTRIBUTION OF SCIENCE

Lately two factors have arisen which are likely to draw interest away from moral suasion as the fundamental and focal factor for the abatement of drinking. The first, already known to the reader, is the medical and medico-social analysis of the drink problem. We have paid some attention in the first chapter to the great progress in our knowledge of the medical, psycho-physical and, lately, psychosomatic factors as they affect alcoholism.[1] As was to be expected, this development raises the question of how far scientific enlightenment can replace the spiritual guidance hitherto given by the temperance movement and the Churches in particular. To the movements concerned with the abatement of drinking by moral suasion, the position of science is clear: they have from their very first beginnings recognised the great significance of scientific elucidation. J. Livesey, in his famous 'Malt Lecture' of 1828, which is considered as a starting-point of the total abstinence movement in Britain, claimed that one of the causes of intemperance was 'ignorance' and emphasised that, by the efforts of the temperance advocates, 'the ignorance long existing respecting the properties of ardent spirits is in a great measure removed'.[2] The temperance movement has accepted 'science' as the 'new ally'. E. C. Urwin has devoted a whole chapter to this point in his recent study on the teaching of temperance (see Urwin, op. cit., ch. vi, pp. 68–79): he speaks of the 'cumulative effect of moral conviction and scientific fact'.

But, while the temperance movement has never failed to make use of scientific knowledge, medicine and pathology have paid little attention to the potential effects of moral suasion on the alcoholic. There is no mention of moral guidance as an assistance to the doctor in his task in that great study on the *Action of Alcohol on Man*; and the connection still awaits the considered opinion of medical men and psychologists. Shall we in future regard alcoholism perhaps exclusively as a pathological condition, as the effect of

[1] As to the psychosomatic factors see a very illuminating recent article by A. A. Carver, M.A., M.D., D.P.M., 'Alcoholism from the Psychosomatic point of view' in the *British Journal of Addiction*, January 1948, pp. 38 sqq.

[2] See J. Livesey, *A Temperance Lecture based on the Teetotal Principle; including an exposure of the Central Delusion as to the Properties of Alcohol*, ed. 1840, p. 33.

disease rather than its cause—and thus its abatement as the job of the doctor rather than that of the preacher? Maybe 'the alcoholist is, before he even touches a drop, an abnormal person'. But Dr. A. E. Carver, who has written authoritatively on many medical aspects of the drink problem[1] and in particular devoted much valuable study to the basic psychology of the alcoholist and to biological factors in the idiosyncrasies of alcoholic effects, quotes with approval the observations of Professor J. T. McCurdy on the importance of the moral element (see Carver, op. cit., p. 47): once an addict-personality has got the affliction under control, 'his only hope of keeping it so is to remain a lifelong total abstainer. Any attempt to become an ordinary moderate drinker leads inevitably to relapse. . . . This shows that a perverse constitutional factor can remain latent and under control and yet ready to be reactivated if its appropriate irritant be not avoided. Ignoring or refusing to accept this fact is in my experience the commonest cause of relapse.' As regards medical treatment of the alcoholic, it is also clear, as Dr. Walter Masters, medical superintendent of a home for inebriates (the Hare Nursing Home, Chislehurst), states in company with numerous doctors, 'for the treatment to be at all effective and permanent, there must be a sincere desire for a cure in the patient.'[2] Putting this condition into practice, some institutions go as far as to refuse to accept a patient for treatment unless this condition—the desire to get cured—is fulfilled, since they believe that failure 'is inevitable without the full co-operation of the patient'. The Voluntary Homes for the Inebriates have to admit many failures and these are largely from that group who never intend to be cured (see ibid., p. 148). It is significant that therapeutic methods used at Caldecote Hall attempt to distinguish between (1) Psychological treatment, (2) General Physical treatment, and (3) Medicinal treatment, and that Dr. Carver observes in connection with the first that, if the patient does not genuinely 'desire a cure, the proper thing for him to do is to admit this and take his departure' (see Alfred E. A. Carver, M.A., M.D., D.P.M., *Modern Treatment of the Inebriate*, publication of the Church of England Temperance Society, n.d., p. 8; see also the Prospectus of Caldecote Hall, n.d., and the list of publications on institutional treatment given therein on p. 2).

[1] See e.g. A. E. Carver, T. Hunt and William Wilcox, *Alcoholism in General Practice*, 1936.

[2] See Dr. Walter E. Masters, *The Alcoholic Habit and its Treatment*, London, 1931, p. 113, see also p. 114.

Moral suasion has a very proper place in inducing the desire for cure and in making cure permanent. Dr. Carvér recognised this in his lecture on the psychosomatic aspects of alcoholism. First, he emphasised again and again that patients must recognise that 'a satisfactory issue out of their troubles, assuming they wish it, can only be achieved if they themselves co-operate whole-heartedly with their therapist. Assuming, on the other hand, that the patient does not wish it sufficiently to make a determined effort, the wishes and work of others will be unavailing' (see Carver, op. cit., p. 58); he then contended that 'the earlier the perverse trend is discovered and tackled in all its ramifications the better the chance for cure'; and finally he explained that the often repeated aphorism, 'prevention is better than cure', carried weight here as in other connections, and that the Band of Hope movement, with its great educational efforts, to which we shall revert later, was 'a most admirable institute for treating [*sic*] alcoholism on these lines': it helps the young, for instance, to 'adjust themselves in body, soul and spirit'. Dr. Carver stressed that 'the medical profession misses much of this preventive side, partly because it is not called in early enough, but partly because of its adhesion to the either-or attitude'. In conclusion, Dr. Carver again emphasised the desirability of considering the 'afflicted organism as a whole' and deprecated the 'either-or' attitude (see ibid., p. 62) of considering the evil of drink as a 'sin' or as a purely physical or psychological matter.

In short, the scientific approach by no means excludes the moral. On the contrary, the approaches are complementary, and medicine should regard moral suasion in the same way as moral suasion considers scientific knowledge, namely as an ally in a common task. Medicine leaves no doubt that willpower, e.g., to reduce the drinking habit, plays an essential initial part in any cure. The psychologist may have an important part to play in this connection. But as long as willpower may be influenced by religion and moral means these remain of considerable importance, and even the psychologist with his own methods of influencing the mind may gratefully accept the help of moral suasion.

Yet moral suasion is not the task of the psychologist, but that of the preacher and the teacher. If the clergyman can successfully persuade a person indulging in too much drink to regard this as an evil from the moral point of view and, if his willpower is not yet sufficient, to seek advice and treatment from a doctor or psychiatrist, moral suasion has initiated the first step towards the application of modern science to the alcoholic. The next step—to the doctor, the therapist, the psychologist or the inebriate home—may then follow. In his Kerr Memorial Lecture, Professor D. K. Henderson observed: 'It has only been in comparatively recent years that psychological components, the drive of the instincts and emotions, have received much attention. Now we know that in assessing any case it is not only unwise but misleading to divorce the psychological from the physiological, the constitutional from the environmental.' (Quoted by Carver, op. cit., p. 39.) This being so, moral suasion is useful wherever the alcoholic is open to it, and should remain medicine's ally; it is for the priest and clergyman to remodel it for this in the light of modern science. Norman Kerr once said that 'in drunkenness of all degrees and every variety, the Church sees only the sin; the World, the vice; the State, the crime. On the other hand, the medical profession discovers a condition of disease.' (See Masters, op. cit., p. 119.) It seems to be time that such partial approaches, which may even lead to opposing attitudes to a joint problem, be replaced by a conception recognising the interrelation of all these factors and seeking their proper co-ordination. In this complex approach moral suasion will play a part perhaps even more important than in the past.

Sociology and the social sciences in general are a recent but already important ally in the fight against drink and drunkenness. There was little systematic knowledge of society at the time when temperance movements began to be formed: for evidence on the impact of alcoholic excess the movements had to rely, as we have seen, on chance exhibition and general impressions from daily life; and these individual examples of the evils of insobriety were always liable to be interpreted as instances merely of exceptional circumstances, possibly exaggerated by the ardent enthusiasts for temperance. This weakness largely persists. But as we have seen, the increased body of social knowledge, increasingly supported by statistics, puts generalisations about the effects of drink on an increasingly sound basis: the effects are shown to recur, and to recur frequently. The collection of private budgets, for instance, was recognised immediately as of importance to the promotion of temperance and no recent study of the drink problem has ignored this valuable source of knowledge.[1] As an example of this, the

[1] See Elster, op. cit., pp. 218–20, for numerous instances of the use of this knowledge in Germany.

Yearbook of the United Kingdom Alliance is full of statistical information, and the Temperance Council of the Christian Churches publishes an annual survey of 'opinions, facts and figures for the use of Preachers and Speakers', in preparation for Temperance Sunday.[2] That the London Diocesan Church of England Temperance Society reprinted in 1941 the 'Drink' chapter of the *New London Survey* for popular distribution is an indication of the importance attached by the temperance movement to the knowledge gained through sociological research.

THE EDUCATION OF YOUNG PEOPLE

The education of young people probably provides the most profitable field for the use of the growing medical, psychological and sociological knowledge of the effects of drink: the dangers are then made known before the habit is likely to be acquired and the knowledge can have a cumulative effect through succeeding generations. Attempts to promote such education have again been earliest in Britain and America. Leaving out of consideration whether they were made by voluntary bodies or by the State, education for temperance began to be systematically promoted in England in the thirties of the last century; in Germany, Belgium, France, Sweden, Norway and Finland this did not happen before 1900 (see Elster, op. cit., p. 229). The early educational efforts in England were closely connected with the temperance movement, of which they have continued to form a part. The 1830's were the period of the worst social conditions of modern times and marked the height of excessive alcoholic indulgence by the working classes. It was then that a great army of mainly unpaid enthusiasts under the guidance of Joseph Livesey and others worked among adults and young people to win adherents to temperance (see Wilson, op. cit., p. 256). In 1847, in all the distress of the 'hungry forties', the Band of Hope movement started; it was extended in 1855 to become the United Kingdom Band of Hope Union (see Waters, op. cit., p. 72). For the first decades the educational functions of the United Kingdom Band of Hope were based more on moral suasion than on scientific enlightenment. Scientific instruction was not given until 1889. That year, the United Kingdom Band of Hope Union inaugurated a more comprehensive scheme of instruction and appointed a number of qualified teachers to visit schools, with the consent of the then

[2] See e.g. 26th Annual Issue on 'The Drink Problem', published by the Temperance Council of the Christian Churches, October 1947.

existing School Boards (see Amulree Commission, A. 29,371 (1–2)). By 1930 its Director of Education, Mr. Thomas G. James, explained to the Amulree Commission that the Union sent periodically approved lesson books to the schools for the use of teachers, arranged conferences of teachers, and appointed its own lecturers, who were, he said, 'skilled and well-informed teachers' and 'not ill-informed, wild, narrow-minded cranks' (see ibid., *sub* 13). He stressed the appreciation of science by the Band of Hope movement: 'The lectures, based upon fully established scientific facts—well illustrated—afford a valuable hygienic guidance, help to build up a sober, healthy race, make for industrial and physical efficiency. . . . The scholars have placed before them the nature and effects of alcohol in the most interesting and forceful way.' The tendency of the movement to develop the scientific side was forcibly backed by the medical profession. Upon the inauguration of the new instruction scheme of 1889 the *Lancet* wrote: 'We wish it every success. There is no doubt that the best hope of greater temperance in this country is the encouragement of total abstinence in the young, who do not need stimulants and are much better without them.'

The progress, particularly, of medical science, greatly influenced action by the State. In 1902 the Board of Education managed to formulate a limited scheme for the regulation of temperance teaching in the face of considerable opposition. In 1903, 14,918 members of the medical profession presented a petition to the Board urging the importance of giving systematic temperance instruction in all schools. In 1904 a Committee on Physical Deterioration (see *Inter-Departmental Committee on Physical Deterioration*, 1904 *passim*) reported that in order to enable them to give sound instruction in the schools and thus to check the fatal effects of drinking on physical efficiency, the practical training of teachers was important. In 1909, the Board issued a syllabus for the teaching of temperance and hygiene in schools. But it was not until 1920 that the Board recommended as a more positive step 'that temperance should be regarded as a separate and distinct subject in the curriculum of elementary schools'. Following the issue of an enlarged and comprehensive syllabus in that year, the Board made a definite recommendation 'that Local Education Authorities should take such steps as were practicable to give temperance an appropriate place in the curriculum of their schools' (see Commission, 29,371 (5)).

The new syllabus embodied the main conclusions of the Alcoholic Investigation Committee of the Medical Research Council and contained the latest scientific knowledge on the subject. It became the obligatory basis of all temperance teaching given in the schools; it marked an important stage in the development of a comprehensive scheme of education in hygiene, and was unquestionably a great step forward in the provision of up-to-date information about alcohol and its effects on man. After its inception, the Board of Education frequently called attention to the importance of instruction in this subject in successive publications (see, e.g., *Handbook of Suggestions on Health Education*, 1928, pp. 34–35). 'Boys and girls', it urged, 'should receive appropriate instruction as part of their general training in health, in the dangers of the misuse of alcoholic drinks, in the current fallacies about the alleged benefits of alcohol, in the results of some of the simpler modern investigations showing its influence on different kinds of people and work, and in the inestimable advantage of sobriety to the individual and the nation. The teaching should be based on the ground of health and fitness, efficiency in work and play, manly self-control, consideration of others and good workmanship.'

The Board of Education's statement was an excellent formulation of the ideal for which the voluntary youth temperance movement had been and still is fighting. The Central Council for Health Education which has so efficiently and successfully worked for the propagation of positive health has unfortunately not yet thought it appropriate to publish on similarly broad lines its own recommendations on the teaching of anti-alcoholic knowledge to youth. Whatever view one may take with regard to instruction on positive health rather than in preventing ill-health—not even medical authorities are altogether agreed on the choice, and it is by no means certain that the two approaches are alternative—there can be no doubt that excessive consumption of alcoholic drink must be regarded as a danger to health, and that is likely to start with a modest indulgence.

We do not know yet how the new Education Act will in practice affect the question. But we may note with appreciation that the Second Report of the Central Advisory Council for Education (England), published in 1948 under the authoritative chairmanship of Professor Sir Fred Clarke, stressed the significance of what 'voluntary organisations have for some time recognised', namely the need for better opportunities for leisure-time activities for young people. It recommended that they should be encouraged to continue the good work which they had begun.[1] 'There are now many organisations, and in great variety, designed to provide for children and young people just this kind of out-of-school training. We would wish them to receive all possible encouragement and support, for not only do they provide healthy outlets for juvenile interests and propensities, they also contribute substantially to the influences making for depth and steadfastness of character.' The Band of Hope movement is one of these: it has consistently supported leisure-time activities. The reading room and the handicrafts room, for instance, are nowadays usual supplementary channels for its teaching among the young people. (See Taylor, *The Hope of the Race*, p. 89.)

DEFICIENCIES OF EDUCATION

Yet the results of all these educational efforts seem far from reassuring. The Amulree Commission was little satisfied even as regards the extent of the teaching. It appeared that teaching on the basis of the Board of Education syllabus was given in a majority of the primary schools in England and Wales, but only in a small proportion of the schools for older children. The services of temperance lecturers were appreciated, but not considered as sufficient (see Amulree Report, pp. 146–8). The Report made it definitely clear that every child ought to receive 'specific and systematic' instruction as to the properties of alcohol as it affected health and that this should be regarded as quite routine to the teaching of health in schools. It was urged that 'every possible step' should be taken to attain the aim of complete and comprehensive instruction in the matter in every school. Yet the Report did not see its way to suggest anything so drastic as making the syllabus compulsory for all children: it considered it wiser 'to leave teachers free'. But it recommended that the Board of Education inspectors should enquire of each school they visited the extent to which instruction on the basis of the syllabus was carried out. There was emphasis also on the need for adequate instruction on the subject in teachers' training colleges: so much obviously depended on the adequacy of this. And the subject was deemed important enough to be mentioned as one of the seven chief recommendations the Report had to offer (see ibid., para. 110 (vii)).

[1] See Ministry of Education, *Out of School*, the Second Report of the Central Advisory Council for Education (England), 1948, pp. 14–15 and p. 22.

A decade later, in 1942, Mass Observation asked its panel of 1,500 'observers' to outline the history of their own attitudes to drinking and the formation of drinking habits, and also incidentally about the attitudes of their parents and generally at home. Only a third troubled to mention their schools, and of these only an eighth mentioned that any form of specific instruction had been given. Expressed statistically the results were (see *Juvenile Drinking*, 1943, p. 20):

No mention of school's attitude ..	67 per cent
No teaching on subject	28 ,,
Some instruction, including visiting teacher	4 ,,
Instruction outside school hours, in Scouts	1 ,,
	100

Even if it could be assumed that the great majority of those who did not mention their school's attitude merely failed to recall that the school had any strong attitude in the matter—this was one of the specific suggestions for inclusion in replies—this would barely improve the results. The Report gave a great number of examples from the evidence taken. They showed that in many cases the attitude of the teachers had been either indifferent and sometimes, indirectly, even encouraging (ibid., p. 22): e.g., '. . . some masters considered that they were connoisseurs of vintage, and others deplored the fact that the practice of serving small beer to the boys had been discontinued for generations'; 'in the VIth form, when staff and pupils meet on friendlier terms still, drinking was regarded—when it was ever thought of, which was rarely—as a pleasant entertainment for those who wanted to enjoy it'; 'I don't remember my school making any statements on drink, but it was more or less connived at on certain communal drinking occasions of pupils'; 'school never expressed any violent opinion, but pubs were never out of bounds at school camps . . .'; 'first introduction was at school, when a party of us had some beer one night at a scout camp . . .'

It is true of course that all educational efforts, and particularly those sponsored officially, have been subjected to heavy and effective opposition from the powerful trade interests to whom their aim can only be anathema; we shall discuss this in some detail later. It is true also that as long as heavy drinking persists outside school, the effects of school education are bound to be limited. As one of Mass Observation's reporters pointed out (see *Juvenile Drinking*, p. 21), 'Consumption of liquor was forbidden in school, and we were not allowed in pubs. Consequently, pub-crawling on the sly was a popular occupation, nicely tempered with excitement. . . . We pub-crawled, not in order to drink beer, but in order to enter the strange and forbidden fairy-land tavern, where the lights were bright and the inmates most extraordinary.'

But some of the deficiencies are definitely in the schools and in the teaching. Particularly significant perhaps are those that arise from the failure to adjust the syllabus and the methods of teaching to new knowledge. As the oldest in this field, the temperance movements themselves are in greatest need of modernisation. While the temperance movements showed early that they considered science as their ally in the field of the enlightenment of youth as in others, the task of harmoniously harnessing both the religious and the scientific drives to the same purpose has presented many difficulties. Again, a writer so favourably disposed to the temperance movement as Urwin emphasises (see Urwin, op. cit., pp. 97–98) that there is great need for some modernisation of methods of instruction: ' . . . workers in the Band of Hope movement might well revise their methods, and learn something from the approach of other organisations to youth. The traditional programme of temperance songs, recitations and dialogues has become threadbare; nor is it essential to have a weekly meeting.' From its latest development it seems that the Movement, which 'is dynamic with imminent reorganisation', is in the process of taking such suggestions to heart: the fundamental principles remain intact; it is aiming at 'modernising' its methods by condensing the devotional part of the sessions in favour of the educational part and by expanding its teaching activities over new fields in which temperance propaganda sees a chance for success.[1]

THE SUCCESS OF TEMPERANCE MOVEMENTS

It is impossible to assess even approximately the total effects of the temperance movement on the abatement of drink: but it is certainly very great and dwarfs the deficiencies. Before the Amul-

[1] See Taylor, op. cit., p. 87, ch. xiii on 'The Modern Band of Hope'; 'Long prayers are taboo'; see also whole ch. xii, 'Things that change and things that remain'.

ree Commission, Mr. George Bailey Wilson estimated the increase in the number of abstainers during the first thirty years of the century at 7,000,000 (see A. 25,641–2). During that period there was a great increase in the membership of temperance organisations and there have been further increases since. The adult membership of the Rechabites, for instance, increased from 168,000 in 1900 to 769,000 in 1935, and their juvenile members from 100,000 to over 300,000; and the adult membership of the Sons of Temperance increased from 50,000 to 253,000 and their juvenile members from 21,000 to 63,000. When the Band of Hope celebrated its fifty years' jubilee its proud achievement was a membership of over 3,000,000 children who were now the members of the movement and the expansion from one society in Leeds to 26,355 societies in the United Kingdom.[1] Even during the second World War, despite evacuations and dislocations of people, the movement was greatly alive; for instance, no less than 151,732 scholars and 4,306 teachers attended its lectures during 1944–5 (see Taylor, op. cit., pp. 49–51).

The numbers of people affected by temperance teaching is of course much larger than the formal membership of the movement. The number of those who, directly or indirectly through moral suasion, have become more moderate drinkers, if not total abstainers, will never be known. For them, direct moral suasion has taken the form of teaching and instruction in and out of school. Indirectly the movement has played a great part behind the scenes, for instance in the attempts to reduce accidents in industry and on the roads, and openly, as a vigorous protagonist for the promotion of restrictive legislation.

TEMPERANCE ORGANISATIONS

Britain is the country for clubs, and there are numerous organisations of one kind or another which have the promotion of temperance as one of their objects. With some, the interest in temperance seems to have been swamped in the pursuit of other aims; working men's clubs seem to be among these. They date from 1862 when the Working Men's Club and Institute Union was founded, and their chronicler, Mr. B. T. Hall, claims that these clubs have done

[1] See Robert Taylor, *The Hope of the Race*, 1946, p. 55 for many interesting details of the movement.

more for temperance than any other agency existent among adults.[1] But the original idea to set up institutes for working men in which the consumption of alcoholic drink would be prohibited, has not been realised (see Amulree Commission, A. 23,508 (2)). It was found that a teetotal club of adult males could not be a success and the ban was removed after three years' experience. When the Amulree Commission was sitting it was reported that only about 1·2 per cent of the total of these clubs were teetotal (see ibid., A. 23,509, table II). The Secretary of the Union stated that, on the average, each member in the Metropolitan District spent 5s. per week—3s. 3½d. was the average in the United Kingdom—on alcoholic and soft drinks, food and tobacco (A. 23,588–9). This suggested a low consumption of alcoholic drink; but we do not know what members spent on alcohol outside their clubs (the point was put to the witness, see Q. 23,816, and agreed), nor how many members out of the total consumed alcoholic drink, nor how heavily they drank. The temperance spirit of most of those clubs is certainly limited: it may be effective here and there; but some clubs were even said to be financed by breweries.[2]

But many clubs and societies have an undoubted interest and importance in the temperance movement. That little is known about them usually means merely that they are confined to limited geographical areas or have only special appeal. The enumeration of county, district and town societies fills many pages in the *Alliance Yearbook* (see for the above and these: *Alliance Yearbook*, 1947, pp. 155 sqq.). Besides there are many organisations of a special character and with special objects, such as the Temperance Unions of Railways, the Society for the Study of Inebriety, the Workers' Temperance League, the Royal Naval Temperance Society and others, and there are life insurance companies which provide a special section for total abstainers, e.g., the United Kingdom Temperance and General Provident Institution, and the Beacon Insurance Company. In 1947 there were no less than thirty-three temperance periodicals.

An impressive array of organisations represents the temperance movement at the national level and it is here that the liveliness of the movement can be studied and assessed. These organisations may be classified into four categories:

[1] See B. T. Hall, *Our Sixty Years*, 1922, whole chapter on 'The Beer Problem'; see also Askwith, *British Taverns*, pp. 248–50.

[2] See evidence by Mr. F. Burrington Dingle, Clerk to the Licensing Justices for the City of Sheffield, A. 3,823 (30) (31).

1. *Religious Societies*

Of these there are as many as twenty important bodies. Among them are the Church of England Temperance Society, the Baptist Union of Great Britain and Ireland Temperance Department, the Church Army, the Church in Wales Temperance Society, the Salvation Army, the Temperance Council of the Christian Churches, the Methodist Temperance and Social Welfare Department, the Congregational Union of England and Wales, and the Friends Temperance Union.

2. *Educational Societies*

To these belong, besides the United Kingdom Band of Hope Union which we have mentioned at some length, the British Temperance League, the National Commercial Temperance Union, the National Temperance League, and the Temperance Collegiate Association.

3. *Orders and Friendly Societies*

We have already mentioned the activities and importance of the most prominent of these Orders, the Independent Order of Rechabites. But of great importance also are the International Order of Good Templars, with the Grand Lodge of England, and Grand Lodges in Scotland, Ireland and Wales; the Order of the Sons of Temperance; the Sons of Scotland Temperance Society; the Templar Institute; and the United Order Total Abstinent Sons of the Phoenix.

4. *Legislative Societies*

They are headed by the United Kingdom Alliance for the total Suppression of the Liquor Traffic by the Will of the People, and the Scottish Temperance Alliance. To this type also belong such well-known bodies as the Central Sunday Closing Association, the National British Women's Tòtal Abstinence Union, the National Temperance Federation, the National United Temperance Council, the Prohibition Party, and the Temperance Legislation League with Mr. B. Seebohm Rowntree as chairman.

CHAPTER X

THE SCOPE OF LEGISLATION

IT will never be possible to state how far the temperance movement and how far restrictive legislation has been responsible for the reduction in heavy drinking and drunkenness: they have been active side by side over a span of many decades. The temperance movement has aimed at generally discouraging the consumption of drink and at getting increasing numbers of individuals to abstain from drink; and legislation has been instrumental in limiting conditions which conduce to heavy drinking and inordinate expenditure by the public. The two agencies have, in short, been complementary.

This proposition—that restrictive legislation has been an effective agency in the abatement of drinking—tends to be denied by two groups of people who are diametrically opposed to each other. The first consists of what may be called temperance 'purists'. They look on legislative restrictions on the consumption of drink in much the same way as nationalisation enthusiasts look on reform in private industry: these developments merely postpone the day, and hence increase the evils, when the problem will have to be really dealt with. They aspire to abolition not reform; and the only legislative measure that will satisfy them is prohibition.

The other group consists of the trade interests. They naturally feel that legislation is a burden on their trade and go on to argue that the achievement of legislation ends there and does not extend to the abatement of drinking at all. It is characteristic that Mr. F. P. Whitbread in his Minority Report to the Amulree Commission stressed that excessive drinking and the amount of drunkenness had decreased, but that he was, at the same time, most anxious to show that legislation had not been very much connected with this tendency: he expressed the view that 'the improvement is due mainly to general social causes rather than to details of licensing and administration' (see Amulree Report, pp. 230–1). He went on to suggest that 'once the need for facilities for temperate consumers is admitted, it is impracticable by licensing legislation to prevent the possibility of overspending', and that 'the inculcation of thrift must mainly rest on better social standards aided by an increased sense of family responsibility'.

PROHIBITION

The experiment with prohibition in the United States of America still remains the outstanding example of this radical form of repression of alcoholic drink. It is sometimes believed that prohibition started in the United States when it came into force for the whole country on 29th January 1920. But this is an erroneous view.[1] The agitation, and, to some part, the enactment of prohibition in at least some of the States of the U.S.A., dates back to a much earlier period. The first step had been a prohibition law passed in the State of Maine in the year 1851. Following Maine's example, other American States almost immediately passed similar laws, including Minnesota, Michigan, Indiana, Delaware, Iowa, Nebraska, New York and the whole of New England (see Heath, op. cit., p. 76). In 1885, however, there came a reaction, partly on constitutional considerations; by 1863 only five States out of forty-eight had retained their prohibition law. But a revival of prohibition followed later in many parts of the country. In 1913, when the population of the U.S.A. was 97 million, more than 46 million people were living in 'dry' States (see John Harrison, op. cit.). The idea of prohibition was therefore well established by the time that the pressure arose to apply it nationally.

In order to achieve prohibition for the whole of the country, the American Constitution had to be amended. By 1917 a national prohibition resolution had been adopted by both the House of Representatives and the Senate; it was submitted to the forty-eight States in the Union and, thirty-six States having approved the method, was finally ratified on 16th January 1919. Eventually forty-six States approved. One year later it became effective as the 18th Amendment to the Federal Constitution, under the name of the Volstead Act, which defined intoxicating liquor as 'all liquor fit for beverage which contains more than one half of one per cent by volume of alcohol' (see Heath, op. cit., p. 76).

Prohibition had in many ways the desired and expected effect.

[1] See John Harrison, 'The Position of Prohibition', *Alliance Yearbook*, 1940, pp. 24 sqq. for some of the following observations.

Drunkenness convictions per thousand of population in New York in 1925 were as low as 14·83, while they were 72 in Edinburgh, 49 in London and 97 in Toronto (see John Harrison, op. cit., p. 36). Arrests for drunkenness in the U.S.A. had been 192 per 10,000 of population in 1916; they receded to 88 in 1925.

Yet despite these trends the whole policy was discarded on 5th December 1933 by the 21st Amendment to the Federal Constitution. The main reasons given for the repeal were that prohibition could not apparently be made fully effective, but that, at the same time, an enormous amount of work had to be applied to control and supervision and to the general prevention of evasion. The Federal Government, partly owing to the repudiation by many States of a part or the whole of their responsibilities, had had to appoint 15,000 agents, that is one agent to every 83,000 citizens; and even this number was not sufficient to suppress bootlegging of liquor and disregard 'for the law by the people generally' (see Harrison, op. cit., p. 37). There was lack of public support for the Prohibition law. There was 'bribery and corruption among those appointed to enforce Prohibition' (see Harrison, op. cit., p. 37). Criminal offences of all sorts were directly connected with prohibition. The 'crime wave' due to prohibition may have been an exaggeration,[1] but the general impression from the experiment was certainly that the law could not be enforced, a feeling which probably further increased the unpopularity of the measure. The American Federation of Labour was anti-Prohibitionist; and the vested interests which lost no opportunity of influencing public opinion in favour of appeal found assistance also in many other quarters of public opinion.

The repeal of the Volstead Act threw the onus for regulating the sale of alcoholic drink largely back upon the individual States. Now there are various systems of control. No State has full prohibition as formerly. Kansas still has constitutional prohibition of 'intoxicating liquors', but this has been construed to permit the sale of beer of a 3·2 per cent alcoholic content, on the theory that it is not intoxicating. Mississippi, Oklahoma and Tennessee prohibit the sale of spirits but allow the sale of beer. There are fifteen States with state monopoly, twenty-five States are under licence, three States have prohibition and local dispensaries, and one State,

[1] See Weeks, op. cit., p. 358: 'Then we were all shocked at what we were led to understand was the moral and criminal outcome of the great experiment, to-day we see that the so-called "crime wave" due to prohibition is still waving under repeal', for which he gives some interesting facts.

Maryland, is under licence and local dispensaries. It is difficult to summarise in concise form the various detailed methods of control adopted by various States (see Cecil Heath, op. cit., p. 37). For instance, in some States which have local licence, local option is permitted; in other States under licence, there is no local option. Again, in some cases the local option is confined to certain alcoholic beverages and others are exempt.[1] As far as the sale of liquor is concerned, almost 20 per cent of the population of the United States now live in areas where it is strictly prohibited (see *Alliance News*, July–August 1948, p. 47).

The repeal must certainly not be interpreted to mean that the evils connected with heavy drinking were not readily recognised then or are not recognised now; and prohibition did lead to social and economic improvement, though some of the statements in its favour at the time must be discounted. The sub-committee of the Committee on Alcoholic Liquor Traffic, for instance, observed in May 1925: 'Our economists assert that Prohibition is a leading factor in our present prosperity. The former expenditure for intoxicants now enters the channels of constructive business'; and 'industrial productivity of labour, decreased industrial accidents, and a multiplied demand for new homes has accompanied a decrease in poverty'. (See also Harrison, op. cit., p. 34.) Between 1920 and 1929 there was a general boom in the U.S.A. due partly to a gold inflation; and after all the widespread introduction of the hire-purchase system, for instance, and the other circumstances which led to what seemed to be rapidly increasing prosperity, came to a sudden and catastrophical end in 1929 (see Hermann Levy, *The New Industrial System*, 1936, p. 247). But the statements undoubtedly contain some truth, and prohibition was certainly, even when bootlegging and its accompanying evils are taken into account, a wholesome factor in the American economy.[2] And there has been much pressure since the repeal for the renewal of prohibition.

But a statute may be said to have failed in its purpose if, after some experience in operating it, it is decided to repeal it even though the avowed evils which led to its enactment are expected

[1] A full description of the legal situation is given by Ernest H. Cherrington, 'The Fight against Alcoholism in the United States since the Repeal of Prohibition', in the *Alliance Yearbook*, 1938, p. 26.

[2] An early appreciation of the good effects of prohibition, in particular as regards the State of Maine, is to be found in C. Helenius, *Die Alkoholfrage, eine soziologisch-statistische Untersuchung*, Jena, 1904; this was based upon personal study in the U.S.A. and represents a scientific piece of research; see also Elster, op. cit., p. 241.

to reappear as strong as they were before. Prohibition in the United States therefore failed. And this failure was due not to an ignorance of the evils of drink nor a lack of appreciation of the benefits of prohibition, but to the increase in lawlessness and immorality and the psychological and emotional cost of what was only a partial enforcement of the law.

This experience in the United States has in many respects been repeated in the other countries that have tried prohibiting the sale of alcoholic drink. Finland and Iceland, which also tried prohibition as an experiment, repealed the laws after some years. In the case of Iceland the repeal may have been due to commercial considerations, as Mr. Heath suggests: Iceland was dependent for some of her foreign trade on exports of dried fish to certain wine-producing countries in South Europe (see Heath, op. cit., p. 78). But in the case of Finland no such considerations applied; yet the prohibition law which had been introduced in 1919 was repealed in 1932 (see Harrison, op. cit., pp. 26–7): it was said that the enactments providing for the enforcement of the Finnish Prohibition law had been singularly inadequate and smuggling from Germany, Poland and Esthonia was rampant. In Canada again development of prohibition was similar. Various provinces of Canada, in addition to Prince Edward Island, tried prohibition experimentally, but the attempts were mostly confined to the first World War and did not survive post-war conditions (see Heath, op. cit., p. 78). During 1921 Quebec and British Columbia discarded prohibition and adopted government control of the sale of liquor. Manitoba followed in 1923, Alberta in 1924, Saskatchewan in 1925, Ontario and New Brunswick in 1927 and Nova Scotia in 1930. Prince Edward Island, which had introduced prohibition as early as 1907 and was the first to 'go dry', is the only province still adhering to the policy of prohibition (see Harrison, op. cit., pp. 28–9).

It cannot yet be conjectured whether this experiment will remove prohibition once and for ever from the scope of anti-drink legislation. The issue is confused because it is never assessed on anything like strict objectivity. In the United States enormous funds were collected to fight prohibition, partly from groups who had been engaged in the drink trade on a large scale, and who were much concerned about the loss of their lucrative business, and partly from other groups of wealthy business men who regarded the sacrifice of revenue from drink and the consequential increase in taxes on large personal incomes to make up for it as obviously adverse to their own interests (see Heath, op. cit., p. 77). Since drink, together with tobacco, represents the most fertile source of indirect taxation, it is natural that whenever this taxation is reduced, vested interests must be afraid that the loss will have to be offset by more incisive direct taxation. It appears from recent ballots that probably one-third of the voters in the United States would be in favour of renewed prohibition.[1] But this does not mean that prohibition can be effective. Every serious writer on the problem of drink seems to have dissociated himself from prohibition simply because it is practically unrealisable. One of the most authoritative scientific writers on the subject viewing the problem mainly from medico-social considerations, Mr. Courtney C. Weeks, M.R.C.S., L.R.C.P., has been anxious to impress on his readers that, despite the grave dangers of drinking revealed in his treatise, he 'is no advocate of prohibition as a solution of our difficulties' (see op. cit., p. 345): and so have many others. The Amulree Report recorded that no witness had suggested prohibition of the manufacture and sale of alcoholic liquors as a practical proposition for present application in Britain.

With such doubts about the efficacy of prohibition, well-wishers of the temperance movement who associate legislative efforts wholly with prohibition may in fact be weakening the movement. They tend greatly to narrow its appeal and its educational effort. If temperance protagonists despair of the possibility of getting prohibition enacted and are not interested in anything short of it, they may relax their efforts generally, in the same way as a substantial section of the temperance movement in the United States of America, who felt that their work was no longer needed when prohibition had become the law of the land, relaxed that intense educational campaign which had always been a feature of American temperance activity (see H. Cecil Heath, *The Control of a Dangerous Trade*, 1947, p. 77). At the same time, they may, through despising or merely ignoring the possibilities of further abating drinking by means of restrictive legislation fail to make use of an agency which, whatever the trade must necessarily say to protect its interests, has been already quite effective so far. This is not denied by many among those who favour prohibition; they feel that it would be neither just nor wise to belittle the effects of

[1] See *The Brewing Trade Review* of April 1948, article by Mr. Rowland Blackburn, 'They are making America dry again'.

repressive legislative measures. As Mr. H. Cecil Heath, the General Secretary of the United Kingdom Alliance, put it (see Heath, op. cit., p. 95): 'Without in any way abandoning the ultimate goal of "Total Abstinence of the Individual and Prohibition for the State", it is practical wisdom to examine from time to time those channels through which the Temperance Movement may be able to achieve progress by conforming to certain legislative tendencies.'

THE EFFECTIVENESS OF RESTRICTIVE LEGISLATION

There are instances where the connection between restrictive legislation and the abatement of drinking is clearly that of cause and effect, and the causal connection is really undeniable when legislative action is followed immediately by sharp reductions, for instance, in convictions for drunkenness. As early as 1911 Lady Bell wrote in her survey of a manufacturing town that she did not see much chance of a drastic reduction of drinking as long as public houses were practically the centres of the social life of the workmen, but immediately added: 'It is consoling, however, to learn that the amount of drinking in public houses has appreciably diminished since the legislation which made the publican as well as the drinker responsible for the drunkenness in the establishment.'[1]

The first World War provided the most impressive example of the immediate effect of legislation on the abatement of drink. In February 1915 the effect of alcohol on efficiency assumed a formidable significance. The passages in Lloyd George's speeches in which he added alcohol to the list of immediate foes (see p. 40) were merely high spots in the sudden and general realisation that the drinking habit was impeding the war effort. That drink was not conducive to industrial efficiency had been long appreciated, but now it was time to do something about it: it seemed to have dire effects in terms of absenteeism in munition factories and delays in transport.

To avert further deterioration in the situation the Central Control Board (Liquor Traffic) was set up in May 1915; Lord D'Abernon was chairman and remained in this position right through the war. Many drastic regulations were introduced by the Board, but none were more far-reaching than those restricting the hours of sale. Before the first World War, the number of hours

[1] See Lady Bell, op. cit., p. 341; the licensee is not allowed by law to permit drunkenness on licensed premises.

during which public houses were open on week-days had been nineteen and a half in London, seventeen in other English towns, and sixteen in country districts. The Board reduced these to five and a half per day in all the prescribed areas (which practically covered the whole country) and made the rule apply to clubs as well as to public houses. On Sundays the number of hours for 'on sale' was reduced to four. It was prescribed that on week-days and Sundays alike there should be a 'break' of at least two hours in the middle of the day to prevent 'continuous drinking'.

It would be wrong to attribute the drop in convictions for drunkenness during the war years wholly to legislation. But the decrease was remarkable: from 184,000 in 1915 to 156,000 in 1916 and 29,000 in 1918; and an observer as cautious as Mr. George B. Wilson regarded restrictive legislation as the dominant cause of this drop, even after taking account of direct restrictions on the output of liquor, the preoccupation of the police, and the considerable withdrawal of men for military service. In the case of spirits Mr. Wilson came to the conclusion that up to March 1917 the restrictions on off-sale, the shorter hours, and the compulsory Dilution Order were effective in reducing consumption. Home consumption of spirits in Great Britain fell from 31,600,000 proof gallons in 1915 to 25,050,000 gallons in 1916, whereas with a rapidly increased wage bill, especially in the industrial districts of Northern England and Scotland, where spirit-drinking was general, an actual increase might have been expected. As to beer and the regulations of the Control Board, Mr. Wilson agreed that the Board's limitations did a good deal at least 'to prevent an *increase* in drinking'. Cecil Heath also speaks of 'the proved benefits of war-time restriction' (see *Alliance Yearbook for 1940*, p. 59). The Southborough Report of 1927 emphasised similarly that 'the restrictions imposed during the war, the reduction of hours during which intoxicating liquor may be sold', had greatly contributed to the reduction of drunkenness (see Southborough Report, pp. 17–18).

In view of these results, efforts were made to use post-war legislation to preserve some of the good which had resulted from the attempts to increase efficiency through reducing insobriety. But the power of the vested interests was too strong to enable legislation to perpetuate all restrictions, and the motive on the part of the State to increase industrial efficiency was no longer overriding. Not all was lost. The Licensing Act, 1921, preserved some of the restrictions, among others the midday break in permitted hours, and so the impetus which had come about accidentally from the war was not entirely lost in the peace that followed. Most important, the inter-relation between certain effects of drinking and industrial efficiency remained an established and officially recognised fact.

The Amulree Commission was on the whole fully satisfied that legislative measures had not been anything like ineffective (see Amulree Report, p. 10): 'Although opinion amongst our witnesses was not unanimous, we feel satisfied that the shorter and broken hours, as fixed by the Act of 1921, have, by restricting the almost indefinite continuity of opportunity for drinking which formerly existed, proved themselves to be an indispensable element in the introduction of insobriety. We have strong evidence of the beneficial results which have followed the cutting off of early morning drinking, particularly among industrial workers, the value of the afternoon break—particularly in checking the continuity of afternoon 'soaking'—and the changed conditions which have been brought about by the abolition of the former late night hours.' The Report was anxious to emphasise these effects in order to obviate the arguments that restrictive legislation had not appreciably served its purpose.

In the longer term the nation undoubtedly profited greatly by what had been achieved through legislative restrictions in the first World War. As the *Alliance Yearbook* stated in 1940 (see ibid., p. 65): 'From the point of view of national sobriety, the nation entered the present war in conditions much more satisfactory than in 1914'; and it went on to mention as the essential factor 'the great improvement in drinking habits effected by the partial perpetuation of restrictions imposed during the last war.'

It is control then, and not prohibition, which constitutes the gist of anti-drink legislation. This legislation does not aim directly at suppressing the consumption of drink—it is therefore limited in scope—but it effectively prevents the most obvious dangers and evils of excess. Cecil Heath chose for his study the illuminating title, *The Control of a Dangerous Trade*. A dangerous trade is exactly what drink is: it requires control on the same grounds as other dangerous trades, and repressive and restrictive anti-drink legislation should be viewed from the same angle as that relating to, for instance, drugs and motor cars.

FORMS OF CONTROL

The forms of control are naturally determined by the nature of the danger, and in the case of drink are particularly difficult to devise. Legal instructions as to methods of labelling and stopping bottles are quite effective in informing people of the poisonous contents of some medicines. But the 'poisonous' effect of alcoholic drink cannot be made clear by a label, because the ill-effects of alcoholic drink are mainly dependent not on its ingredients but on the degree of consumption by the individual and on the way the individual may react to alcohol. A definition of drugs was once made by an advisory committee which classified a large number of substances into: (*a*) never a drug, (*b*) always a drug, and (*c*) sometimes a drug, (see Hermann Levy, *National Health Insurance*, 1944, p. 189). Alcoholic drink could span all three categories: it may not be hurtful at all, if taken in small quantities and occasionally, or on medical advice in prescribed doses; it may become immediately hurtful if taken in larger quantities; and the same quantity taken may react very differently on different persons and have very different effects on their occupational efficiency and safety: motor drivers, for instance, may run great risks by a relatively small intake of beer. A bottle of medicine marked 'poison' very definitely warns the patient of the inherent dangers and so does the label which contains the exact prescription of the dose of a 'dangerous' medicine to be taken: the person who takes more might die through doing so. The person who becomes drunk may kill himself or another in a state of intoxication, but he is not warned by a label: the state of intoxication may arrive against his own wish and quite gradually. The motorist is aware that when he is taking a certain curve at a certain speed he runs the risk of a grave accident; but the person who is induced to drink more than he can digest without intoxication may never be aware of this possibility of drunkenness, because his consciousness is gradually reduced and his power of judgment slowly impaired. While in other cases of dangerous trades and drugs a clear warning may suffice to prevent disaster, the danger line is blurred in the case of alcoholic drink. It is for that reason that it has been recognised as necessary to protect the drinker against his own failings by different kinds of legislative controls.

PUNISHING DRUNKENNESS

Punishment of drunkenness is one line of action. Though the effect of a fine or a non-monetary penalty on the abatement of drinking is indirect, it may in many cases operate as a strong deterrent and thus have a repressive effect. Any sort of disqualification from driving 'under the influence of drink', for instance, can be regarded as a legal measure to reduce the frequency of accidents through drunkenness or excessive drinking. The significance of this type of legislation has been increasingly recognised of late since the attempts at educating motorists can no longer be regarded as having been anything but disappointingly unsuccessful. Sir H. M. Vernon wrote some years ago (see H. M. Vernon, *Road Accidents in War Time*, 1941, p. 99): 'Though some reduction of accidents can be brought about by the education of road users, by propaganda, and by other methods . . . there remain a large number of motor drivers and other road users who are not amenable to mild persuasion. They react only to more direct and drastic treatment, such as the imposition of legal penalties. If the penalties imposed by the authorities are relaxed, they are only too ready to take advantage of the relaxations, and to drift into their old bad habits.'

Penalties for driving 'under the influence of drink' are thus recognised to have a prophylactic effect. In some countries no licence will be delivered to any person who, within a certain period prior to his application, has been convicted of drunkenness. This is the case in Norway, where the period fixed is three years.[1] Similar legislation exists in Denmark. In Switzerland no driving licence may be granted to any person known as an abuser of alcoholic beverages. The view that mere presence on the roads 'under the influence of drink' should be considered as an offence even when no accident has occurred is widely accepted: it has been adopted by legislation in Sweden, Norway, Denmark, Finland, Switzerland, Holland and Great Britain. An increased criminal responsibility is also affirmed by the growing severity of penalties (see ibid., p. 45): they vary greatly from country to country, but in the most recent legislation in Sweden, Norway, and Denmark, a prison sentence is considered normal punishment for drunken motorists. There can be hardly any doubt that the recent tendency towards severer penalties for driving in a drunken state, or for

[1] See the interesting article, 'Alcohol and Traffic Safety', by Dr. Thorkild Dahlgren, insurance director of Malmö, Sweden, in *Alliance Yearbook for 1938*, p. 41.

causing injury through drunkenness, has been largely influenced by the fact that legislation is not only regarded as necessary punishment of the offender, but also as an effective preventive measure.[1]

Legislation to put persons addicted to alcohol under tutelage is of a similar kind. The German law is very explicit here; according to para. 6 of the Civil Code a person may be subjected to tutelage who through alcoholism is not able to administer his own affairs, or exposes his family to distress, or endangers the safety of others (see Elster, op. cit., p. 233 for more particulars). This clause is intended to provide the condition necessary for compulsory institutional treatment of inebriates.[2] In Britain, homes for habitual drunkards were established under the Habitual Drunkards Act of 1879, which was amended in 1888 and again in 1898. The Inebriates Act of 1918 followed as an important experiment; under it detention could be made compulsory on account of addiction to drink, irrespective of an incidental offence. Up to 1921 between 500 and 600 cases were treated annually under the Act,[3] but by that date the authorities were forced to arrive at the conclusion that the treatment of the unwilling was too seldom successful to justify the continuance of compulsion, and it was consequently allowed to drop. Inebriates' homes still exist in Britain, but they are organised under voluntary management.[4] Their patients for the most part attend voluntarily, e.g., after pressure has been put upon them by relatives or friends. But there are also people who committed some offence incidental to drink, and were released by the magistrates under a probation order which included in its terms the condition that the offender should reside at an inebriates' home.

In recent years British magistrates have been increasingly inclined to send the offender back to live at his own home, under the general supervision of the probation officer. This trend does not seem to apply generally to other countries. In Sweden, for instance, legislation on the treatment of inebriates was first intro-

[1] See also H. Cecil Heath, 'Alcohol and World Road Safety' in *Alliance Yearbook for 1939*, pp. 53 sqq.

[2] The course of this procedure has been criticised before the Ninth International Congress against Alcoholism of 1903, by Professor W. Endemann, of the University of Heidelberg, who suggested that treatment of alcohol addicts should precede the putting under tutelage.

[3] See Charity Organisation Society, *How to help Cases of Distress*, June 1940, p. 188.

[4] Such homes are Caldecote Hall, Nuneaton, licensed for treatment of male inebriates; 'Coningsby', Women's Shelter Home, London; Spelthorne St. Mary, Thorpe, Chertsey, Surrey, licensed.

duced in 1913 and extended in 1931 by a new Act. The provincial governor can, at the request of the communal temperance board, or in certain cases at the request of the police, order an inebriate to be compulsorily detained in a public institution for the treatment of inebriates. This action is dependent among other things on proof that the inebriate has become a danger to himself and the community, that he has become negligent of his domestic duties, or an encumbrance to the parish, or that he has been convicted during the preceding two years more than three times for drunkenness. In 1936 the number of admissions to inebriate institutions was 864 as against 265 on the average between 1920 and 1924, a high figure for a country with some six million inhabitants, when compared with the English figures. The difference is probably largely due to stricter enforcement, and in particular to the existence of an official temperance movement which finds expression, for instance, in the temperance boards which constitute local organs for supervising Swedish legislation relating to intoxicating liquor legislation.[1] What does appear to be general in this type of legislation is the increasing severity of the penalties for drunkenness, particularly on the roads.

CONTROLLING SALES ESTABLISHMENTS

The main focus of restrictive legislation is the control of the establishments which sell drink. As alcoholic drink is mostly consumed in public houses, in catering establishments, retail establishments and clubs, it is here that there is the widest possible scope for the repression of its abuses. The method applied is, in Britain, to control the trade by the enactment of certain restrictive regulations and to safeguard the enforcement of such regulations by licensing the vendors or suppliers.

In Britain as elsewhere (see for early action on the Continent, Elster, op. cit., pp. 208–9) the first legislative regulation of establishments selling drink is of early date. Regulation of the sale of intoxicating liquor is older than Parliament itself. Before Parliament intervened, regulations were imposed by local bodies such as municipalities and enforced by their charters and manorial courts.[2] These early regulations were of course merely local in their operation and varied from place to place. London alehouses and

[1] See for further details, the Royal Social Board, *Social Work and Legislation in Sweden*, Stockholm, 1938, pp. 252 sqq. and p. 204.

[2] We follow here the very instructive description in Appendix 2 of the Amulree Report: Notes on the History of Licensing Regulation, pp. 259 sqq.

taverns had to be shut before curfew; in Nottingham they had to be shut at nine o'clock; in Canterbury the brewers were to sell no beer or ale by retail except to 'such as be of good disposition and conversation'.

The first Parliamentary and general regulations took the forms of Assizes or Ordinances for Bread and Ale, and were at first mainly devised to safeguard the quality, measures and prices of the alcoholic drink supplied. 51 Hen. III, st.1, 1266; 4 Edw. III, c. 12, 1330 and many statutes followed this line. Up to the time of Henry VII, there were no restrictions on the number of alehouses and taverns in any area, and no qualification was in general required for an alehouse or tavern keeper. It was only towards the end of the fifteenth century that Parliament began increasingly to turn its attention to legislative restriction of the drink trade itself (see Heath, op. cit., pp. 3 sqq.). An Act of Henry VII of 1494 (11 Hen. VII, c. 2, 1494) brought this innovation and marked the beginning of the licensing methods in their more modern form with its general attempt to regulate the number of alehouses.

The purpose of this and immediately following statutes was in line with the general attempts to reduce vagrancy and lawlessness by idling persons—a problem which was one of the great worries of legislators and social reformers of the fifteenth, sixteenth and seventeenth centuries. In the opinion of Parliament, the excessive number of public houses and inns was bound to have some connection with these evils and certainly was not likely to have a wholesome influence on them. The Act of 1494 provided among other things that 'it shall be lawful (for two Justices of the Peace) . . . to reject and put away common ale-selling in towns and places . . . and to take surety to innkeepers on their good behaving'. This provision was re-enacted in 1503. An Act of 1552 became what Heath has called 'the basis of our present licensing system' (5 and 6 Edw. VI, c. 25). Perhaps the power to reject the common selling of ale had not been enough, or the Justices had failed to exercise their powers with that full warrant which the circumstances admittedly required, or the remedy itself was insufficient. In any case, the new Statute complained of the daily growth of 'intolerable hurts and troubles to the Commonwealth', and that they increased through abuses and disorders arising in common alehouses and other places 'called tippling houses' (see Amulree Report, p. 261). Justices of the Peace were accordingly empowered 'in the open sessions' *inter alia* to license alehouse-keepers, requiring them to enter into a bond or recognisance of 'good order', which included the prohibition of unlawful games.

The Amulree Commission noted in 1932 that 'this Statute of 1552 is the foundation of all our legislation concerning the sale and consumption of intoxicating liquor, and subsequent legislation is mere amendment'. It would therefore be of mere historical interest and not within the scope of our study to record the large number of the subsequent enactments dealing with licensing. What is noteworthy here is that during the first half of the nineteenth century there was a decided relaxation of the licensing laws, which found expression in the Ale House Act of 1828 and the Beer House Act of 1830, and was to some extent the result of a campaign for 'free trade in beer'. The result of this was appalling. Beer houses grew like mushrooms. It is reported that a Birmingham brewer's agent opened two hundred houses in one year (see Wilson, op. cit., p. 204). Within less than six months there were no fewer than 24,342 new establishments selling beer. In 1831 there were 30,978; by 1838 the number had increased to 45,717 (see Amulree Report, p. 272, also Heath, op. cit., p. 6). Brewers' agents travelled from village to village to persuade all and sundry persons to start selling beer, advancing the two guineas fee and supplying beer on credit. According to the Amulree Report, indescribable orgies occurred 'accompanied by gambling, brutal amusements and licentiousness'. By 1860 the number of beer houses had topped the 50,000 mark.

It was not until 1869 that legislation began, after some minor enactments in the early sixties, to undo the unwise deeds of 1828 and 1830. In that year the Wine and Beer House Act was passed,[1] which, though it was regarded as a makeshift until some more complete measure could be introduced, marked the beginning of a new era of more effective legislation. This was followed in 1871 by an attempt to effect much stronger legislation, but the Bill introduced by Mr. Bruce (afterwards Lord Aberdare) was not welcomed by the temperance movement, and the trade denounced it as a 'Robber Bill'; it was therefore withdrawn. But one year later, in 1872, a Licensing Act was passed which provided that grants of new licences by the justices were required to be confirmed by a separate authority, and abolished appeals to Quarter Sessions against the refusal of new licences. It was a mild measure compared with the 1871 Bill, but a definite step forward (see Amulree Report, pp.

[1] Wine and Beer House Act (Amendment) (33 and 34 Vict., c. 29).

267–77). The Royal Commission of 1896–9 was the next important measure towards further control. Its immediate legislative outcome was the Licensing Act, 1902. This was followed in 1904 by an Act popularly known as the 'Balfour Act', which had as its avowed object a large reduction in the number of licensed houses. This piece of legislation is still operative, incorporated in the Licensing Act of 1910, which consolidated all the previous legislation which had become extremely complicated to administer (see Heath, op. cit., p. 7). Since then licensing legislation has concerned itself more with questions of sale. This is the case, for instance, with the Licensing Act of 1921 by which the restriction of hours in operation during the war was made a permanent feature of licensing legislation and with the Licensing (Permitted Hours) Act (24 and 25 Geo. V, c. 26, 1934), which so far has remained the last of the long list of Acts of Parliament dealing with the control of alcoholic drink through licensing.

THE TWO DIRECTIONS IN ANTI-DRINK LEGISLATION

The licensing system presents to the student of the drink problem, and to politicians and administrators, a host of complex regulations shot through with technicalities which are the constant object of heated criticism from those who wish to see a further abatement of drinking and from those who, for trade reasons, wish the contrary. To arrive at a conclusion as to its real significance, it is necessary to concentrate on the point that the licensing system serves to control the actual execution of anti-drink legislation: and as the abuses are overwhelmingly connected with the consumption of drink in public houses, it seems most expedient to lay the responsibility on those who sell the drink. Viewed from this angle, the licensing system resembles the application of qualifying tests by some retail trade associations.[1]

The Assistant Legal Adviser to the Home Office, Mr. O. F. Dowson, summarised before the Amulree Commission the effects of the provisions 'in the form of principles'. One of these in his words was (see Amulree Commission, A. 36): 'The imposition of penalties in respect of illegal transactions in intoxicating liquor and the improper conduct of licensed premises, and of other penal provisions relating to e.g. drunkenness, imposed in the interests of good order and public welfare'; another was: 'The general lim-

[1] See Hermann Levy, *Retail Trade Associations*, 2nd ed. 1944, pp. 173 sqq.

itation, subject to variations at the discretion of the licensing justices, of the times during which intoxicating liquor may be sold or supplied and consumed in licensed premises and clubs.' These two points, one relating to good order, the other to the limitation of drinking hours, are indeed the main purpose of the licensing system. But in a way one may regard the second as included in the first, just as Mr. Dowson did when he stated, in reply to the question of Lord Amulree whether 'the main objective of justices' licences' was in his view 'for the preservation of good order', that this 'certainly is their main objective' (see Amulree Commission, Q. and A. 37).

A second objective, but one that has in general not been considered very much in recent British licensing legislation, is the reduction in the number of public houses for the purpose of preventing their superfluity. This purpose plays the main role in the retail traders' policy of licensing and registration (see Hermann Levy, *The Shops of Britain*, 1948, pp. 235–6 and *passim*). In the case of drink, the renewal of a licence may be refused on the ground of 'redundancy', a term in the words of the Assistant Legal Adviser to the Home Office of rather 'wide significance', possibly meaning that 'the licences are no longer required for the needs of the neighbourhood'.[1]

Regard to the economic demand for establishments serving drink is further developed in some other countries. In the German law, for instance, licensing depends on compliance with three conditions: (*a*) adequate personal qualification of the licensee; (*b*) the existence of an establishment conforming to the requirements of the police regulations; and (*c*) the existence of a local need. As to the latter the number of the inhabitants and their personal and social conditions are to be taken into account.[2] In the United Kingdom the accent of licensing still lies on the qualification of the licensee, though this does not preclude attempts by those who oppose an application for a new licence or support the removal of an existing one to get some sort of 'distance limit' established.[3] Linked to this aim is the official control of licensed premises in certain parts of

[1] See Amulree Commission, A. 198; the Justices may *inter alia* institute preliminary enquiries on the renewal of old licences as to the amount of public-house accommodation in the locality, see Heath, op. cit., p. 52.

[2] See Elster, op. cit., p. 236; the technical term is 'der Nachweis eines vorhandenen Bedürfnisses'—proof of an existing need.

[3] Heath, op. cit., p. 47, advises the 'leader of the opposition' that, *inter alia*, 'the distance from the site of all existing on and off licences in the neighbourhood should be ascertained'.

Britain, which represents one of the most interesting experiments in administrative action towards the abatement of drink.

These two objects then, the preservation of 'good order' in public houses and the control of the number of trade outlets, are the main features of legislative action. Both found expression in the Central Control Board (Liquor Traffic) which was set up in 1915, as we have already had occasion to mention. In March 1915 the great private shipbuilding firms had asked the Government to impose total prohibition and the Transport Workers' Federation promised their support 'in any drastic restrictions provided they affect all districts alike and all classes alike' (see Wilson, op. cit., p. 128), and on the 29th April 1915, Mr. (later Earl) Lloyd George brought in an elaborate scheme to defeat the ill-effects of drink. It was enacted as the Defence of the Realm (Amendment) Act, 1915, and provided for regulations to be laid down for state control of the supply of intoxicating liquor, 'for the purpose of increasing directly or indirectly the efficiency of labour' and 'preventing the efficiency of labour . . . from being impaired by drunkenness, alcoholism, or excess'.[1] The Central Control Board (Liquor Traffic) was the executive body. Under the Regulations of 10th June 1915 the Board was given power in many important directions,[2] such as the closing of licensed premises and clubs, the limitation of the hours during which drink could be sold, the prohibition of 'treating' and the regulation of the introduction of intoxicating liquors into certain areas and its transport within them; the Board was empowered also to prohibit the sale or supply of liquor except by themselves, to establish refreshment rooms, and to acquire premises or businesses by agreement or compulsorily. It was, indeed, a most drastic and far-reaching system of control. Formally the Board and all its orders came to an end with the Licensing Act of 1921, but in fact the main features of its regulations were retained, and to this day underlie legislative action for the abatement of drinking in Britain.

[1] See Wilson, op. cit., p. 129; also H. Cecil Heath, 'The Drink Problem in War Time', *Alliance Yearbook*, 1940, pp. 58 sqq.

[2] See for many details Henry Carter, *The Control of the Drink Trade in Britain*, 1919.

CHAPTER XI

THE MAINTENANCE OF 'GOOD ORDER'

THAT there is much legislative action which has some effect on the consumption of drink is manifest, even if consideration is limited to action which is aimed specifically at influencing the distribution of drink. Not all measures that influence the consumption of drink have the abatement of drinking as their main purpose, nor do they all react on the repression of drinking in the same way. The main motive for action may be a moral one; or it may be intended mainly to prevent the ill-effects of alcoholic drink on health or safety. The legislator and administrator may achieve, intentionally or unintentionally, a reduction of drinking and, in particular, of excessive drinking in his pursuit of other objectives. Legislation relating to the compulsory treatment of inebriates in institutions for instance may act as a direct deterrent and so also reduce the expenditure on drink. In the same way, the imposition of fines on drivers 'under the influence of drink' may indirectly reduce the consumption of alcoholic drink: drivers may avoid indulgence in excessive drinking through fear of the possible consequences. But these secondary and indirect effects hardly justify treating their legislative bases as part of the legislation directed at the abatement of drinking. It is generally assumed that anti-drink legislation proper is imposed mainly on the retailer and has three aspects of outstanding importance: (1) that he is not allowed to serve children or young persons; (2) that he is forbidden to serve drunken people; and (3) that the hours during which drink may be sold are limited by law. We will in the main also confine ourselves to an examination of these three.

Of least importance in the abatement of drinking is the prohibition to serve drink to drunken people. It has no doubt played some part in the reduction in drunkenness, but, as we have seen, this is no indication of the effect on quantity of drink actually consumed. Nor can this provision be strictly enforced in the prevailing pressure of competition between public houses and on the publican himself by the owners: there are strong incentives for the publicans not to obey the instructions of the law and to serve customers who have already had enough to drink. It is said that for every fifteen hundred cases of drunkenness only one licensee is prosecuted for permitting drunkenness or for selling intoxicants to a drunken person; and though not all these cases may relate to drunkenness which had its origin in the public house or club, the overwhelming majority undoubtedly do. (See *Alliance News Summary*, 27th September 1948, p. 1.) The main reasons for maintaining this aspect of legislation are that its effects, though limited, are in the right direction and that it supports certain aims of moral conduct and acts as a safeguard to the drinker as well as to those who might be endangered by the excessive consumption of drink by others.

JUVENILE DRINKING

The prohibition of juvenile drinking is of much greater importance. Though it is inspired by moral, educational and hygienic aims rather than by the wish generally to reduce the consumption of drink by eliminating from the public houses a substantial part of the population, the effect of the legislation has certainly been to abate the consumption of drink. In its stricter form special anti-drink legislation in respect of children is of a recent date (for early beginnings see Heath, op. cit., p. 23): the Metropolitan Police Act of 1839 prohibited the sale of spirits in London to any boy or girl under sixteen for consumption on the premises, and it was not until 1872 that this prohibition was extended to the whole country. In 1886 the sale of all kinds of liquor for consumption on the premises was forbidden to persons under thirteen years of age. In 1908 a Bill was passed which included provision for the exclusion of children under fourteen from the drinking bars of licensed premises. The Licensing (Consolidation) Act of 1910 again forbade the sale of spirits for 'on' consumption for young persons, 'apparently' under sixteen, and it is only twenty-five years ago that the Intoxicating Liquor (Sale to Young Persons) Act forbade the supply to young persons under eighteen of intoxicants in a public bar.[1] It still remains a fact that any person between the ages of sixteen and eighteen can be supplied with beer, porter, cider or perry for consumption with a meal.

[1] See for interesting details of the problem, Mass Observation, *Report on Juvenile Drinking*, June 1943.

In 1943 the Home Secretary, then Mr. Herbert Morrison, sent out a letter to the Brewers' Society, as representing the owners of the great majority of public houses in England and Wales, and to the National Consultative Council of the Retail Liquor Trade, to make arrangements for the prominent exhibition in all public houses of a notice setting out, briefly and simply, the provisions of the Act of 1923 relating to juveniles. He enclosed a copy of the proposed notice which the Trade had already promised to display (see Heath, op. cit., p. 25). In this notice, signed by the licensee, customers were asked for their 'co-operation' in 'securing the strict observance' of the juvenile regulations.

The regulations are formally nearly watertight. There are perhaps two legislative loopholes of some importance: Young persons of between fourteen and sixteen are allowed to be in any part of licensed premises, even in the bar; it is merely an offence for the licence-holder knowingly to sell, or allow any person to sell, intoxicating liquor to them. And it is not an offence for a young person of this age actually to supply liquor to other people, so that there is nothing to prevent any person over fourteen years of age being employed as a barman or barmaid; in fact, there are regulations, issued and approved by the Ministry of Labour, which lay down the rate of remuneration for barmen and barmaids under eighteen years of age. A more remote possibility is mentioned by Heath (op. cit., p. 26): the law does not prohibit consumption of intoxicating liquor on licensed permises, provided that the liquor has not been purchased there. Thus, if a person under the age of eighteen were to bring a flask of whisky into a public house and consume it there no offence would be committed, provided that the room where the whisky was consumed was not a bar; but this is hardly likely to happen.

But enforcing the regulations is difficult. Mr. Morrison recognised this in asking the trade to appeal for the co-operation of the customers. In the same year as his letter, Mass Observation published the findings of their study of juvenile drinking. They revealed, *inter alia*, that three-quarters of the children between seven and fourteen years of age said that they had tasted beer at one time or another, and it may be assumed that a considerable proportion of them had done so in a public house (Mass Observation, *Juvenile Drinking*, 1943, p. 5). The word 'knowingly' in the regulations leaves open possibilities of evasion, as the licensee has hardly any means to check whether the 'young person' is really over eighteen years of age. In cases which have been brought before the Courts it has often been successfully pleaded by the licensee that the person to whom he supplied the liquor looked over eighteen years, or, alternatively, that the liquor had been supplied by a servant of the licensee who had disobeyed instructions. As a field-investigator reported in an article in the *Times Educational Supplement* in February 1942, '... all judgment as to age has to be guesswork, since, however insatiable one's curiosity and however good one's interrogatory technique, it is impossible to obtain very definite information about people's age even when one spends several evenings in the same company'.[1] And the licensee cannot apply anything like an 'insatiable curiosity' to the younger guests. But even this loophole has certainly not prevented a decline in the present and potential consumption of drink through legislative action in respect of young people.

There is continuous pressure for further increases in the minimum age of customers. Many witnesses before the Amulree Commission were in favour of greater restriction. Sir Edgar Sanders, speaking as a former General Manager of the Carlisle scheme of State administration, declared that he would like to see persons under the age of twenty-five, male and female, prohibited from drinking spirits: 'This would largely stop the cocktail habit amongst young people' (see Amulree Commission, A. 20,122–3) He referred to the fact that prohibition up to eighteen was started under the Carlisle scheme and then became the law of the land. Mr. Courtney Weeks emphasised that in his view the regulation that no child under five may be supplied with drink of an intoxicating character, except on medical orders, should be replaced by the order that alcohol should not be given to any child under fourteen (see ibid., A. 24,850). Mr. G. B. Wilson agreed that it was difficult to prohibit young persons of over twenty-one earning the wages of adults the consumption of alcoholic drink and that might merely lead to 'wholesale evasion' (see ibid., A. 26,016 sqq.); he thought in any case that at the present time 'drinking', or at any rate, heavy drinking, is drinking by mature persons rather than by the young (see ibid., Q. and A. 26,029) as interesting a reflection on morals as possibly on trends—so that further restriction of the age-limits would therefore mean perhaps only a slight advance in the abatement of the consumption of drink. But this

[1] See *The Times Educational Supplement*, February 1942; see also London Diocesan Church of England Temperance Society, *Young People in Public Houses*, n.d., p. 5.

does not eliminate the case for further restriction: restricted opportunities to develop an early taste for drinking might be preparatory to further reduction in heavy drinking among the adults of the future and thereby be an important element in reducing consumption. It is not unfortunately possible to do more than merely speculate on the results of an enquiry made by the Salvation Army amongst 2,158 men living in their institutions in England and Wales, in particular that 994, or 46 per cent, took first to drink when they were between fifteen and nineteen years old: how many would have avoided drink altogether if they had not taken to it then?[1]

The Amulree Report was anxious to emphasise that the Commission had been 'impressed' by the evidence put before them on the growth of the 'cocktail' habit amongst young people of both sexes, and that it regarded it 'with apprehension'. But it recognised that 'it is hardly possible to touch the considerable amount of cocktail drinking which takes place in private houses' and came to the conclusion that 'any further raising of the minimum age for the sale or supply of intoxicants must present enhanced difficulties of discrimination and enforcement' (see Amulree Report, para. 585). Even Mr Weeks, who as a witness for the Organised Temperance Forces of England and Wales cannot be suspected of bias against restrictive legislation, suggested to the Royal Commission that 'after fourteen up to eighteen' discretion should be left to the parents (see A. 24,850). Mass Observation found that 'the great majority of children are first introduced to alcoholic drinks by their parents' (see Report on *Juvenile Drinking*, 1943, p. 9). It is, then, at them that further action in this matter must be directed; and with parents it becomes a problem of conviction, one of education and moral suasion.

THE LIMITATION OF HOURS OF SALE

While the age limit considerably reduces the number of people who may consume alcoholic drink in public, the limitation of hours of opening public houses attempts to curtail drinking among adults. This is certainly a more complicated task. The immediate aim of this type of regulation has been to reduce drunkenness; and, judging from the trend of convictions for drunkenness, it has certainly met with success. We have already mentioned some of

[1] See Evidence of Commissioner David C. Lamb, Amulree Commission, p. 1958, Appendix I.

the regulations. Before August 1914, the hours had been, on week-days, nineteen in London, seventeen in other English towns and sixteen in English country districts. The Board reduced these to five and a half per day in all prescribed areas—which covered practically the whole country—and made the rule apply to clubs as well as public houses. The hours ended at 9 p.m. or 9.30 p.m., according to the character of the district. Similar restrictions were placed on the 'off-sale' of liquor, except that the hours were one hour less per day than those for 'on-sale' and ended one hour earlier in the evening. On Sundays the number of hours for 'on-sale' was reduced to four. It was prescribed that on week-days and Sundays alike there should be a 'break' of at least two hours in the middle of the day, in order to prevent 'continuous drinking'. The main features of these regulations were kept in being when the new Licensing Act of 1921 (section 15) made all orders issued by the Central Board redundant, and abolished the Board itself. The normal permitted hours became eight in the provinces and nine in London with the proviso that magistrates had power to extend the hours in the provinces to eight and a half where they were satisfied that the special requirements of the district rendered such an extension desirable.

Scientists look to the time limit to lessen the possible physiological ill-effects of alcoholic drink, and here also it has been successful. They rightly point out that alcohol had better be taken at longish intervals, and this has determined the principle on which permitted hours have been distributed over the day (see Sir Henry Dale, Amulree Commission, A. and Q. 11,541–2): the idea is to give access to public houses in the first place in the middle part of the day about mealtime, then to have an interval in the afternoon during which public houses are closed, and to restore access after work in the evening. The purpose of the time limit therefore is by no means only that of reducing the hours in which alcoholic drink is available in public houses; perhaps more important even is the aim, stressed by physiologists, to reduce the consumption of alcohol on an empty stomach. Sir H. M. Vernon told the Amulree Commission in a Memorandum (see Amulree Commission, 32,343 (19)) that the closing of public houses until midday under the Board's regulations was important, since round about that time most people had their dinners. As some food taken at a meal remained in the stomach for about three hours, drink taken in the opening hours between 12 and 2.30 p.m. was likely to be taken along with food. For the same reason he maintained that the afternoon closure should not be shortened: '. . . it is desirable that the public houses be not reopened at an earlier hour than 5.30 p.m., for if they open at 5 p.m., workmen are apt to get a drink on their way home from work, and postpone their return home for a long time. It is better for them to go home first and have a meal, and visit the public house later on if they wish to do so.' It is from this point of view also that the later opening of public houses has been mainly discussed.[1]

How far this attitude and the resultant restrictions have reduced the quantity of drink consumed, it is difficult to say. It may well be that once the workman has got home for his meal he may not be inclined to go out again for a drink later. It should certainly be clear that longer opening, or opening earlier in the afternoon, would mean a greater consumption of alcoholic drink. One may agree with Mr. B. T. Hall, when questioning Dr. Roche Lynch, that a pint of beer which the miner takes when 'coming out of the pit does not do him so much injury that he should be deprived of the pleasure and gratification of ordering and drinking it' (see Amulree Commission, A. 11,976), but the question how far this habit should be encouraged is a different one when regarded from the point of view of the total consumption of alcoholic drink. Here it can only be said that it appears that the earlier the access to public houses, the more drink is consumed. On Saturdays people not only spend more time and drink more in public houses than on other week-days, but they also come earlier (see Mass Observation, *The Pub and the People*, p. 192): time permits them to do so. The same effect would probably be observed during the week if they had access to public houses immediately after coming from their work.

The Amulree Commission, which had questioned a large number of witnesses of all shades of opinion for and against the restriction of permitted hours, found 'a remarkable consensus of opinion in favour of restriction' (see Amulree Report, para. 456). It cautiously added to its 'approval of the present permitted hours' that 'restriction, in a matter of this kind, depends on the sanction of public opinion'. The Report said: 'We think that to a vast section of the public, including public house clients, the present

[1] See among others Weeks, op. cit., p. 219: 'It is universally admitted that the habit of taking solutions of alcohol, such as beer, on an empty stomach between meals is very bad for the individual'; see also Dr. Roche Lynch, then Senior Official Analyst to the Home Office, before the Amulree Commission, A. 11,973.

scheme is acceptable, and is becoming more, and not less, so.' In view of this and the other statements relating to the beneficial effects of restricted hours which we have already encountered, it is surprising to find Mass Observation taking a rather different view. They say (see op. cit., p. 233) that 'it is difficult to believe that in limiting the hours during which pubs are open you limit drunkenness, any more than forbidding abortion prevents some 90,000 working-class women aborting per annum. First, people do not go to pubs to get drunk. Second, their drinking is limited by their spending capacity. Thirdly, as our timings show, they could easily get drunk in the available hours if they wanted to do so, by coming earlier instead of during the later hours of opening time.'

All these arguments run counter to the findings of other studies. The Buckmaster Report, whose methods of taking evidence came nearest to those used by Mass Observation, came to the conclusion that 'restriction of hours in which the sale of drink is permitted' was one of the outstanding causes of the progress in sobriety (see *Aspects*, pp. 48–9). Turning to the Amulree Commission, we may omit statements by witnesses who would as a matter of social or ethical convictions favour every sort of restriction. But evidence from those judging the matter obviously without bias and even from those from whom one would expect a bias against restrictions shows the same picture. Dr. Alfred Salter, M.P., with his extensive knowledge of drinking habits in Bermondsey, left no doubt that 'restricted facilities of drinking' were 'due to reduced hours of opening and particularly the earlier closing hour' (see Amulree Commission, 26,041 (*sub* 21)). Mr. Arthur Shadwell, the authority on many social questions, declared himself against an increase of restrictions (see A. 32,563–4) and enumerated many factors which had led to 'a great diminution of excessive drinking'; but he put restrictions of hours, after changes in social habits and the increase of prices, as the third main cause of greater sobriety: 'If you diminish the restrictions', he claimed, 'you would at once get an increase of drunkenness, but I would not advise increasing restrictions.' But perhaps even more persuasive is the evidence of those who are connected with the trade itself, or at least have first-hand experience of it; they indeed should know. There is, for instance, the evidence of Sir Edgar Sanders, later the Director of the Brewers' Society (see A. 20,033 (7)): 'Present Opening Hours. I consider these have met with extraordinary acceptance by the British public. . . . The earlier closing hour has been a reform of first magnitude for the whole country. The last hour in the evening is always the worst, whatever the period of opening is . . .' Perhaps the most illuminating evidence was that of Mr. Harry Rogers, a member of the General Council and a District Representative of the Licensed Victuallers' Defence League of England and Wales (see Q. and A. 13,866 and 13,905–9):

Mr. Arnold: Would there be difficulty about rearrangement of hours, if longer permitted hours were given?

Mr. Rogers: There would be no difficulty; probably an extra hand would be employed.

Mr. Arnold: How would those extra hands be paid?

Mr. Rogers: According to the terms agreed upon.

Mr. Arnold: Where would the money come from?

Mr. Rogers: Out of the alleged profits of the trade.

Mr. Arnold: So you expect extra profits through longer hours to pay for that further labour?

Mr. Rogers: That would contribute to it.

Mr. Arnold: Your idea is, there would be extra consumption?

Mr. Rogers: Naturally, there would be extra consumption.

This last point should surely settle the matter.

Mass Observation is, of course, right in its view that shorter hours as such do not prevent drunkenness: we have already heard in a previous chapter that people get drunk in very different ways, and that with some it takes longer and with others it happens in a very short space of time. But the chances are that the longer a person stays in a public house, the more he will be exposed to the inducements to heavy drinking. His ability to spend money on drink has certainly something to do with drunkenness. But it does by no means exclude other factors and the possibility of staying in a public house, possibly, as in former days, almost to the next morning, is one of them. The initial point of Mass Observation's argument is perhaps the least ingenuous: of course people do not go to public houses to get drunk, just as motorists do not intend to incur accidents. But the time restrictions aim at reducing the risk of getting drunk. A person might drink too much in the last twenty minutes of any 'last hour'; but the chances are that any additional hour increases the risk that he will drink more than he otherwise would, perhaps could, have done. Not even drinking in clubs alters this position. Clubs are required by law to conform to the permitted hours operative in the neighbourhood. The absence of police inspection may make it difficult to enforce the law, and it may not be an offence to be intoxicated on club premises, but (see Heath, op. cit., pp. 27–8) it has never been contended that the possibilities of evasion seriously diminished the importance of restricted hours. As the Amulree Report put it (see para. 44), shorter and broken hours, as fixed by the Act of 1921, have 'proved themselves to be an indispensable element in the reduction of insobriety'.

SCOPE FOR FURTHER RESTRICTION

To review still existing problems it may be necessary first to state the present position of permitted hours in some more detail than the reader already knows from our description of the general scope of restrictive legislation.[1] We have, for instance, used the term 'permitted hours' but have so far omitted to render its particular meaning. The term dates from the Act of 1921. In this Statute 'closing hours' were no longer mentioned, and the new phrase of 'permitted hours' appeared for the first time. The intention of this alteration was that the hours of the day when the sale of liquor was permitted should be distinct from the hours when the public house or the premises might be open and sell refreshments other than intoxicants. The general scheme of the distribution of the permitted hours is that public houses may sell alcoholic drink for a limited number of hours on weekdays and Sundays and that these hours must commence at some time in the morning and must end at night, subject to the legally required break of at least two hours in the permitted hours after 12 noon. Within these limits, and subject to the 'break', the licensing justices in each licensing district are free to vary permitted hours for their licensed premises. (Licensing will be discussed in some detail in the next chapter.) In the case of registered clubs, the permitted hours may be fixed by the members in accordance with the rules of the club, but are subject to the same statutory limits, i.e. that the hours shall not begin before a certain time in the morning and not continue after a certain time in the night (the significance of both these limitations on greater sobriety was stressed by the Amulree Report, see para. 45), and that there is an afternoon break, to ensure that there is no continuous sale of intoxicating liquor for more than four or five hours.

[1] We follow here the authoritative and most recent description provided by H. Cecil Heath, op. cit., pp. 15 sqq., 53 sqq.

The number of permitted hours for the sale of alcoholic drink in the Metropolitan District of London is nine hours on week-days; elsewhere it is eight hours, though in special circumstances the justices may extend the permitted hours in the provinces to eight and a half per day.[1] On Sundays the permitted hours in London are five, of which two hours must be in the afternoon between 12 noon and 3 p.m., and three hours in the evening, between 6 and 10 p.m. The hours are fixed by the licensing justices. Since the enactment of the Sunday Closing (Wales) Act, 1881, there is no sale of liquor on Sundays in Wales and Monmouthshire; only clubs are permitted to supply.

There is certainly no uniformity of permitted hours over the whole country, and this presents a problem. According to Wilson (see Wilson, op. cit., pp. 158–9) out of nearly 40 million people living in England and Wales in 1936, 59·5 per cent lived in districts with 10 p.m. closing, 39·5 per cent with 10.30 and 1 per cent with 11 p.m. closing. In the County of London the figures were 76·7 per cent with 10.30 closing, 13·9 per cent with 10 p.m. closing and 9·4 per cent with 11 p.m. closing—the latter being mostly in that small part of London commonly called 'theatreland'. (See Amulree Report, para. 458.) The effect of these differences has become painfully obvious, especially in the Metropolis. The Amulree Report heard 'a good deal of evidence in regard to the disorder which results in London at and after 10 p.m. on the margins of the 11 p.m. areas through persons streaming across the boundary from 10 p.m. areas'. For instance, after remarking that 'hundreds and thousands of children get to bed earlier now as a result of legislation', Mr. Frank Briant, J.P., stated that he regarded it 'as extremely dangerous that there should be a variation of the hours in different parts of London, thus creating an inducement to extend the hours of drinking by crossing into what may be a contiguous borough' (A. 30,575). The Report did not wish to exaggerate this unpleasant matter, but it could not deny that it was of 'local importance', and suggested that general permitted hours should end at 10 p.m. for the whole County of London. It was six years later that Robert Sinclair described the 'tipsy pilgrimage' which could be witnessed in certain London areas between the hours of 10 and 11, and added that 'each departure from a pub, each arrival at another, means another ceremonial round and another tinkle from

[1] But there are some other exceptions of minor importance to our subject, see for them Heath, op. cit., p. 53.

the cash register'.[1] The Amulree Report suggested uniformity of hours over the whole country. It said that there was 'no real need' anywhere in the provinces for licensed houses to be open for business in intoxicants after 10 p.m. And in rural districts, especially in winter, it was possible that there was no significant public demand for even so late an hour as 10 p.m. (see Amulree Report, para. 460).

CLUBS AND BOTTLE PARTIES

Another problem is the enforcement of permitted hours in clubs. That it is only occasionally that an infringement is brought to light may point to nothing more than that the police and magistrates have no right of inspection: whereas a constable does not require a search-warrant to enter licensed premises and detect violations of the law, he needs a search-warrant to enter a club. This means that the police have to go to a magistrate; that the magistrate may grant a search-warrant to a constable if he is satisfied by evidence on oath that there is reason to believe that the club in question is so managed as to constitute a ground for striking it off the register, or that intoxicating liquor is sold or supplied on the premises of an unregistered club; and that it is not before a search-warrant has been granted that a constable will be authorised to enter a club (see Amulree Commission, Q. 482). The employment of an 'agent provocateur' to get the necessary evidence was much criticised before the Royal Commission.[2]

There can be no doubt that the club provides an opportunity, and a temptation, to break the law relating to permitted hours, and that it is difficult to detect the offence. Whether the increase in the numbers of clubs has been due to any considerable extent to this possibility is not known for certain. But Mr. J. C. Swinburne-Hanham, Chairman of the Licensing Committee for Dorset, told the Royal Commission that, of the seventy clubs in the county, most had sprung up 'out of extinguished licensed premises'. (See A. 4950.) There has certainly been a substantial increase in the

[1] See Sinclair, op. cit., p. 124; see also Heath, p. 16: 'The lack of uniformity leads in some districts to undesirable social results, particularly where two contiguous areas close at a different hour in the evening. There tends to be an exodus of undesirable persons from the earlier district to the later district, and drunkenness in the later district becomes aggravated by this exodus.'

[2] See e.g. Mr. James H. Hudson, M.P., A. 28,751: 'It is highly desirable that we should get away from the practices which are now often adopted by the police, those surreptitious means of acquiring evidence which often lead to the employment of young constables and even of agents actually outside the police, friends of the police, who break the law in order that facts may be discovered regarding general breaches of the law.' See also Q. and A. 24,309–11 for the same criticism.

number of clubs in Great Britain serving drink, i.e., from 9,295 in 1913 to 16,497 in 1946 and 18,370 in 1948 (see *Alliance Yearbook for 1950*). By the time the Amulree Commission reported the club had already become 'in many instances . . . a formidable competitor to licensed premises'. One of the reasons for this was the ease with which a club could be registered under current law; this, the Commission thought, offered 'a strong temptation'; the Commission was satisfied that 'there are many clubs in all parts of the country which have been brought into existence solely for the purpose of supplying intoxicants' (see Amulree Report, para. 508). It has been estimated that some 7 per cent of the total bill for alcoholic drink is incurred in clubs (see Wilson, op. cit., p. 143), but even if the proportion were smaller, it would not provide an argument for maintaining the privileges of clubs. The same applies to the fact that clubs concern mainly the wealthier classes. We shall return to the licensing aspect of the matter in the next chapter on licensing. In connection with permitted hours and the difficulty of enforcement in clubs, it may be worth reiterating that it is the gap in the law and not its statistical significance which seems the important pointer to action.

'Bottle parties' seem to be particularly open to criticism. Lord Goddard, the Lord Chief Justice, discussed their legal position in a recent appeal case to the King's Bench:[1] 'As was common knowledge, the object of those parties was to enable alcoholics [*sic*] and others to continue drinking after licensing hours, and the way it was done, or supposed to be done, was that orders were placed with a wine and spirit shop during the day and the shopkeeper was supposed to sell there and then and appropriate a bottle or bottles of drink to the particular customer, but postponed delivery until it was asked for. Then when public houses were closed the purchaser called, or more probably sent, for the whole or part of his purchase, which he then consumed on unlicensed premises. So long as the sale took place at the shop and not at the bottle party there was no breach of the law, unless, indeed, as actually happened in the present case, the sale and delivery at the shop took place out of permitted hours.' His Lordship described in detail what had happened in this case: an excise officer entered the gates of the club; he told the waiter that he had an order with a firm carrying on a wine merchant business and asked him to get

[1] Report of the case which came before the King's Bench Divisional Court in January 1947 in *Alliance News*, March–April 1947, p. 17.

a bottle of Gordon's gin. The waiter thereupon produced a bit of paper 'dignified', as His Lordship put it, by the title of 'delivery instructions', filled in the name of the wine merchant and the kind and quantity of liquor required and asked the officer to be good enough to sign forthwith. It read: 'To . . . Please deliver to me at . . . the undermentioned goods, being part of the order you hold on my behalf.' The waiter told him that the price would be £3 10s. which the officer paid. The Quarter Sessions had found that the document constituting the order was 'colourable only'—which meant nothing more or less, as the Lord Chief Justice explained, than that the 'process of getting an order in advance and pretending to appropriate goods in advance to it was pure humbug' and that the wine merchant firm in question 'paid just as much attention to it as one would expect, which was none'.

The Lord Chief Justice took pains to explain that 'blameless sales' could happen and did happen because Parliament 'had not seen fit to legislate against those parties', and had left judges to decide on nice points under the Sale of Goods Act as to the 'passing of property'. This was not for lack of attention, for instance, on the part of the Amulree Commission. The Report mentioned that 'there are clubs where the hours chosen have been so sandwiched between the hours fixed for licensed premises as to enable members to have practically continuous opportunity for obtaining intoxicants'. The Commission thought that this was 'wrong in principle'; it urged that 'where the hours have been selected for the sole purpose of providing such continuous opportunity—which we are satisfied is true in some cases—we regard it as an evasion, in spirit not in letter, of the Statute' (see Amulree Report, para. 484). The Report said that clubs ought normally to comply with the permitted hours obtaining locally. No doubt, there were clubs and clubs. There were many clubs, such as golf clubs or athletic clubs, for example, the objects of which were bound up with particular hours, and whose active life normally ended with the onset of darkness; but though some discretion might be left to the registration authority to vary permitted hours in special cases of clubs, the latest hour should, in the view of the Commission, not be later than 10 p.m., i.e. the latest general permitted hour. This would itself only do little, of course, to prevent the other forms of evading the law.

Another difficulty arises through the extension of permitted hours of serving drink with meals. This concerns restaurants and hotels. In the case of clubs serving food, the Amulree Report recommended (see para. 486B) that the registration authority should be entitled to grant the right to serve intoxicants with meals until 12 midnight in London and 11 p.m. elsewhere, if satisfied that they fell within the category of a hotel or restaurant. But what is a 'meal'? The refreshment may be of a quite subordinate nature and only be served to comply with the ruling. It is with a view to this difficulty that the Amulree Report stressed the need to specify a meal as 'a substantial refreshment'. The Commission had got no further than this even after receiving a good deal of evidence on this point. The most illuminating was probably that of Mr. O. F. Dowson, an assistant legal adviser to the Home Office, who was asked whether a biscuit or a sandwich served with alcoholic drink was a 'meal' in the legal sense; he had to reply that 'the question had been raised in the summary courts', but that there was no agreement on the point. His interpretation of a 'meal', however, was far from reassuring; he went so far as to contend that 'one sandwich appeals to one's common sense as not being a meal; with two sandwiches you get a little nearer to it being a meal; and in proportion as you increase the number you increase the chances of it being a meal' (see A. and Q. 550 sqq.). Sir Robert Wallace, Chairman of the County of London Sessions and Licensing Committee, was asked (see ibid., A. and Q. 637 sq.): 'Can you enlighten us at all as to what is a *bona fide* meal?' to which he replied: 'I think if you were to apply to the members of the Commission here you would get twenty-one answers to the question.' Yet it seems hardly appropriate to make the supply of alcoholic liquor beyond the generally permitted hour dependent on whether a client will consume one or four sandwiches.

It is for this reason also that the proposal of the Amulree Commission to restore the closing hour principle in the old sense, i.e. closed only for the sale of drink, must meet with criticism (see para. 462): if licensed premises were to be allowed to remain open, 'except for the sale of intoxicants', during the afternoon, the temptation to evade the law was bound to be greatly increased. A member of a club may order, during a time when the sale of liquor is generally prohibited, a few sandwiches or a small hors d'œuvre with a roll and thus get the drink for which he came. Such possibilities are, of course, far greater in clubs than in restaurants whose business depends on serving substantial meals.

It seems to us that no solution to this problem can be found from a definition of the 'substantial' meal. At once more necessary and probably also possible is the alteration of the law to make the ordering and dispatch of liquor, as distinct from its appropriation, unlawful during non-permitted hours. If this cannot be effected by legislation, for reasons which may be outside the scope of this enquiry, the simplest way would be to prohibit altogether the consumption in clubs of alcoholic drink during non-permitted hours, without any regard as to whence and by what 'steps' the drink was provided.

The Royal Commission was, as we have heard, decidedly for a maintenance of the existing closing times and permitted hours, and expected rather an extension of the restrictions than a relaxation; but the actual development in the next fifteen years was somewhat different. During the years immediately before the second World War a substantial number of licensing districts throughout the country had permitted hours ending at a time later than 10 p.m. during the whole or for part of the year: in 1932 the number of districts throughout the country—excluding London—that had closing hours later than 10 p.m. was not more than thirty; the Licensing (Permitted Hours) Act in 1934 enabled magistrates to fix later permitted hours for part of the year; and by 1939, as a result of trade applications at brewster sessions, whole-year extensions to 10.30 p.m. had been secured in ninety-eight licensing districts, and part-year extensions to 10.30 p.m. in 350 districts. Out of a total of 990 licensing districts outside the Metropolis, therefore, 448 had extensions either for the whole or part of the year (see Heath, pp. 53–4). The second World War caused the withdrawal of a considerable number of these extensions. But their revival is a very real probability, and may only be one sign of a trend in what many would consider to be in the wrong direction.

CHAPTER XII

LICENSING AND THE SUPERFLUITY OF OUTLETS

LICENSING, by which we mean in this connection the grant, upon certain conditions, of Justices' Licences,[1] is still the main means of ensuring that the retailer carries out the legal restrictions imposed on the sale of alcoholic drink. The Amulree Report called this objective the 'preservation of good order' (see para. 21), but this definition is rather too narrow if it suggests that licensing is merely a matter of 'policing'. There is also a forward-looking aspect in licensing: through it attempts are made, for instance, to improve standards by testing and certifying the qualification of the licensee or the would-be licensee, and by specifying the physical condition of the drink and the place in which it is to be taken. Nor is this aim restricted to hygienic purposes; aesthetic considerations, for instance, may also be involved.[2]

But licensing has another major purpose besides enforcing the various regulations: this is to influence what may be called the economic superfluity of sales outlets. Here the test is not one of standards of morality, safety, or efficiency, but primarily numerical: are there 'too many' public houses or other sales outlets? The question may be raised in the same way as in the case of shops in general. But there is a difference in the considerations affecting the answer. With retail outlets in general Adam Smith's words still retain their social significance: '. . . shopkeepers and tradesmen . . . can never be multiplied so as to hurt the public, though they may so as to hurt each other' (see Adam Smith, *Wealth of Nations*, book ii, ch. v). As Adam Smith saw it, and we still see it—

[1] The object of Excise Licences is strictly confined to revenue purposes—their practical effect on the sale and manufacture of alcoholic liquor is that no person without an Excise Licence can make or sell liquor, i.e., a solution containing more than 2 per cent of alcohol.

[2] See e.g. evidence of Mr. A. K. Wilson, Chief Constable of Plymouth, before the Royal Commission, A. 20,862: '. . . the houses taken to new districts should be made to harmonise in every way with the architecture of other houses and be modern . . .'

excepting, of course, trade associations with restrictive purposes—more competition may mean lower prices, and through this a larger consumption of goods which is in the interests of society. With alcoholic drink the problem is different, though the analysis is the same, because an increase in the consumption of drink is by no means free of social dangers and economic disadvantages. There is a fundamental difference between 'too many shops' and 'too many public houses'. The competitive struggle between too many public houses can be an inducement to publicans to violate legal restrictions. The story of the 'long pull' is an instance of this from bygone days. 'Long pull' was the term used for the licensees' practice at one time of giving overmeasure to their clients in order to attract their custom. The man who asked for a pint got more than a pint, and naturally sought the house where this 'long pull' was practised (see Wilson, op. cit., p. 165). This form of illegitimate competition was so prevalent early this century that the Licensing Bill of 1908 sought to empower justices to impose the penalty of non-renewal of an on-licence in connection with 'the supply to any person, as the measure of intoxicating liquor for which he asks, of an amount exceeding that measure'. But it was not until the Central Control Board began its operations that the practice was effectively prohibited, and by section 9 of the Licensing Act of 1921 it was provided that 'no person shall either by himself or his servants, etc., sell or supply to any person as the measure of intoxicating liquor for which he asks, an amount exceeding that measure'. Other offences however persist. Throughout this chapter there will be instances of breaches in the regulations by publicans, more often in spirit than in the letter, owing to the pressure of competition.

The less conspicuous type of drinking outlets, the clubs, could probably also provide numerous examples. How far, in fact, does a superfluity of drinking outlets counteract the aims of legislation to reduce rather than to increase drinking, and heavy drinking in particular; and how far should licensing legislation have regard to purely economic superfluity quite apart from any other considerations?

In principle the possibility of restricting the number of sales outlets is included in the present legislation. The term 'redundancy' may well be applied here. Justices may ask the police to make enquiries when applications for the renewal of licences are made in order to be able to take account of the 'amount of public-house accommodation in the locality'.[1] The difficulty is to decide what redundancy means. It is relatively easy for authorities to find out whether certain establishments are out-of-date and a possible danger to hygiene, and therefore 'redundant'. But those who are opposed to measures intended to abate the consumption of drink in general are justified in contending that the position is far more difficult when redundancy becomes a question of economic superfluity, or of the possible discrepancy between the number of outlets and the demand for them. A question put by Mr. Frank Whitbread to Sir Robert Wallace, K.C. before the Royal Commission made this clear. Mr. Whitbread suggested rightly that before any procedure can take place under the law 'there must be redundancy'. He continued: 'But I am not quite clear in my own mind, and I do not think anybody is quite clear, as to what a redundant house is. . . . I am bound to say from the commercial point of view and from the common-sense point of view, the mere fact of the payment of compensation of some £20,000 or £30,000 in respect of an individual licence raises considerable doubts in my mind as to whether it can really be regarded as redundant. My view always was that the object of the Act was to provide means by which, without grave injustices, the superfluous licence which might be said to be not in a position to command a living trade, that is to say, a trade out of which a man could make a living, might be done away with.'[2] From the commercial angle this was indisputable. But if the purpose of legislation is to abate the evils of excessive drinking, consideration of 'redundancy' of outlets is not excluded by the mere fact that they are a profitable business proposition. The question seen from the angle of excessive consumption, or of an undue encouragement of it, is how far there are more establishments than the population really requires.

REDUNDANCY AND THE CONSUMPTION OF DRINK

The assumption underlying this question is that a superfluity of establishments is conducive to more drinking, quite apart from the possibly undesirable effects of over-competition. The Amulree Report unfortunately avoided consideration of this issue. It said that it had 'long been a subject of discussion whether the mere

[1] See for the same question in connection with general retail trade, Hermann Levy, *The Shops of Britain*, *passim*.

[2] See Q. 570: see also Mr. W. Warney Webb's evidence, A. 8,842: 'The whole point is, what is redundancy. I do not know what it means. I have never found anybody who does.' Mr. Webb was Chief Constable of Cambridgeshire.

superfluity of licensed premises is in itself a bad thing. The stock arguments *pro* and *contra* were fully entered into by our predecessors, and we do not feel it necessary to do more than express our conviction that their conclusions were right, and that superfluous licences do no good but may do much harm' (see para. 126). But while the Report was fully convinced that 'a much more rapid reduction of licences was desirable' (see para. 110), it did not feel inclined to scrutinise more closely what redundancy in one case might mean in contrast to others—for instance, in the case of mere economic superfluity as contrasted with redundancy for hygienic or similar reasons. As to the former the Commission was apparently so much impressed by the difficulties of stating what economic or social superfluity exactly was that it refrained altogether from probing deeper into the position; so that the point of how far a multiplicity of outlets for alcoholic drink was *per se* conducive to more widespread and heavier drinking was not discussed by the Report at all.

It is difficult enough to separate the influence of the numbers of public houses from the many other factors affecting the consumption of drink. One warning may suffice. From the evidence once submitted to a Swiss Commission it emerged that the highest degree of inebrity and alcoholism prevailed in localities which had the smallest number of drinking places; the point was that there the drink generally consumed was ardent spirits. This was confirmed by the findings that the greatest sobriety prevailed in places where drinking facilities were most plentiful, but where the beverages consumed were fermented liquors. (See Julian L. Baker, *The Brewing Industry*, 1905, pp. 170–1.) The size of the public house and general environmental conditions are clearly also immediately relevant. But 'other factors being equal', it can be taken as a matter of course that multiplicity of public houses is conducive to heavy drinking or, reversely, that a reduced number of public houses leads to less drinking.[1]

There is the argument that the closing of public houses does not reduce the consumption of drink but simply leads to overcrowding of other houses. This point came up before the Royal Commission in connection with the closing of a public house in Plymouth, in an area where no less than eleven public houses were situated within a radius of 200 yards. (See Q. and A. 3,003 and 3,111) Mr. R. A.

[1] See e.g., Royal Commission, evidence by Mr. A. K. Mayall, Chief Constable of Oldham, p. 440, under 'Probable Reasons for increased Sobriety: Reduction in the number of Licensed Premises'; also Dr. Alfred Salter's evidence, p. 1441, A. 26,041 (21).

J. Walling, J.P., at that time Chairman of the Licensing Justices of Plymouth, was asked: 'Are you quite satisfied that when you close down one house you do not overcrowd another?' Again: 'Take the instance of the "Rifleman's Arms". Presumably the people who were in the habit of frequenting that place are not going to abandon their habits straight away. . . . They go somewhere else. How do you satisfy yourself that they do not overcrowd some other place . . . ?' If people merely transferred their custom to another house, one might argue that the closing down of some pubs on the grounds of superfluity might lead to undesirable conditions in other public houses in consequence of overcrowding. But the witness was of that opinion that this just did not happen: his reply was that if such overcrowding had happened the authorities would have been informed, and this was not the case. He added: 'I think that when you have an area with a large number of licensed houses—and that is the kind of area we chiefly tackle—it would require a very large public house for its clientele to overflow all the others when it was divided up amongst them.'

To the extent that multiplicity of public houses means greater proximity to people's homes, the temptation to have a drink must be greater. The public house just round the corner may in many instances stimulate consumption beyond what would otherwise occur, simply because it is so near. This does not only apply to drinking in the pub, but also to the custom, more prevalent in former days, of sending round to the nearest public house for draught ale from the 'jug and bottle' department. Fetching beer by jug has been to some extent replaced by the buying and storing of bottled beer.[1] The greater use of bottled beer similarly was to some extent explained by Mr. A. Chaston Chapman to the Royal Commission: people living in flats find it simpler 'to put a certain number of bottles in a corner than, as was formerly the case when people had houses, to have casks in the cellar.' (See A. 38,647.) In close proximity to people's homes the public house has a good chance also to have strong social ties. So strong becomes the custom of visiting the pub 'within a few minutes' stroll' from their homes that sometimes workers retain the habit of visiting it even when they have moved farther away (see Mass Observation, *The Pub*, p. 129).

But in general the great multiplicity of public houses is found in the centres of towns and in main roads. Mass Observation found

[1] See Sir William Crawford and H. Broadley, *The People's Food*, 1938, pp. 74 sqq.

that 11·1 per cent of the area investigated contained 48·3 per cent of all the public houses. Even more strongly marked was the relative density per square mile: the density of public houses in the central quarter-mile was seven times the average density for the whole area. The oldest part of the town had most public houses, and the newest the least. As the town developed and spread outwards, pushing tentacles of built-up area along the main roads, the number of new public houses built in the newer areas became proportionately much less than in the older districts. The immediate explanation for this was the progressively stricter application of licensing laws and a growing unwillingness to grant new licences on any pretext (see *The Pub and the People*, 1943, pp. 67–71). But, while 'the age of the district' is an important factor in indicating the relative frequency of public houses in different areas, this observation should not lead to rash conclusions as to the interconnection between drinking and the multiplicity of public houses. Town centres cater for many other people than just those of the immediate vicinity, or even of the town itself. The purpose of visiting the houses in the centre may be different from that of visiting regularly a public house round the corner in an outlying district of small streets. A new public house in a central district may attract very few new drinkers of that district; but a new public house in a smaller street, where otherwise no public house would exist, may lead to very much more drinking (Mass Observation overlooked these differences, see p. 74). 'Density' is not a sufficient indication of the incidence of drink.

The value of a formula comparing the effects of a few large with many small public houses is also limited. We agree with Professor F. Zweig when he says that 'the public house is not a statistical unit which can be dealt with adequately by numbers. One large public house can be equivalent to five or ten small ones' (see Zweig, op. cit., p. 24). The points we have so far mentioned do not exhaust the complexity of the problem. The Amulree Commission, which also emphasised that it did not 'consider it possible to estimate by any sort of statistical calculation whether there is or is not in any area a superfluity of licences' (see para. 126), explained that 'not only have areas of different types different requirements, but within the range of a single area there may be under-licensed parts and over-licensed parts, such variations remaining unrevealed by statistics covering the whole area'.

The question, so the Report urged, was essentially one to be decided from case to case. 'If there are more licensed houses in a given area than are reasonably needed for the service of the public, resident and non-resident, then there are redundant houses. That there are still such areas we are convinced.' But what is 'reasonably' needed? This is the crucial question, only in another guise. The Report did not attempt, as it might have done, to give some general indications as to what constituted reasonableness, even if the essential relativity of the term had been taken for granted. It is not sufficient merely to draw from the difficulties of arriving at some absolute indication as to what constitutes economic redundancy the conclusion that Professor Zweig draws, namely (see op. cit., p. 24) that 'all generalisation in respect of public houses is false'. On the contrary, there are some definite conclusions of a general nature to be drawn from experience.

SOME CRITERIA OF REDUNDANCY

There can be no doubt, for instance, that a multiplicity of drinking outlets is more conducive to excessive drinking than a smaller number. In Germany the 'Bier-Reise'—a more refined term than 'pub-crawl', but the same thing—is an established institution; some people go from one inn to another just for the pleasure of frequenting a number of public houses on a single night. Less formally, a person may have left home with the object of having just a few glasses of beer, but finding it a dull evening in one pub, may be tempted to try another one and have there some more beer. The 'Bier-Reise' is certainly not altogether alien to Britain. 'On the way back the coach stopped at several pubs', says one of Mass Observation's descriptive passages (see *The Pub and the People*, p. 271). It became evident in the course of that survey that 'some people were regulars in two or three pubs, sometimes going from one to another on the same evenings, and sometimes visiting different ones on different evenings' (see ibid., p. 133). Lady Bell tells of one man (see Lady Bell, op. cit., p. 349) ' who had to pass five public houses on his way home from his work . . . had to make a separate effort at each one; he had succeeded one winter's after noon in passing four, and if the fifth had not been there he 'would have got home alright', but at that last one he succumbed and went in, cold, wet and tired, to sit in the warm and cheerful room, with the incidental subsequent result that may be imagined'. The liquor trade of course does not tire of asserting that 'because there are a lot of locals around you, that does not mean that you drink more' (see Whitbread & Co., *Your Local*, 1947, p. 42). But they know better: on the very next page of the book just quoted it is urged that distances between public houses and the home should be shortened so that 'no one need complain of having too far to walk' (see ibid., p. 43). It cannot be consistently contended that people would drink as much as they do now if there were fewer public houses at their disposal.

A multiplicity of drinking outlets is also likely directly to promote heavier drinking even in the same pub. The evidence of the Bishop of Kingston before the Amulree Commission was illuminating in this respect (see A. 26,783). The Bishop was satisfied that a reduction in the numbers of public houses in a strongly competitive area enabled publicans to 'be rather more independent in dealing with their trade'. For instance: 'A customer went to the "Henry the Eighth" and asked to be served, but he was not in a condition to be served and so the licensee refused to serve him. The man walked twenty-five yards down the street to the "Water Mill", got what he required, took it back to the "Henry the Eighth" and drank in the presence of the publican and said, "I will not get any more from your house". Naturally that discouraged the licensee of the "Henry the Eighth" from taking rather a strong line, knowing that he was surrounded by a lot of little beer-houses. When a lot of them were weeded out it gave a better chance for a man to carry on his trade properly.'

The formula, then, which Professor Zweig seems to have in mind, namely that one large public house may be equivalent to five or ten small public houses and thus cannot itself contribute to a reduction in the consumption of drink, is not really satisfactory. The five or ten small houses may, indeed, offer more inducement to drink than one large house with the same number of potential customers. This point appears to be more weighty than the possibility that the temptation of drinking in 'company' may be less in small public houses, and this is the reason by virtue of which heavy drinking and drunkenness is sometimes associated particularly with the large public house.[1] That the small houses are generally those selected for reduction is therefore likely to be the

[1] Cf. e.g., the *Alliance Yearbook for 1938*, p. 128: 'The smallest houses, and those doing the least trade, are almost invariably singled out for assault, whilst those which are playing infinitely more conspicuous and deadly a part in the demoralisation of the respective neighbourhoods are severely left alone.' But see evidence of Mr. J. C. Swinburne-Hanham, J.P., to the Amulree Commission, A. 4,979–80: 'Some of the superintendents of police rather favour a number of small houses as against a few large ones . . . there is not the same encouragement to drink in a small house, and you do not get a large company of people there at a time as you do in the larger houses . . .'

correct policy in many cases;[1] the multiplicity of small drinking outlets is probably *per se* conducive to more consumption and thereby possibly also to an excessive expenditure on drink on the part of working-class people.

The reason which may lead to the closing down of public houses or to the refusal of new licences, indeed the entire administrative attitude concerning redundancy of outlets, is naturally more complex than this. In one case it may be that redundancy is clearly indicated by the number of outlets. The Royal Commission had, for instance, the evidence of the Chairman of the Licensing Committee for Dorsetshire who was troubled by the fact that in one division, Sturminster, there was actually one licence for every 200 inhabitants (see A. 8839), a clear case of redundancy because of unquestionable excess. But in most cases it is a combination of reasons which leads to the closing down of public houses. Even with regard only to economic factors, 'the numerical one, the character of the population, the density of the population in a given area', may all lead to different attitudes on the part of the authorities in different districts (see Amulree Commission A. 30,821; see also A. 2,742 and 2,818).

Even when the decision has been reached that there is redundancy in a district there arises the need to choose which house or houses to close. This choice has to be made according to additional, and not altogether economic reasons. Mr. R. A. J. Walling, the Chairman of the Licensing Justices for Plymouth, which had as many as one licence to every 423 inhabitants and, therefore, a 'considerable degree of redundancy', told the Commission (see A. 3,068 and 3,112) something of the many conditions which were taken into account before declaring any house redundant: 'It is no good to try to close a house on the ground of redundancy purely and simply. You cannot do it. You have to have some relevant consideration in addition to the redundancy of the house. When you have half-a-dozen houses and you think one of them is redundant, you naturally take the one which is worst designed and worst conducted, or worst equipped for the purpose.' Another witness, Sir Robert Wallace, declared that he could not tell the Commission 'the hundred different ways' in which the final conclusion was arrived at (see ibid., A. 723). In some cases it could be simply the fact that some public houses

[1] See ibid., Q. 20,858: 'redundancy meaning, as I understood you to say, a large number of small houses rather than the total area being too large'.

showed a downward trend in the sale of beer and could therefore be declared redundant (see ibid., A. 724). In others, lengthy consideration of numerous possibilities was necessary. As regards new licences, anyone may oppose an application, and need not give any notice of the intention to the appellant or to anyone else. Temperance workers are therefore exhorted by their leaders to oppose 'every application for a new licence', and are instructed in detail how to select their arguments and to prepare their opposition (see for this Heath, op. cit., pp. 45–8). With the brewing interests in general well prepared to back the new licence by all possible means, the licensing authorities are often in the little-enviable position of having to deal with two opponents equally biased in the matter, the bias of high idealism on the one side, and one dictated by business motives on the other.

The relative ease with which a drinking place can be managed, and the fact that managing a public house is often merely a business side-line, may help to explain how the local excess of houses has come about and provide an important consideration for redundancy. Yet so far it has received little attention. We know from a study of the superfluity of shops how much the relative ease of managing a retail outlet can be responsible for an economically unjustifiable increase in the number of certain shops (see Hermann Levy, *The Shops of Britain*, pp. 10 sq. and *passim*). The Royal Commission was told that in Cambridgeshire 90 per cent of the publicans followed some other calling; they 'could not live on the house'; they have it 'for the sake of a roof over their head' (see Royal Commission, Q. and A. 8,831 sqq.). As a result there was in some rural districts a public house for every 120–130 inhabitants. To the Commission this seemed a case of obvious superfluity. It may be difficult to close public houses on the ground that they provide merely a business 'side-line'. But the fact that they often do so undoubtedly contributes to an excess in outlets.

It is not unusual for a multiplicity of drinking places to entail the social disadvantages of unemployment, particularly in places subject to considerable seasonal fluctuations in demand. In the years 1935 to 1939 the average unemployment in Great Britain in the hotel, public house, restaurant, club, and similar services varied in the summer and winter by 57 per cent for men and 71 per cent for women. In holiday resorts the fluctuations were no doubt greater. Figures showing the relative sizes of catering establishments and other retail outlets were quoted in a recent survey of the County of Worcester which is increasingly frequented by holiday-makers. In Worcester City, 381 persons were employed in hotels, inns and public houses, while 1,069 people were employed in retail establishments dealing in 'consumers' necessities' for daily wants; and in five towns, Worcester, Cheltenham, Gloucester, Dudley and Burton, the number of persons employed in hotels, inns and public houses exceeded the number of those employed in retail groceries and provisions.[1] We may therefore take the relation of unemployment in drinking places to employment in other trade outlets as a useful indication of superfluity.

Even when the manifold difficulties are recognised and the differentiations of local conditions taken into account—which may justify one number of licences in one place and another number in another—one cannot avoid the conclusion that a series of criteria should be by now available, or at least be emerging, out of the experience with redundancy and superfluity to date. It is indeed desirable, as the Amulree Report (see para. 128) stressed, that the problem of superfluous licences should be approached in a comprehensive way, and public-house statistics cannot give the complete picture. And 'the needs of the public in any district cannot be altogether static', so that, on that account alone, no settlement can be regarded as final. But a comprehensive and general scheme dealing with redundancy 'would enable a wise and judicious selection of the houses to be extinguished to be made; it ought not, even if it involved a considerable measure of reduction, to be wholly unwelcome to the trade if it freed it from anxiety to which the present system subjects it; and it would do the work more cheaply by avoiding the operation of betterment under which a certain element of trade may be the subject of repeated compensation'. The Amulree Commission apparently did not feel that it could make immediately practical suggestions as regards the criteria to be employed for testing superfluity. But it proposed that licensing justices in all districts should within a short period of time, say two years, review their areas and prepare provisional plans for reduction, and that these surveys should be considered as supplying the material for redundancy on a national scale, carried out possibly by a central authority (see paras. 137–9).

These very useful recommendations were not implemented. But even if they had been carried out, the need remains for some measure of superfluity for general guidance. George B. Wilson has

[1] See *County Town, A Civic Survey of the Planning of Worcester*, 1946, pp. 193 and 81.

proposed some. He suggests 'one on-licence to every 400 persons as a maximum allowance in rural petty sessional divisions', and one on-licence to every 600 persons in municipal boroughs having licensing benches.[1] There would thus have been, in 1931, a redundancy of 2,978 on-licences in 102 districts and one of 5,977 in 382 areas; in the case of boroughs there were in 1931 twenty-seven with a surplus of 663 on-licences, 90 with a surplus of 2,332 on-licences, and 28 with a surplus of 348 licences. For London, Mr. Wilson reckoned with a maximum allowance of one on-licence for every 800 persons: on this basis there were 13 areas with an excess of 1,597 on-licences, 31 with an excess of 3,244 and 17 with an excess of 973. All in all, Mr. Wilson came to the conclusion that in 1931 the 'surplus' for all England and Wales was no fewer than some 18,000 on-licences. We do not know what the figures would be now. For one thing, bombs have been less unscrupulous in reducing the number of public houses in the London area than the authorities were before the war. Large numbers of public houses have been destroyed; and town planners are of the opinion that 'it is obvious from any standpoint of social welfare that they should not be rebuilt in their previous form'. (See C. B. Purdom, *How Should We Rebuild London?*, 1945, pp. 93–4.)

THE OBSTACLE OF COMPENSATION

But the reduction in the number of public houses before the war was retarded not merely, or even perhaps mainly, by the difficulties of finding adequate criteria for deciding how many and which houses to declare redundant: even on the basis of standards vaguely recognised in the early thirties, the Amulree Commission reported that 'in a number of licensing districts there is still considerable redundancy'.[2] Mr. G. B. Wilson, it should be noted, prepared a table for 1936 in which many towns in England and Wales were shown to have an average of one licence for fewer than 300 persons. Compensation is the major difficulty here. It does not

[1] See Wilson, op. cit., p. 112. We use here the term 'on-licence' for the first time. The great majority of licensed premises fall into two main categories, both of which require the production of a Justices' Licence before the appropriate Excise Licence can be obtained: 'on-licences' authorise the sale by retail of the liquor to which the licence extends for consumption 'on' or 'off' the licensed premises; and 'off-licences' authorise the sale by retail of intoxicating liquor for consumption 'off' the licensed premises only. For further details see Heath, op. cit., p. 9.

[2] See G. B. Wilson, op. cit., p. 112, and his instructive and detailed table on pp. 443–5.

arise in regard to licences granted since 1904, for the justices were then given absolute discretion to refuse renewal without compensation. With regard, however, to licenses issued before 1904, any refusal of renewal, except on certain specific grounds, is referred to the Compensation Authority, who decide on the amount of compensation that is to be paid to the owner of the licence. The compensation fund is not provided by the public, but by all the licensees in the district in accordance with the rateable value of their premises—on the understanding that the extinction of any licence will automatically increase the trade of other licensees in the neighbourhood and that the owners of these ought, therefore, to make some recompense for the extra custom they derive from the disappearance of a competitor (see Heath, op. cit., p. 38).

The compensation arrangements of the Licensing Act of 1904 were hotly opposed by the Liberal opposition: they said it destroyed the centuries-old discretion of justices to refuse renewal of on-licences, and as Wilson puts it (see op. cit., p. 110), looking back on nearly forty years of its operation, gave 'to the trade a security of tenure not hitherto enjoyed'. The intention of legislation was that the licensee—as distinct from owner and brewer—should receive fair compensation. In fact, compensation came to involve very substantial indemnities. The discrepancy arose from the judicial construction placed on the compensation clause by Mr. Justice Kennedy, who decided in a Revenue case that the award must represent the 'market value' of the licence at the time of refusal, and that such market value must be arrived at on the basis of the brewers' profit on the barrelage of the house, adding thereto a certain number of years' purchase of the property income, and deducting from the sum of these figures the value of the premises unlicensed.

The effect of the judgment was to raise the compensation far beyond the trade's most sanguine expectations, and greatly to retard the process of reducing the number of public houses. Mr. Walter Foster, for instance, reported to the Royal Commission (see A. 3,173) that the Licensing Committee in Leeds regarded many on-licences 'as suitable for extinction on payment of compensation', but the the compensation fund, even though imposed at the maximum rate, was inadequate to provide for the process of speeding up the reduction of licences. In addition the change in the value of money has really called for a revision of the maximum rate of charges to the compensation fund to maintain its value, but this has not been done. The result was inevitable. Another witness also remarked (see evidence of Mr. R. A. J. Walling, J.P., A. 3,083) that his activities in reducing licences are limited by the amount of money he had available: 'You know that if a licence is costing your city an average sum of so much you cannot hope to reduce by more than so many licences in a given year.' (For further complications of the compensation question, see Q. and A. 1,284 sqq.). The Amulree Commission was in no way satisfied with the existing scheme of compensation. It considered 'it to be a serious weakness in the present scheme that the measure of reduction is governed by the amount which can be raised under the compensation charge'.

The logical policy would be to divorce the consideration on merits of the question of extinction from any financial adjustments which may be thought necessary. It would then be possible to leave to the renewal authority, with or without appeal, the actual decision as to extinction, and to the industry itself the task of compensation. Whether 'market value' is the correct basis for compensation is also questionable. The Amulree Report thought that the enhanced trade of neighbourhood houses would be a fairer basis and this would be influenced, as we have seen, by the greater remoteness of public houses consequent upon redundancy. The 'ideal scheme' would be that only that part of the business which was lost absolutely would be made the subject of insurance; the value of the rest, namely of the business dispersed over the neighbouring houses, would be paid to the losers by the gainers unless the persons were identical, in which case no money at all would need to pass (see Amulree Report, p. 29). But this solution would meet, in the view of the Report, with many 'practical difficulties', in particular with regard to the element of trade which upon the extinction of a house just failed to reappear elsewhere, so that each closure entailed a measure of absolute loss. For this and some other more technical reasons, the Report did not make any radical recommendations to change the arrangements. It suggested that the proposed National Licensing Commission might reach a solution which would result in a payment of 'much less than if it were left to a public body to assess'. (See Note to ch. iv of the Report). Be that as it may, here we are less concerned with the fair evaluation of compensation than with the fact that its cost at present is high enough to act as a check on the speedier reduction of licences. As George B. Wilson put it in 1940 (see op. cit., p. 112) 'the market value of refused licences has so greatly increased that the local funds available have been totally insufficient to pay for an adequate reduction of licences'.

LICENCES IN NEW AREAS

Licences in new residential areas present special problems. Do the people want public houses in their vicinity at all? And if they want some facilities, how many outlets should there be? The Amulree Report discussed these questions under the heading of 'Local Option', and they gain new significance in view of the current development of new communities on a large scale. In 1947 *PEP* conducted an enquiry into the Watling Estate, founded in 1927 by the London County Council, and housing a population of about 18,000 people. It is said that this estate with its associations provides a 'signpost' for many other new communities and that experience here can be regarded as characteristic. The apparent attitude of residents to public houses was particularly interesting. A Community Centre had originally been designed for licensed premises. But officials of several organisations on the estate, and ordinary residents, particularly women, were 'firmly convinced after twenty years' experience that it was sound not to have public houses within the boundaries of the estate': 'That's what we came here to get away from'. The feeling was that the estate would not have risen above the conditions of a slum if a demand for easily accessible public houses had been transplanted along with the tenants.[1] Nothing could better illustrate the moderating effect which good housing and domestic surroundings can have on the drinking habit. Though the *PEP* investigators apparently regretted the 'lack of easily accessible places' where people could meet, they apparently could not supply stronger evidence in favour of 'more accessible licensed premises' than that these 'would also do something to meet the loneliness of old people'—a point which confirms the view that in so many cases the pub is merely a substitute for a home or a good home.

It is perhaps not accidental that people who follow the enthusiastic Lawrence Wolfe in believing that in new garden cities the old conception of the 'house' being the 'home' should be abandoned in favour of a 'social community' with all sorts of new community facilities, do not regard with disfavour the provision of opportunities for drinking. Mr. Wolfe even extols this possibility,

[1] See *PEP*, Broadsheet of 15th August 1947, 'Watling Revisited', pp. 71–2.

saying that 'a rich man's home is "fully licensed", in the sense that he can get drinks at any hour from his cellar. There is no reason why the Community Centre, being an extension of the home, should not be in a similar position, if the residents desire it.'[1] He recalls the time before the Industrial Revolution, when 'the vast majority of English people lived round village greens, with all the residents knowing each other and meeting at the village inn' (see ibid., p. 143). He thus ignores entirely the evils of excessive drinking as they characterised Britain all through the eighteenth and nineteenth centuries in a way hardly paralleled anywhere else, due to the very existence of those inns and their use for general social and formally organised purposes. To transplant drinking at home, which is likely to be less excessive, to drinking in public with all its inherent risks, should be dismissed as dangerous advice. Much as one may welcome any suggestions to relieve the isolation of family life by fostering communal and co-operative social activities, one can hardly support suggestions which might give a new impetus to the 'a home from home' evil which better housing is expected to abate and has, indeed, so happily reduced.

Meeting places other than public houses should be available and have been made available on many estates. Since a corporation is not always able to provide such social amenities in addition to its contribution towards the cost of the houses, Lord Winterton's plea for State grants merits consideration (see Amulree Report, A. 33,869). The size of the community is very important in this connection. At the present high level of costs, financial and technical resources are required in such measure that only a fairly large organisation can cope with them even when they are provided out of public funds. But, as *PEP* emphasises, management benefits from being local and organised in small units. The fostering of community life is usually most satisfactorily undertaken by tenants' associations.[2] It will therefore be in general up to them to provide the proper substitutes for public houses, and to decide whether or not village halls and similar amenities will be merely drinking places in a new cloak.

The Royal Commission took the view that, as regards new communities, 'there are many such areas where a large number of inhabitants, not necessarily themselves abstainers, are anxious to

[1] See Wolfe, op. cit., pp. 102–3; he supports 'the abolition of the kitchen'.

[2] See *PEP*, Broadsheet of 21st May 1948, *Councils and their Tenants*, pp. 333–4 and 339.

avoid the establishment of licensed premises near their residence', and concluded that 'development areas are *sui generis* and that there is a special case for giving to their inhabitants direct control, by vote, over the licensing of premises within the area' (see Amulree Report, p. 39). Mr. Whitbread opposed this suggestion for control of licence in his Minority Report.[1] They discussed the ways in which the purpose of licensing could be obstructed in new areas (cf. pp. 39–40) and made some recommendations to fill the gaps. It was apparently possible, for instance, for enterprising brewery companies to secure sites, erect premises, and obtain a licence for them in advance of housing development. So the Report thought fit to recommend that the licensing justices should not normally entertain the grant of new licenses in 'special areas' until a substantial number of the residents had arrived; and the same ought to apply to the removal of existing licences to new areas. In both cases they suggested that the principle of local option should be employed, though only in a consultative way; in other words, the residents should be consulted as to whether they wished a licence to be granted or not. But in 1947 Cecil Heath could still draw attention to the fact that it had never been authoritatively decided whether the justices had power to refuse a 'special removal' on the grounds that the new premises were so far removed from the old site that they could not possibly cater for the previous trade and that the premises, therefore, were not 'fit and convenient' (see Heath, op. cit., pp. 59–60). There are thus grave loopholes in the licensing legislation as it exists. The Licensing Act, 1948, may provide the proper remedy through the introduction of State management in new areas.

STATE CONTROL

Like much other legislative effort in connection with the drink problem, local State control of the liquor trade dates from the first World War. The Central Board was then vested with the right to exercise State control wherever in its view the public needs required it. It used these powers in acquiring direct control by purchase at Enfield Lock, in the Cromarty Firth Area, and in the Gretna and Carlisle districts. In April 1916 the Board acquired the licensed premises at Invergordon and Cromarty in Scotland,

[1] See p. 239: '. . . an informative vote in the new development areas ought not to be established'.

after special problems had arisen through the establishment of a naval base at Cromarty Firth. Later in the same year the Board took over the Gretna and Carlisle districts with breweries and licensed houses on both sides of the Solway Firth, covering about 500 square miles and a war-time population of about 140,000. This still provides the leading example of State control. After the war, the Licensing Act, 1921 (section 15) provided that the schemes of State management established by the Board in the four districts might be continued by the Home Secretary, so far as England was concerned, and by the Secretary of State for Scotland, for districts in Scotland, 'until Parliament otherwise determines' (see for further details, Wilson, op. cit., pp. 113, 131 and 175).

In some respects the Carlisle venture resembles the much earlier and already long famous Gothenburg system of control (see Elster, op. cit., pp. 238–9). In this Swedish town the supply of alcoholic liquor has been controlled since 1865 by a society called 'Bolag', and in time similar and interlinking societies have sprung up in places over the whole country, as also elsewhere in Scandinavia.[1] We should stress that these societies are not interested in the volume of sales of alcoholic liquor. They rent from the municipality all drinking establishments and the publicans whom they employ are interested in profits only in so far as these accrue from the supply of meals which they are urged to offer. The members of each society get not more than 5 per cent of the net profits, of which a certain percentage is distributed for communal and charitable purposes, in particular to organisations connected with the fight against alcoholism.

The Carlisle system emanates from the same aim of organising the drink trade on the basis of commercially 'disinterested ownership'. Even in this respect it is distinctive in Britain. For though the Public House Trust Companies, for instance, operate under the same label, and do not pay their managers on the basis of turnover, they work within the limits of the ordinary licensing system. They are not definitely built up on a non-profit-making plan. This was also the view of the Amulree Report (p. 77): 'The fact that a manager's remuneration is not based upon his sales of intoxicants is not of vital significance if, because of his owner's interest, he has to maintain sales of intoxicants in order to keep his job. The attitude of the owner is then the really vital matter;

[1] See for interesting details and comments, Lord Askwith, *British Taverns*, 1928, pp. 101–3.

and the value of "disinterestedness" must, we think, in the end depend on the extent to which the owner's policy is reflected in the practical conduct of the business.'

The Carlisle undertaking has other unique features. It is, unlike the Trust Companies, a wholesale and retail concern, brewing its own beer and supplying its houses with that beer. It is exempt from certain of the requirements of ordinary licensing law; in particular, it may open new or alter existing premises, without magisterial consent. For all practical purposes it is, except in the outlying areas, a monopoly, whereas the Public House Trust movement, aiming at establishing 'disinterestedness' through having salaried public-house managers, always remains a private trade system under the stress of competition. The Carlisle undertaking, as the Amulree Report was anxious to emphasise, 'might be regarded as a working model of monopoly run on 'disinterested' principles (see Amulree Report, para. 367). As such it has managed to eliminate abuses which may be largely due to competition between public houses. For instance, to the extent that 'there seems to be good reason to think that an appreciable proportion of excessive drinking may arise from a licensee's anxiety lest refusal to supply a customer who had already had sufficient may offend him and lead to permanent transference of his custom to a more pliant competitor', excessive drinking has probably been directly reduced by the 'elimination of competition' (Amulree Report, paras. 401 and 397). The Departmental Committee on the 'Disinterested Management of Public Houses' which reported in May 1927, under the Chairmanship of Lord Southborough and with Mr. (later Sir) Henry Holman Gregory, Sir Frederick Sykes, and Sir Montagu Barlow as members,[1] emphasised therefore that under the Carlisle system the promotion of the general manager depended principally upon the standard of conduct which he succeeded in establishing, and 'not upon the amount of intoxicating liquor which he can sell'.

The whole policy of the Carlisle scheme administration has been definitely aimed at the abatement of drinking and of excessive drinking. On behalf of the Home Office, Sir John C. G. Sykes described the general policy as follows (see Amulree Commission, A. 19,197 (20)): 'The general object sought in the schemes is to conduct the supply of liquor in such a way as to meet the public demand under the best possible conditions, and to assist the prevention of

[1] See *Report of the Committee on Disinterested Management in Public Houses*, 1927, p. 12.

excess and the promotion of sobriety. The methods employed to attain this object comprise the closing of superfluous houses and the improvement of the remainder, the adoption of the principles of disinterested management, and the provision of food and non-alcoholic refreshments in public houses.' There is no advertising of drink. The Carlisle administration tried 'Sunday closing' and the 'spiritless week-end', though both were dropped in 1919. It is quite true, as Mr. James H. Hudson, M.P., has pointed out, that such measures, which he regarded as an 'undoubted advantage', did not require that the licensed premises of Carlisle should be socialised (see op. cit., p. 105) and might have been done without State management. But the plain fact is that the Carlisle scheme put into practice what others did not dare to attempt. One of its special organisational features, reminiscent of the Swedish schemes, is the Local Advisory Committee, which consists of a number of representatives of local authorities and other interests appointed by the Home Secretary.[1]

'Temperance purists' are opposed to the Carlisle scheme (see e.g. ibid., pp. 100 and 106) on the grounds that it has not done enough for the abatement of drinking. Mr. Cecil Heath suggests that the Carlisle 'experiment', 'having built up a reputation of spectacular progress in very abnormal times, still attempts to draw upon that reputation in spite of its steady departure from grace'.[2] But the Amulree Report did not regard the scheme as an 'experiment'[3] and stressed that 'the results of the Carlisle scheme have had a definite value in furnishing an example to trade elsewhere', and 'that a further demonstration, preferably in an area exhibiting different characteristics, would be valuable' (see ibid., para. 407). It concluded that the system was 'likely to reduce excess, while meeting the requirements of the moderate drinker', and 'that monopoly under public ownership was likely to effect a much more rapid development of the policy of public-house improvement than is probable, or indeed, possible, under the existing system'.

[1] It consists of twenty-four representatives of the City Council, the Watch and Licensing Committee, the Carlisle Trades Council, the Joint Cumberland Standing Committee and the County Council, Maryport U.D.C., Licensing Justices of various divisions and three women members. The Committee meets regularly at Carlisle and discusses questions of policy and administration; see James H. Hudson, M.P., in the *Alliance Yearbook for 1947*, p. 115.

[2] See Heath, op. cit., p. 72.

[3] See Amulree Report, para. 385: 'It has been freely—but quite incorrectly—spoken of as an experiment.'

THE 'OCCASIONAL LICENCE'

Within the major framework of licensing policy and execution there are numerous specific aspects which present special problems. One of these is the 'occasional licence', which is an authority granted to the holder of an on-licence to carry on sales at some place other than his ordinary business (see Licensing (Consolidation) Act, 1910, section 64). In 1930 15,500 occasional licences were granted to cover some 21,500 days. By 1940 the number of licences had risen to 36,500, and represented 43,700 days. The sharp war-time reduction (13,250 in 1945) could not be regarded as permanent, and by 1948 the number of licences was back to 35,745, representing 46,285 days. If the occasion is a public dinner or ball, the authority may allow sales at any hour; if not, it may only authorise sales between sunrise and 10 p.m.; and in no case can an occasional licence authorise sales over a period exceeding three consecutive days. The authority is granted by the Board of Customs and Excise, with the previous consent of a petty sessional court, or, in certain circumstances, of two Justices of the Peace, and may be refused if the Board do not consider it conducive to public convenience and order.

Occasional licences are therefore not subject to the general rule that facilities for the sale of intoxicants are under the control of the licensing justices. The Amulree Report said that 'this inroad was represented by some to be serious'. (See Amulree Report, para. 618–9.) The Commission was satisfied that occasional licences were to a large extent necessary: without them all public dinners, dances and the like would require to be held in licensed premises, which, even when available, were not always suitable for the purpose. But the Commission also felt 'that there has been some abuse in the use of occasional licences. For instance, it was not necessary to define exactly what should be understood as being 'occasional' to be satisfied that sometimes the sale of intoxicants had been authorised in cases where no element of occasionality was present, and where the proper solution would have been the grant—always providing the licensing justices thought fit—of a suitably conditioned justices' licence'.

Though the Report recommended that the law should be so amended as to guard so far as possible against such misuse of the occasional licence in the future, it is difficult to be satisfied that it attached to the matter the importance that it already then deserved. It is true that at that time occasional licences increased normal facilities for drinking by less than 0·1 per cent (see Amulree Report, para. 619). But the simple statistical computation is likely to be, as usual, misleading. For the figure does not reveal the fact that occasional licences entail the danger of very heavy drinking, particularly of spirits, and of drunkenness, and an obviously greater risk of evasion of the law than under normal licensing conditions. Feasts of all sorts call for occasional licences and result in heavy drinking.[1] Leniency shown to persons when under the influence of drink on festive occasions confirms that it is officially accepted that heavy drinking is a corollary to rejoicing. For instance, a London evening paper recently reported: 'Found hanging on the railings of Chester Square, a porter was asked by Mr. Daniel Hopkin at Marlborough Street: "Did you get drunk because Glamorgan won the championship?" "It had a lot to do with it," replied Morgan. "Then it is a good excuse," said Mr. Hopkin. He dismissed the case under the Probation Act' (see *Evening News*, 30th August 1948). The relative importance of additional facilities through occasional licences is not an adequate guide to their relative importance in terms of heavy drinking and drunkenness.

The signs are, moreover, that any occasion seems good enough to request an occasional licence and that often the reason given is something of a sham. From Annual Reports of Chief Constables presented at Brewster Sessions a good deal of evidence may be gathered in that respect. Of Oxford it was said that 'it will be observed that the number of occasional licences and extensions granted in each year shows a considerable and progressive increase, and one wonders whether they are not granted too freely and without sufficient necessity for them being always shown'. In York, instances had come to the notice of the Chief Constable where the liquor licence had for some reason not been allowed and the dances had simply not taken place, 'leaving the obvious conclusion that it is not so much the dance and its object that matter as the occasional licence. There is a definite tendency and danger of dance halls becoming licensed premises, so habitual is the grant of facilities.' From the same source it was reported that 'it was abundantly clear' that abuses were taking place. Of Nottingham it was said that 'there have been cases of disturbances outside

[1] See the article 'A Blot on the Coronation' in *Alliance Yearbook for 1938*; where a considerable number of cases relating to deaths, motor accidents, manslaughter, fight and assault are recorded which happened under the influence of drink during the coronation period and were directly related to patriotic celebrations.

dance halls when drink licences have been granted for longer periods than two days'.[1] There is danger that any two people may get together and call themselves a club, saying they will hold a dance. One magistrate, turning down the application from one club, said that 'that sort of thing is not to be encouraged . . . in one month this club had five occasional licences, and in another four. These cannot by any stretch of imagination be called occasional events. They are habitual events, and to my mind do not come within the category of occasional licences' (see Heath, op. cit., p. 62). Mr. H. Cecil Heath sums up the position when he says: 'As to what constitutes a public dinner or ball, it is obviously a matter where differences of opinion can arise, and it seems difficult to believe that the legislation when originally framed was intended to permit all sorts of clubs and institutions, many of a purely commercial character, to avail themselves of this facility with the co-operation of some holder of a justices' licence.'

The Amulree Report was of the opinion that greater caution should be applied to the grant of occasional licences, but on technical grounds could not agree to the recommendation that the power to grant occasional licences might be transferred to the licensing justices (see Amulree Report, para. 622). But it made an important recommendation in connection with offences: in accordance with comments made by the Board of Customs and Excise, it recommended that selling liquor outside the hours specified in an occasional licence should not remain merely a revenue offence but that the police should be enabled to institute proceedings instead of the Department (see Amulree Report, para. 624).

In the absence of more detailed national regulations concerning occasional licences, it has been left to the magistrates to frame rules for their districts. In 1938, a stipendiary magistrate, Mr. Frank Powell, framed in collaboration with a colleague, Mr. L. R. Dunne, detailed rules as to handling such licences in Woolwich. One rule specified that if the event is to be held on the licensee's own premises, he must satisfy the court that the grant of an occasional licence would not give him the right to do something which his justices' licence forbids him to do; for instance, if he is normally only licensed to sell drink with meals, he cannot have a less restricted occasional licence for the same premises. Among the

[1] See Annual Reports of Chief Constables presented at Brewster Sessions, 1938; also *Alliance Yearbook for 1939*, pp. 96–7.

other rules are that the licensee must also disclose to the magistrate whether or not licensing justices have refused to license the premises on which the event is held, that a public dance is not to be treated as a public ball unless those attending it are brought together by some common interest other than the desire to drink and dance, and unless the event possesses some formality, and that there must be an interval of at least three months between grants to the same promoters. Other districts have elaborated their restrictive rules in the same way as Woolwich. At Birmingham, Bristol, and Smethwick, it is stipulated that the drink licence shall not be advertised. At Winchester, licences are not granted where money is taken for whist drives and dances. In Lincoln Borough, no tickets may be sold at the door after 9 p.m. Coventry rules that no person may be admitted after the time of closing public houses. In Croydon the total number of occasional licences for public dances is limited to 50 per annum. In Smethwick special proof is required from the licensee when an occasional licence is said to be connected with a charitable purpose: the organisers must hand the magistrate within twenty-eight days of the event a statement of the receipts and payments, showing the net balance handed over to a particular charity.[1] The importance of this rule is shown by the fact that it has been reported by many Chief Constables that sometimes '. . . dances have been held and drink licences applied for, where the function is supposed to be held for some deserving charity. In actual fact practically the whole profits have gone into the proprietor's pocket and a miserable sum allotted to charity'.[2] In Chester the magistrates decided in 1947 to impose a number of restrictions on the premises covered by occasional licence: for instance, 'no person in a state of intoxication shall be allowed in a dance hall', and the 'consumption of liquor shall cease half an hour before the end of the dance'.[3] Nevertheless in the absence of legislation it remains with the public to make representations to the Justices that local rules to restrict occasional licences should be framed at Brewster Sessions, or by a letter to the Clerk. But it would seem that the existing magisterial practices could provide an ample basis for some codifying national legislation.

[1] See, for these and other rules applied by magistrates, the interesting description in Heath, op. cit., pp. 62–4.

[2] See *Alliance Yearbook for 1937*, H. Cecil Heath, 'A Survey of Magisterial Practice in Relation to Occasional Licences', p. 97.

[3] See *Liverpool Evening Express*, 13th March 1947; see also the article 'Magistrates and Occasional Licences' in the *Alliance News* of May–June 1947.

BOTTLE SHOPS

'Bottle shops' are another source of confusion and difficulty. In Britain the retail trade in bottled drink cannot be carried on just anywhere, as in Continental countries like Switzerland where a bottle of brandy or Chartreuse can be obtained at most Konditoreien—tea-rooms—or grocer's shops. But trade in bottled spirits can be carried on without a justices' licence, and the same applies to wholesale quantities of beer: only an Excise licence is required. The crucial effect of these facilities is that persons may carry on retail sales of intoxicating liquors without the approval of the licensing justices.[1] The holder of a spirit retailer's off-licence may sell single bottles of spirits, but he may not sell it in open vessels, nor in any quantity less than one reputed quart bottle (this is two-thirds of an imperial quart—the normal bottle), nor wine in any quantity of less than one reputed pint bottle (this is two-thirds of an imperial pint—the normal half-bottle). The number of off-licences in Great Britain for spirits increased from 14,310 in 1930 to 15,405 in 1939, and for beer fell slightly from 19,659 to 19,297.

Some protagonists of temperance, including H. Cecil Heath, the Secretary of the Alliance, wish to see a distance limit introduced for bottle shops[2], and in this suggestion they are sometimes joined by the trade. This alliance of basically conflicting interests is less odd and more dangerous that it seems. Demands for distance limits from any trade are generally animated by the desire to get rid of competition rather than to protect the consumer. It is hitherto only with newspapers, which are next to bread the most 'perishable' commodity, that distance limits have found general acceptance. Otherwise they are in general, and rightly, to be considered as restrictive measures propounded by quasi-monopolistic trade associations (see Hermann Levy, *Retail Trade Associations*, 2nd ed. 1944, pp. 163–72). Generally they contend that the 'requirements' of the public are already 'adequately' met, while it is really the reduction of the competitive struggle which is the target of the promoters of distance limits. It is characteristic that Mr. Walter

[1] This anomaly in the Licensing Law has ceased to exist. By the Licensing Act (1949) the authority of the Justices was extended to cover all retail sales of alcoholic drink. All bottle shops in existence prior to the introduction of the Bill were granted a Justices' licence on application.—*Editor*.

[2] See op. cit., p. 34: 'There is certainly a very strong case for limiting the distance over which any particular licence may operate.'

H. Jones, speaking as Vice-President of the Licensed Victuallers' Defence League of England and Wales, considered bottle shops a 'form of unfair competition' which he would like to see removed.[1] It should also be observed that the agitation against bottle shops from this side goes hand in hand with a similar opposition against clubs, of which the trade interests also claim that they represent 'unfair competition' to the licensed victuallers (see ibid., A. 14,047 (10 and 11)). Mr. Henry Charles Hunt, an off-licence holder, told the Royal Commission in a memorandum that it was the intention of the Licensing Acts to enable wholesalers in wines and spirits to supply retailers with small quantities of alcoholic drink, but that they were used now for the purpose of opening shops and selling in retail; any person having obtained a dealer's wholesale Excise licence for wine and spirit could apply for a dealer's Excise retail wine and spirit licence. Having explained this, the witness regretted that 'the so-called monopoly that the licensee is supposed to possess is entirely gone'; (see Amulree Commission, A. 37,735, *sub* 57–62). Some of the opposition to 'grocers' licences', i.e., justices' licences which allow the sale of beer in conjunction with business in groceries and the like, springs probably from the same source; but the Commission did not regard them as dangerous (see Report, paras. 615–16). The fear of competition is much the same the world over. In Bavaria a tax on bottled beer was avowedly enacted as a measure for the 'protection' of public houses; the trade in bottled beer was considered as one of the 'distasteful trades' which, like that of hawkers, was threatening the old-established trades of innkeeper and retailer.

It is therefore very necessary to be wary of restricting the number of bottle shops. There can be hardly any doubt that buying in bottles for home use is less conducive to heavy drinking and drinking abuses than frequenting public houses. Pernicious habits like that of 'perpendicular' drinking (see for this Amulree Report, para. 208) are certainly less likely to grow at home. Also there is the housewife who may keep a closer eye on expenditure on drink. A greater or lesser number of bottle shops in the street will hardly incite heavier consumption, unlike a superfluity of public houses within easy reach of the homes of workers which may well stimulate drinking that otherwise would not exist. There is the danger that the pavement outside the bottle shop may be used

[1] See Amulree Commission, A. and Q. 12,936 and 12,937: 'I think it would reduce competition very much.'

as a 'drinking place',[1] but this is exceptional. The Amulree Report supported the suggestion, made by off-licence holders, that the minimum amount of spirits which they should be entitled to sell should be lowered to half a bottle on the grounds that 'there are many customers who wish to obtain spirits who do not wish to or cannot purchase as much as one bottle at one time. They must either go without or go—which they may not like to do—to an on-licensed house.' (See para. 605.) This observation contained a possibly unintended reference to the competition between drinking at public houses and at home.

The conclusion to be drawn is that retail sales of spirits should be regarded mainly as a potential means of keeping people from public houses, inns and bars. This was agreed by the Finance Act, 1937, which permitted retailers henceforth to sell less than one reputed quart of spirits, and took the further useful step of restricting the concession to retailers holding justices' off-licences (see Wilson, op. cit., p. 179). Much as one may wish to see excessive drinking reduced wherever it takes place, it should be a cornerstone of policy to draw people away from public houses, where the danger is greatest. Recommendations to reduce the competition between bottle shops and public houses need therefore to be regarded warily, and no approval given by the authorities to proposals of trade interests which have as their main though camouflaged purpose the enhanced strength of the position of public houses as against retail shops. The superfluity of public houses is always likely to be a source of more and heavier drinking; but competition between retail shops selling spirits is not likely to increase the craving for drink so much as to reduce it through weaning consumers away from the public house.

[1] Mr. Henry Charles Hunt, an off-licence holder, gave an example, see A. 37,911: 'A man comes into my place and says: "Give me half a pint of ale in a bottle." He gets it. That man takes it outside and drinks it on the pavement outside the premises. A policeman comes up immediately and says to me: "You ought to have asked the man what he was going to do with that beer."'

CHAPTER XIII

THE POWER OF THE TRADE

THE developing processes of manufacturing alcohol into food make an intriguing study. For instance, the history of the distillation of spirits since the times of the Alexandrian School and ancient Greece is full of scientific perseverance and industrial skill (see *The Action of Alcohol on Man*, pp. 6–8). Were we concerned with the industrial and business achievements of the trade, we would also have to refer with praise to the high efficiency of British brewers and distillers, their effective techniques resulting from long tradition and a keen appreciation of new research, and the financial soundness of the enterprise: their trade undoubtedly belongs to the outstanding successes of British industrial and commercial development. But to us the problem of 'drink' lies in its relation to consumers and consumption. In that it does not differ from many other problems. In its general sense 'sport', for instance, also relates to those participating in the activity, and not to the trade in sport and games equipment. Only there is more reason in the case of drink to stress the distinction between consumption and production.

In other trades greater technical and commercial efficiency generally spells benefit to the consumers: one expects an improvement to react favourably on cost and prices, and thereby increase the purchasing power of the consumer's income. The particular social and economic problems connected with drink counteract these possibilities, though the business process may be much the same. Viscount Astor was indeed right when he stated emphatically that 'the drink trade differs from practically every other business which provides articles of consumption. It is to the interest of the community to increase and stimulate the consumption of milk, bread etc. It is not to the interest of a community to stimulate and increase to the maximum the consumption of alcoholic—particularly the stronger drinks.' (See Amulree Commission, *sub* 29,476(3), p. 1,644.)

Sometimes, though with a somewhat different emphasis, the same point has been stressed by brewing trade interests. Thus the *Brewers' Gazette* once wrote: 'Anyone may sell general provisions, anyone may vend greengrocery, under conditions which he is almost at liberty to determine for himself, and if the sale of alcohol were as innocuous as that of biscuits or oranges, similar liberties would obtain for the licensed victualler as for the retailers of other commodities. It is axiomatic that it is because of the potentiality of drunkenness—that unfortunately is a corollary to the sale of alcohol—that restriction exists' (see *Brewers' Gazette*, 25th September 1913). We may add that drunkenness is not the only kind of objectionable excess. 'Excess' may also be viewed and deplored from the angle of the impact on working-class budgets. While, therefore, other trades are constantly stimulated to increase turnover, and any of their technical or commercial improvements and any efforts in salesmanship are officially welcomed as the means to increase sales further, the same achievements by the trade in alcoholic liquor encounter the opposition of all those who oppose the further increase in the consumption of drink for social and economic reasons. A trade does not exist immediately for purposes of social and economic welfare, but often its own interests and those of welfare coincide. In the case of drink, an increase in welfare means a reduction in the scope of the trade; indeed, as we have seen, a vast amount of legislation and a continuous and successful effort on the part of administrators and voluntary organisations has been effectively at work to bring about just such a reduction. Between them and the commercial interests of the producers and retailers of alcoholic liquor there is a direct, head-on conflict of attitude and action.

The degree to which the trade is able to support and finance its fight against the abatement of drinking is obviously largely dependent upon its political and economic power. A feature of the very first importance is the great width of its activities. They stretch over a wide field and embrace a great number of separate business units. Where a trade can speak for a multitude of individual businesses its political influence can be considerable, and this is all the more likely to be so when some units are of substantial size. This is so in the drink trade. Figures relating to the war and post-war years were of course subject to special influences, but the great number of business units in the trade, and the long-term trend towards greater size is not in doubt. The numbers of brewers 'for sale' in

Great Britain was 703 in 1945 and 602 in 1949 (figures, if not otherwise stated, from *Alliance Yearbook*). These exclude the far less important, though more numerous, body of 'brewers not for sale' who hold what is called home-brewing licences and are licensed houses with a brewery in the back yard (see Amulree Commission, A. 14,724): their number had been over 12,000 in 1930; but by 1945 there were only 3,734, and in 1949, 2,987, and they play a quite secondary role in the brewing industry. The number of distilleries is far smaller: 104 were in operation in 1939 against only 44 in 1944.[1] As to the wholesaling side, a pre-war estimate gave the figure of 1,300 wholesale wine and spirit merchants and of 300 wine and spirit agents (see ibid.), 55,000 public houses, 22,000 off-licences, over 7,000 licensed hotels, and about 15,000 grocers with wine, spirit and beer, or wine and spirit licences (see ibid.). In 1945 there were in Great Britain 18,158 'off' beer and 13,737 wine retailers, and in the United Kingdom alone, 23,272 'on' beer and 4,558 'on' wine retailer's licences. Dealers numbered 4,173 for spirits, 3,550 for beer and 4,089 for wine. The number of clubs was 16,611 in 1946. The number of publicans' licences has remained around 60,000 over the past few years.

But, as we already know, drink flows not only through what are technically called 'single trade outlets', that is, specialised sales outlets, such as public houses or wine merchants or clubs, but also through outlets where drink is only a part of the trade or service. Just as chocolates are sold by bakers, tea shops, grocers, greengrocers, tobacco and newspaper shops apart from genuine confectionery shops (see Hermann Levy, *The Shops of Britain*, under 'Compound Shops'), so drink is sold as part of compound businesses. This explains the discrepancy between the number of beer and wine retailers, both 'off' and 'on', and the number of liquor licences, which was as high as 161,265 in Great Britain in 1945. The reduction in the number of liquor licences to 141,244 in 1948 was the result of numerous mergers of separate beer and spirit licences applying to the same place, rather than of a reduction in the number of retail outlets. Occasional licences numbered over 13,000 annually in the last few years, but some 35,000 before the war. And there are in addition the retail excise liquor licences

[1] A rather different figure was given by the *Manchester Guardian Commercial* of 9th December 1938, which mentioned the existence of 190 distillers, including over 100 whisky blenders alone; 'the Distribution of Spirits, Wines and Beers'.

for restaurant cars and passenger boats (see Wilson, op. cit., p. 398). In the drink trade the existence of so-called 'commodity outlets' as distinguished from 'single trade outlets' plays an exceedingly important part. In short, the retailing of alcoholic drink pervades a long list of vendors and suppliers quite apart from the business exclusively devoted to it; and its distribution in public, as in the case of charitable and associational occasions, is not even limited to business purposes.

CONCENTRATION IN THE INDUSTRY

We have become accustomed to regard the degree of concentration of establishments as a significant indication of the strength of an industry. The tendency to concentration may be inherent in essentially modern industries like electrical supplies, chemicals or rayon. In the older industries it may come about in the process of amalgamating firms over a period of years. And even where there still exist a large number of firms, the modern trade associations may attain domination of the industry.[1] The liquor trade in Britain presents a picture of progressive concentration in large concerns, though as regards the quasi-monopolist effects of this, the distilling industry should be distinguished from the brewing industry. In distilling, there is definitely a quasi-monopolistic organisation, but brewing belongs to the 'non-monopolised' industries.[2]

The number of distilleries actually at work in Great Britain and Northern Ireland declined from 209 in 1900 to 104 in 1939. The decline in consumption of spirits was far more severe (see *Alliance Yearbook for 1947*, p. 149), but this is less important than the fact that the number of active producers is small, and through war conditions was actually reduced to 10 in 1944. The distilling industry was among the first prominent in the history of trustification in Britain. The beginnings of this development can be traced as far back as the end of the seventies.[3] By 1925 the trust, the Distillers' Company, combined the three greatest distilleries in England and Scotland—Dewar, Buchanan, and Walker. The 'policy of expansion', as it was called then, resulted in an augmentation of capital and reserves of the Distillers Company

[1] See for details, Hermann Levy, *The New Industrial System*, 1935, and *Retail Trade Associations*, 2nd ed., 1944.

[2] See W. Arthur Lewis's authoritative essay, *Monopoly in British Industry*, 1945, p. 20; calculations are based upon the investigations of H. Leak and A. Maizels of the Board of Trade.

[3] See Hermann Levy, *Monopolies, Cartels and Trusts in British Industry*, 2nd ed., 1927, pp. 236–7.

from £6·8 millions in May 1925 to £13·6 millions in May 1926. By 1948 the issued capital, plus capital reserves, revenue reserves and unappropriated profits, amounted to approximately £50 million, and a further 'programme of expansion' was reported by the Chairman. This expansion, apart from embracing firms in the drink industry but hitherto outside the trust, relates also to industrial undertakings producing margarine and cooking fats, a part of which are sold to the United Yeast Company for the bakers' sundries trade; further to the acquisition of chemical works producing bakers' requisites, and to the manufacture of penicillin.[1] The industrial section of the trust alone, with its new interests in chemicals, plastics and biochemicals, and its ramifications in the petroleum industry, represents one of the most successful giants in British industry. The close association of production of spirits for human consumption with the production of spirits for industrial purposes has certainly assisted concentration and amalgamation. A striking factor recently added in connection with whisky, the most important of the home-produced spirits, is the emergence of a small number of brands which now dominate the market (see *Manchester Guardian Commercial*, op. cit.). This development has been made possible by the fact that the secret of whisky production does not lie in the distilling alone, but in the subsequent blending of the single whiskies. Unless great skill is applied to this task, and unless the blender has access to a wide range of single whiskies, there is little hope of reasonable uniformity being achieved in the final result. The Distillers Company is said to control 80 per cent of the trade. According to Mr. Lewis, some efficient independents remain, and 'appear to be able to exercise a restraining influence'. (See Lewis, op. cit., p. 14.)

The number of brewers has been reduced more quickly than the volume of consumption, and this holds true irrespective of whether we compare present times with the beginning of the century, or with the position in 1930;[2] the most marked trend of recent years has in fact been an increase in production and a simultaneous decrease in the number of brewers. This development, unlike that in the spirits industry, has not been entirely, and perhaps not even mainly, due to amalgamation of firms of more or less

[1] See Report on Seventy-first Annual General Meeting of the Distillers Company Ltd., *The Economist*, 2nd October 1948, pp. 553–4.

[2] In 1930 there were over 1,148 brewers 'for sale' in Great Britain as against 703 in 1945 and in 1946; but beer produced in the United Kingdom was over 32,600,000 bulk barrels in 1945 and in 1948 as against 25,000,000 in 1930.

similar industrial and financial type, but to very decisive changes in the structure of beer consumption. Until recently a brewery was expected to serve the area in which it is located. To some extent this is still so, for instance, the main breweries in Edinburgh, the centre of the brewing industry in Scotland, still exhibit the local characteristic of the brewing industry; they are clustered round the Abbey locality, where a plentiful supply of water suitable for brewing is found in wells sunk in the old red sandstone.[1] The new development replacing this older practice is the supply of beer to outlets all over the country by a small number of well-known brewers (see *Manchester Guardian Commercial*, op. cit.).

There has been a progressive development towards amalgamation and large business units in the brewing industry in the last sixty years. In 1887 Sir Edward Guinness floated his great business as a limited company—the first large brewery flotation. The capital was £6,000,000 and was twenty-eight times over-subscribed. Allsopps followed, and many brewery firms offered some of their business for public subscription. George B. Wilson suggests that this movement had to some extent a deliberately 'political significance'. One of the big firms admitted that a great number of shareholders would 'add to the influence of the Company' (see Wilson, op. cit., p. 86). Bass; Truman, Hanbury and Buxton; Courage; Watney, Combe, Reid & Co.; Meux; and Whitbreads are to-day among the principal representative of 'big business' in the brewing industry. According to the *Manchester Guardian Commercial* of 1938, 'competition is still very real', despite amalgamation (see *Manchester Guardian Commercial* of 9th December 1938). But that amalgamation has not led to monopolistic organisation in the brewing trade does not mean, as we shall see in more detail in the next chapter, that the relatively small number of giant concerns do not use their great financial strength in a powerful way.

Brewery interests have, of course, interpreted the significance of amalgamation as consisting mainly in the desire to introduce economies and to reduce overhead charges. It is certain that the elimination of smaller companies with their licensed properties does allow a larger outlet for the product of big breweries with all the advantages of bulk distribution (see e.g., *The Brewery Manual for 1929*). As an argument in favour of the buying up of

[1] See Dr. Mary Rankin, 'The Brewing Industry of Edinburgh', in *Further Studies in Industrial Organisation*, Nuffield College Social Reconstruction Survey, 1948, p. 209.

firms this line is familiar, and, as an economic explanation, to a large extent correct. It is significant that even smaller brewery companies are willing to-day to buy up small chains of country shops and achieve control in those areas purely in order to obtain the sales of liquor passing through the off-licences.[1] One of the immediate motives of this policy is to maintain quality (see ibid.): 'Inexpert handling may destroy the reputation of a certain brand, and loss of goodwill may ruin the brewer. This is why most brewers in this country have always considered it of paramount importance that they should control distribution right up to the point of sale to the consumer.'

Another advantage of size is that a wide spread of 'tied' houses gives to the brewery greater flexibility to make good for a slackening demand in one district by brisker trade done in others. The consumption of beer is by no means the same in all districts. There is, for instance, a particularly great strength of demand in the Midlands and in the North, which is to be explained by the heavy concentration of industry there and possibly by the great amount of overtime worked. And the demand for drink is not even over the year. Amalgamation on a nation-wide scale may finally be considered as an important means of stabilising profits between the years.[2]

But amalgamation is also pursued as a means of acquiring financial and economic power; and if one considers that one firm may control, as a famous Midland brewery does, no fewer than 800 public houses the position becomes abundantly clear. The difficulties under the licensing legislation, the increasing difficulties of opening new public houses, give remarkable protection to existing outlets. With their amalgamated financial resources brewers are able to acquire important local outlets. The quasi-monopolistic value of these houses is shown by the difference in terms of capital value of the premises when licensed and their value if they were not licensed (see Amulree Report, p. 38). This difference has led to the requirement that no new licence should be granted without the public securing this 'monopoly value' (see Licensing (Consolidation) Act, 1910, section 14). And this very requirement has

[1] See for this 'Britain's Biggest Multiple Shop Business' in *Business*, November 1948, pp. 42–3.

[2] See *Financial Times*, 11th December 1948, 'Changing Markets for Breweries': 'Although at present local requirements would absorb their full output, a widespread trade is in their the [Burton breweries'] favour should the recession in sales touch the Midlands.'

demonstrated the significance of the financial strength of the big amalgamations: as the Amulree Report emphasised, this strength 'tends to accentuate the advantage enjoyed, in the matter of obtaining new licences, by those with large capital resources, e.g. the large brewery undertakings, over their competitors' (see ibid., para. 168).

Amalgamation, then, is by no means due wholly to the desire to achieve economies: it is inspired mainly by the ambition to acquire greater competitive power through the acquisition of quasi-monopoly positions. This aim of the large establishments has naturally caused other undertakings to be constantly confronted with the alternative either to succumb to the grasp of the octopuses or else to seek combination and amalgamation among themselves. The combination in the Scottish brewing industry has been recently described by the Nuffield College Social Reconstruction Survey: 'combination among brewers in Edinburgh has not been in order to reduce production costs but to keep the trade from getting into the hands of outsiders' (see Rankin, op. cit., pp. 216–18); the combination of Edinburgh's two largest firms was not to achieve economies by co-operation, but the 'chief motive was to keep control of the firms within the families, and to stop any powerful extraneous influence from entering the Edinburgh trade'. In brief, it was simply due to the desire to answer might with might.

The fact that there is no national quasi-monopolist organisation in the brewing industry has not therefore prevented quasi-monopolistic domination of the trade by big brewing interests. It has merely taken a form other than cartel or trust, namely that of domination of the retailing of beer in public houses. Here, as we have just seen, is a genuine monopolistic condition, based upon the local significance of the vendor and enhanced by the limitation of competition through the licensing legislation. And this monopolistic condition has become a welcome field for exploitation by the financially mightiest establishments. The *Manchester Guardian Commercial* correctly expressed the position before the war, when it explained: 'As the vast majority of drinkers of beer are not concerned with the one that made the beer, the control of retail outlets is the obvious key to improved turn-over—or even maintained turn-over—on the part of any individual brewer.' Advertising of the 'goodness' of certain brands may be a useful means of stimulating their consumption. But it is far more effective to secure, through purchase or otherwise, domination over the key-points of retail distribution, and then restrict these houses to selling only that brewery's products. Hence the 'tied house' system.

THE 'TIED HOUSE' SYSTEM

The essence of a 'tie' is that the tenant of the licensed premises undertakes to purchase either all his beers, or all his beers and also some other commodities such as wines, spirits, and tobacco at agreed prices from his landlord, the brewery-owner, and from no one else. Tied houses may be run either under management or under tenancy. In the former case, the manager is a salaried employee who has no financial stake in the business; in the latter case, the tenant takes the premises on lease or under a tenancy agreement from the brewer. (Amulree Report, pp. 65–6). The system may be coupled with the granting of a mortgage to some suitable person who uses it to buy the premises. But this is less and less the case, for the brewery is no longer able to insist on preferential treatment by the licensee when the mortgage is paid off.[1]

The bulk of the on-licensed houses in England are now owned by brewers, for this seems the most certain method of securing permanently an exclusive sale of their beers. At the time of the Amulree Commission, estimates placed the proportion of tied houses in England and Wales as high as 95 per cent. 'Free houses' have become rare.[2] The *Manchester Guardian Commercial* found the exact number of 'tied' houses difficult to estimate in its survey of 1938; its correspondent added that 'it is not, perhaps, without significance that in the details given of many individual breweries in the *Stock Exchange Yearbook* appear the words "Information as to the number of licensed houses owned withheld".' (See *Manchester Guardian Commercial*, 9th December 1938.) The position is somewhat different in Scotland, where brewers do not sell through their own public houses, but give considerable credit to those public houses whose customers demand their beer on draught. Scottish public houses are, therefore, also to some extent tied to brewers, but if they pay off their mortgages they can go elsewhere (see Rankin, op. cit., p. 215).

[1] In a law case where a brewery sought to enforce a condition in the mortgage that it should receive preferential treatment even after the mortgage had been paid off, the Court held that such a condition was 'a clog or fetter on the equity of redemption'. See Noakes v. Price, 1902, and *Manchester Guardian Commercial*, op. cit.

[2] See Amulree Report, para. 295; see also Lord Astor's evidence, p. 1169: 'There are very few "free" houses left in England.'

The tied-house system is perhaps the first example, certainly one of the first examples, of attempts on the part of producers to combine their business with that of retail distribution. We hear of it already in 1817 in the Report of a Select Committee on the State of the Police in the Metropolis and Licences of Victuallers, where it is mentioned as a 'practice which seems to have gradually grown up and increased considerably within these few years. . . .' (See Wilson, op. cit., p. 82). In our own days, the prevalence of the system seems to be in line with what is now called the 'composite business', that is, a business which exercises two or more of the three functions of manufacturing, wholesaling and retailing. The trend towards such organisation has greatly increased in the last decades. An outstanding example is Lever Brothers and Unilever Ltd., the combination of soap and margarine manufacturers, which controls indirectly also a great number of multiple grocery concerns, retail establishments in the fish trade, and the distribution of certain ice creams.[1]

There is hardly a trade which can offer so complete and exclusive ties in retailing as the trade in beer. Beer represents the great bulk of the turn-over of the normal public house whereas, with other commodities, retailing is a far more compound business; the scope of commodities sold in the normal shop is wide and heterogeneous. How important this factor is can be seen from trades, where, as with beer, sales are limited to one single product. There, a 'tie' is also more easily effected. We find, therefore, similarly exclusive selling arrangements in the shoe trade through the multiple chains of big manufacturers, or through similar chains in the bespoke tailoring establishments. The beer trade has enjoyed the additional advantage of having concentration fostered by the constant limitation of licences. As Mr. F. P. Whitbread suggested to the chief witness of the Brewers' Society before the Amulree Commission, 'Where you have a body of competing manufacturers of any class of goods and the only channel or outlet for those goods is severely restricted under a monopoly, and the extra channels which are granted do not keep anything like pace with the extra progress of the produce, those manufacturers are inevitably bound to buy up those channels of output in order to preserve their identity'. (See Amulree Commission, Q. 15,079.)

[1] See Hermann Levy, *The Shops of Britain*, p. 146; also Levy, 'The Composite Combine' in the *Banker* of December 1943; see also Lever Brothers and Unilever Ltd., *Progress*, Autumn 1948, in particular the 'Story of Walls', pp. 24 sq.

Recent progress in the tied-house system has stemmed very directly from the increase in the financial strength of brewery establishment. The conversion of breweries into limited liability companies in the late eighties and the early nineties gave a special fillip to its development (see Amulree Report, para. 293). The prosperity of the beer industry laid the foundation for the accumulation of capital which could be used for acquiring more and more retail outlets. It enabled the leading firms to buy up public houses even at soaring prices. It gave them the opportunity to interest themselves in the acquisition of prospective development schemes. And each of these steps at the same time further increased the financial strength of the firms. Profits have increased rapidly, also over recent years. In 1913–14 the profits of the brewing trade as returned to the income tax authorities, less allowances for wear and tear, were £9,970,000 (see Wilson, op. cit., p. 89); in 1938–9, after allowing for wear and tear of plant and machinery and after deducting the National Defence Contribution, Excess Profits Tax and Profits Tax payable, but including profits arising from trade ancillary to the main business, there were £27 million, and in 1946–7 £49 million (see H.C. Debates, 3rd May 1948, *sub* Brewers' Profits). As an example of the powerful financial position of the distillers, the total revenue of the Distillers Company reached £12,621,000, in 1947 (see *The Economist*, 2nd October 1948, p. 553).

Of the many angles from which the tied-house system may be discussed, e.g., the relationship of tenants to brewers, or the prices and profit margins for public houses, or its effects on public house improvement, the point which interests us most in this book is how it affects the consumption of drink. For instance, can the tied-house system be regarded as a factor which counteracts the attempts to keep drinking within reasonable limits? Or is it the opposite? It is immediately clear that an unlimited multitude of public houses and an absence of exclusive restrictive agreements on the tenants might well entail as much danger of exaggerated sales as the present system of restriction by licensing and domination by the manufacturers' tied-house system. The pressure of competition under complete freedom might well reduce the profit levels of public-house owners so much that there would be permanent pressure and temptation to increase turn-over by trespassing on the laws, for instance, of permitted hours, or by offering customers all sorts of inducements to stimulate the consumption of alcoholic liquor. We have already seen that such practices are frequently the outcome of a multiplicity of drinking outlets. On this consideration alone one might expect the tied-house system, linking as it does the individual tenant or manager to large and highly reputed industrial concerns, to have counteracted such tendencies and thus reacted favourably on excessive drinking.

The Amulree Commission gathered a good deal of evidence in connection with the tied-house system and its effects on the consumption of drink. But since the evidence came simultaneously from those interested in the trade and also from others interested, for moral or social reasons, in its abatement, it was contradictory. The Report tried to draw the balance between the sharply opposed views. But the trade relationship between landlord and tenant is, of course, represented as ideal and the financial strength of the brewing trade as of the greatest benefit to the publicans.

The following appeared under the caption 'The Tie' in one recent trade publication (see *A Monthly Bulletin*, September 1948, p. 67): 'A "free house" has a fine generous sound, implying that the licensee of it is his own master and deserves to be admired for his brave independence and thanked for his unrestricted service to the public. But all this is misleading. It often happens that this kind of "master" is by no means master of his circumstances; the financing of himself through a lean time is a torment; and in the same circumstances repairs or improvements cannot be attempted. In a tied house the tenant always has the brewery behind him; he is invariably "seen through" a crisis if he deserves to be.' Another article specifies further advantages (article in *Business*, November 1948, pp. 42–3): 'The advantages enjoyed by the publican-tenants are manifold. They pay a rent which is far lower in most cases than the house would command as a "free house". Often the brewers pay part or all of the rates, and also Schedule A income tax and the licence duties, and the cost of maintaining premises in good repair. It would not have been possible for the thousands of fine new public houses built up and down the country in the last thirty years to have come into existence had they not been paid for and equipped by the breweries to operate as tied houses.'

The Amulree Report did not dispute that the tied-house system might have these advantages. But the Commission considered that they probably only presented one side of the picture. It said (paras. 307–10) that 'under a good and careful brewer-owner' the tied-house system may certainly operate advantageously and even 'produce excellent results'. He will 'tie the tenant for malt liquors only, and even in the case of malt liquors will furnish him with supplies of special brands for which there is a public demand . . . ; he will lend, where need be, part of the capital which the incoming tenant may require, and advise and assist him in the conduct of the business until the tenant becomes a capable and successful innkeeper'. But the Report also stated that quite 'unsatisfactory' conditions could result from the 'tie'. The 'tie' could include all beers, spirits, wines, tobaccos, and other commodities. Supplies of articles which the public demand, but in the sale of which the brewer has no interest as a producer, could be withheld or be offered at prohibitive prices. Most important, the margin within which the tenant has to buy from the brewer-owner and sell to his customer may be a narrow one, and he may be required, by implication if not expressly, to push the trade and the sale of intoxicants to the utmost and may thus be able to keep within the law only with difficulty: and if he commits an offence his tenancy may be brought to an end and he may lose, it may be, the whole or greater part of the money he has put into his business and very likely his livelihood as well.

The Amulree Report emphasised that 'between these two extremes is a great variety of instances'. If the publication of the trade interests from which we have just quoted contends that the Amulree Commission 'accepted the tied house principle as an established thing that was better left alone', it ignores the main point which the Report was at pains to stress. For the Report said that only if the tied-house system had nothing but the advantageous arrangements which were possible under it, things could be left as they were. But the undesirable possibilities were much in evidence, and the undesirable 'class' of tie had become more prominent during the depression and its effects more obvious. For instance, 'the turnover of the industry has diminished considerably; nevertheless brewery profits have been maintained or even, as a whole, have increased. We cannot doubt that the brunt has fallen upon the licensee.' (See para. 310.) The position changed somewhat in the years that followed immediately, when brewery profits dropped from £25 million in 1929–30 to £16 million in 1932–3; but after that break, brewery profits showed an upward tendency quite independent of trade fluctuations. (See H.C. Debates, 3rd May 1948.) Undesirable also are certain practices concerning the payments to be made by an incoming tenant to his predecessor on taking over a tenancy. In some cases he pays a fair sum, fairly calculated, for the fixtures, together with a sum, openly set down, by way of premium for what is called goodwill. In other cases he makes a payment for which the justification is not shown in any detail, but which, while nominally representing the valuation of the fixtures, is in reality much higher and includes what one may call a concealed goodwill payment. This may be bearable as long as prosperous times prevail; but it may prove very dangerous to a tenant leaving his business in slack times and involve him in much loss of money. The Amulree Report was quite clear in deprecating any sort of possibility of 'inflated valuations'.

On balance there can be little doubt that the tied-house system increases the consumption of drink, and this is, after all, just what brewers desire. This does not mean in the least that brewery companies shut their eyes to the evils of excessive drinking and drunkenness, but only that these are the undesirable outcomes of their normal activities. The position resembles in some respects that of industrial assurance agents and their employers. While industrial assurance companies are not in favour of policies that lapse, they have done little to prevent agents using pressure on people to persuade them to take up policies, even though millions of policies started by this high-pressure salesmanship lapse annually to the great loss of the insured (see Wilson and Levy, *Industrial Assurance*, 1937, *passim*). One cannot of course weed out beforehand all policies that are liable to lapse from those which are going to last. But just as insurance companies do not feel inclined to ease the pressure put on agents to get more business—even though business with a high rate of lapses—so the brewery companies will not generally feel inclined to take drastic action to relieve the tenants who for one reason or another, e.g., the unfavourable circumstances connected with the tenancy, have little option but to make use of every possible inducement to increase turnover. To what peculiar methods of propagating drink some public houses may resort in addition to the more straightforward serious devices may be gathered from the *New London Survey*. The *Survey* found some public houses organising children's outings, day-trips to Southend and other resorts by charabanc, or dart teams under the name of the public house to play against other public-house teams in their public bars (see the *New London Survey*, op. cit. (reprint), p. 17). By using their financial power to acquire domination over the main retailer, the public house, the large brewing interests have now the most efficient instrument for increasing the consumption of alcoholic liquor. Inasmuch as this instrument may be used with high-pressure methods, it represents the most powerful weapon against attempts to abate the drinking habit.

TRADE ORGANISATIONS

The economic might of the trade does not find expression only in the existence of powerful companies. It is also supported and strengthened by associational bodies, generally known as the 'defensive organisation of the liquor trade'. These organisations have a long history and are well established. The principal body, the Brewers' Society, was established in 1822, and various retailers' societies were also in existence early in that century. The first retailers' societies were associations of licensed victuallers—publicans with spirit licences—but after the Beerhouse Act of 1830 separate beer retailers' societies were formed. Trade organisations became more active after the middle of the century, when legislative changes of importance began to be introduced. The associations became naturally more elaborate and federated into more powerful bodies to resist the encroachment of the law. As the temperance movement developed, the organisation of brewers' societies and licensed victuallers' associations was readjusted, and increasingly large federations of societies were formed to represent both brewers and licensees. (See Amulree Report, pp. 75–6.)

The National Trade Defence Association, founded in 1888, is representative of all sections of the trade in alcoholic liquors in the United Kingdom. Affiliated with it are the Brewers' Society; the Licensed Victuallers' Defence League of England and Wales, formed in 1873; the Licensed Victuallers' Central Protection Society of London, Ltd., founded in 1833; and the Scottish Trade Defence Association, founded in 1879 (see Wilson, op. cit., p. 184). These are the pivots of the defensive organisations of the trade. There are about 600 local societies of the wholesale and retail trade throughout the United Kingdom. Mention may also be made of the Allied Brewery Traders' Association, the Licensed Grocers' and Vintners' Protection Association, the National Federation of Off-licence Holders' Association, the Northern Districts League of Beer and Wine and Spirit Trades Defence Associations (see *Alliance Yearbook for 1947*, pp. 185–6).

We are not concerned primarily with discussing the political implications resulting from a cluster of so many organisations working on the behalf of powerful trade interests, but one can hardly overestimate their influence as regards the trade's policy, which will be discussed in the next chapter. They are the organised representatives and mouthpieces of all traders interested in the fight against abatement of drinking, whether pursued by the temperance movement or by legislative enactments. This policy is not in conflict with the fact that the organisations do not support any of the blatant evils of drink: as the late Lord Rosebery once said, 'The trade naturally wants drinking—drinking short of excess'. (See Wilson, op. cit., p. 185.) But apparently they have not been able to exercise that sort of influence which would have relieved the publican's anxiety to increase the consumption of drink by all possible means. In his elaborate Memorandum to the Royal Commission, the Right Hon. Lord Balfour of Burleigh stated quite plainly, and interestingly enough in connection particularly with the tied-house system, that 'public expression is . . . rarely given to the real feelings of the retail trade, owing to the predominant position of the Brewers in the trade defence organisations, including the Licensed Victuallers' Societies. Such societies are not in a position to advocate any policy contrary to the wishes of the Brewers; the societies are largely financed by the Brewers and individually the members dare not take a line which will bring them into conflict with the Brewers.' (See Amulree Commission, A. 27,992 (9)). If it is true—and in many cases it is certainly true —that 'the tenant has the work, the worry, and the risk' (see ibid., *sub* (8)), and if this condition must necessarily lead the public-house tenant to push the consumption of liquor at his premises up to the highest level short of deliberately promoting drunkenness, it is not to be wondered that systems of 'disinterested management' have gained increased approval and that there is pressure for the prohibition of the present systems of control.

CHAPTER XIV

THE POLICY OF THE TRADE

In addition to its powerful organisation backed by ample finance the drink trade has the advantage of a coherent policy with a clear and simple aim—a strength which comes naturally from knowing well one's enemies as well as knowing well one's interests. We may distinguish here for convenience between the essentially defensive manifestations of that policy, that is, the strong and immediate efforts to resist all encroachments on the affairs of the trade, and its offensive manifestations which are directly aimed at increasing the consumption of drink.

THE FIGHT AGAINST RESTRICTION

The trade becomes very active whenever legislative administrative or educational measures threaten its interests. Every move for the abatement of drinking is immediately countered. The trade may object to and fight regulations dealing with licensing, with permitted hours, with the tied-house system and such related matters as monopoly value; with magisterial jurisdiction, regulations by transport services, taxation issues, planning schemes, the composition of alcoholic liquor and of beverages like medicated wines. All these and many other matters give constant rise to an assertion or an extension of trade policy because they inhibit already the volume of drink consumption or may restrict it in future. And the volume of consumption is as important to producers as it is to those engaged in the distribution of drink.

The trade will use virtually any argument that will serve this purpose. For instance, in opposing the Child Messenger Bill of 1901 which raised the age-limit for the sale of beer to children to fourteen years, the *Licensed Victuallers' Annual* went out of its way to praise the healthy atmosphere in which the children of publicans were growing up: 'Why, then,' so concluded the article, 'the atmosphere being so wholesome to the publican's child, should his neighbour's child be excluded from such a school of manners?' (Quoted Wilson, op. cit., p. 161.) In interrogating a witness before the Royal Commission, Mr. Whitbread had this answer to the suggestion that it would be good to 'get the workman home first' rather than give him the opportunity to call at a public house on the way back from work: 'What particular good purpose is served by getting the workman home? Is it the theory that he is never to get out of his home again, or is it that the longer he stays about his home the more he dislikes the idea of ever having anything stronger than water? . . . I am afraid I do not agree, with all due respect to your suggestion, that there is necessity for getting the man straight back to his home.' (See Amulree Commission, Q. and A. 4,029–30.) It is quite obvious that persons holding these views deprecate the absence of drink facilities on new housing estates. Mr. Whitbread was apparently much discomforted by the fact that in a housing estate where no licence had been granted, people were 'obliged to travel some distance in order to get reasonable facilities' (see ibid., Q. 4,024–5) and he suggested to the witness that inhabitants on the estate 'would be likely to go into a public house, supposing there was one handy. . . .'

Education of young people in the dangers of drink is a particularly dangerous intruder on trade interests, particularly in view of its likely prophylactic effect in later years. Three instances from the trade press will illustrate the tone of the trade's opposition (for the history of that opposition, see Amulree Report, p. 1666). The first is from *Harper's Wine and Spirit Gazette* of 1924: 'We understand that Mr. C. P. Trevelyan, the Minister of Education [later Sir C. P. Trevelyan] is being urged to make a notorious intemperate pamphlet issued by the Board of Education in 1921, which we have frequently denounced in these columns, part of the *compulsory* syllabus in all elementary schools. Will our trade associations in all parts of the country be good enough to meet and denounce any movement of this kind?' The second is from Ridley's Wine and Spirit Trade Circular of the following year: 'Our readers are familiar with the nauseating syllabus put forward under the recent Radical Nonconformist regime in H.M. Board of Education during the Puritan degradation of the English Civil Service. . . . Millions of little victims who by force of their poor circumstances were committed to a Board School Education were to be made the vehicles of Puritan Manichaeism by being continuously instilled with the Albigensian doctrine that the spirit of evil resides in certain forms of matter, namely alcoholic liquor.'[1] And another periodical of a similar kind which purports to promote, among other things, the 'determination inside and outside the brewing industry to improve public houses' recently warned its readers that 'boys may even be tempted to condemn their own parents for not accepting a rule of living insisted upon by the teetotal lecturers' (see *A Monthly Bulletin*, vol. 18, No. 9, September 1948, p. 70); to the author it would apparently be a tragic thing if children disagreed, say, with the spending of money on drink which might be urgently needed for other expenditure, for instance on their own education.

These essentially defensive aspects of trade policy find expression in the official aims and structure of the trade organisations. The Brewers' Society, which has at present a membership of 360 firms, has a Parliamentary Committee appointed annually for the purposes of (1) considering Bills and all matters affecting the Trade in Parliament; (2) taking such action as may be necessary to their support, or defeat, or amendment; and (3) placing the views of the Society, as occasion may arise, before Ministers and heads of public departments. The Licensed Victuallers' Central Protection Society—the word 'Protection' alone characterises the defensive attitude—has as its object, *inter alia*, to aid in securing to the trade such parliamentary, municipal and parochial representation as is necessary for the protection of its interests. The National Trade Defence Association—note 'defence'—proclaims as one of its purposes to secure by all legal means, and regardless of party politics, the return to the House of Commons and other elected bodies of candidates favourable to trade interests. And the Licensed Victuallers' Defence League wants generally to 'place the Trade in the best possible position to defend its interests, when assailed, to resist encroachments when attempted, and obtain legislative redress of grievances' (see *Alliance Yearbook for 1947*, p. 186).

The policy of the drink trade must indeed always be largely defensive. But it is important to note that if 'restrictive' is the label applied to this, the word means something utterly different from what it is usually meant to convey in other trades. Generally we are accustomed to seeing trade organisations, such as cartels or retail trade associations, eagerly trying to control and to limit the possibilities of excessive production or competition. But in the

[1] See also Lord Astor's evidence before the Amulree Commission ,A. 29,828–9.

liquor trade policy must necessarily concentrate on the fight against all official or semi-official measures which are likely to counteract the expansion of drink consumption. Policy is thus not restrictive in the usual sense: on the contrary, restriction is the greatest enemy and official restrictions the main target. While retail trade associations have frequently advocated such measures as distance limits or restriction of the number of shops by registration and licensing,[1] the drink trade works with the opposite idea, on the contrary, to prevent such restriction, particularly as regards the number of public houses and other retail outlets, and far from supporting licensing, proclaims the advantages of a multiplicity of drinking places. 'Under-licensing does not promote sobriety' is the headline of a publication issued in connection with the London Brewers' Planning Exhibition of 1947, and the same view is put forward by Whitbread and Co., Ltd., in a recent booklet.[2]

It is therefore not surprising that one finds the drink trade emphasising its preference for unlimited 'freedom' and 'liberty' in contrast to the policy of trade organisations in most other fields. This has been the trade's consistent policy ever since it agitated for 'free trade in beer' and thus greatly influenced the Ale House Act of 1828 (see Heath, op. cit., p. 5). In those days the licensing system was attacked on the ground 'that the demand for goods ought to regulate the number of vendors', and that this principle should be applied to this trade as well as to every other' (see Wilson, op. cit., p. 97). The slogan is still much the same in our days when restriction of drink is attacked as an infringement of 'individual liberty' and of 'people's fair play'.[3] And a press devoted to trade interests constantly supports this policy.[4]

ADVERTISING DRINK

The remainder of trade policy is devoted to the effective promotion of greater sales of alcoholic drink, and centres on attracting drinkers by the widest possible use of publicity. Advertising is a leading means to hand. The Amulree Report stated as a 'conservative estimate' that the figure of annual expenditure on

[1] See Hermann Levy, *Retail Trade Associations*, 1944, and *The Shops of Britain*, 1948, *passim*.

[2] See *The Licensed House, its Human Importance in Town Planning*, 1947, issued in connection with the London Brewers' Planning Exhibition of 1947, p. 5; also Whitbread and Co., Ltd., *Your Local*, 1947, p. 42.

[3] See interesting documentary material in Lord Astor's Memorandum to the Amulree Commission, A. 29,476 (26).

[4] For an enumeration of trade newspapers and publications, see ibid., Appendix I.

liquor advertisement alone was £2 million (see Amulree Report, p. 156). A study carried out by the National Institute of Economic and Social Research in 1946 gives the advertising expenditure for drink in 1935 as £3,391,000.[1] Advertisements in the press constitute a high proportion of this total. In 1938 it cost £1,438,000—a greater sum even than the press advertising of cigarettes (see E. A. Lever, *Advertising and Economic Theory*, 1947, p. 37). The study estimated the total advertising to represent 7 per cent of the sales value of drink to the final consumers. This is a relatively small percentage if compared, for instance, with medical goods where it was 42·6 per cent (ibid., pp. 122–3), and prompts the conclusion that the manufacturers of drink can indulge in a large expenditure on advertising without very greatly burdening the value of turnover. Sky-writing has been drawn into service, and ingenious use has been made of rail and tram tickets; and one enterprising firm had, when the Amulree Commission reported, placed an advertisement of its wares on the walls of a hospital which occupied a commanding site (see Amulree Report, para. 735). Large-scale advertising may also have advantages in addition to the direct promotion of drink. The Amulree Commission mentioned that (see ibid., para. 733) 'as regards press advertisements, it has been contended that certain sections of the press are likely to shape their policy so as, at least, to give no offence to an industry which supplies them with much advertisement revenue'.

The Amulree Commission rejected the contention that the 'effect' of some advertisements was merely competitive, that is, that their whole purpose was ' to transfer demand from unadvertised to advertised beverages. . . . That admittedly is one of the results, but all advertising experience establishes that the advertisement of goods of any particular brand tends to swell the total demand for all goods of the kind. Support for this view may be found in the strong advocacy by leading Trade Journals of bulk advertisement of intoxicants.' (See Amulree Report, para. 731.) This tendency is clearly expressed in the growing significance of what the National Institute of Economic and Social Research termed co-operative press advertising and its study drew special attention to it; in 1938 the Brewers' Society alone promoted £68,000 worth of press advertising (op. cit., p. 17). Co-operative advertising immediately and obviously does not even attempt to

[1] See National Institute of Economic and Social Research, *Statistics in Advertising*, 1946, p. 10.

promote certain branded and proprietary commodities but is designed to persuade the public to consume more of any and all of the commodities which fall into the advertised group. Such slogans as 'Say it with Flowers' or 'Eat more Fruit' indicate that the tendency to co-operative advertising in the drink trade conforms to the modern trends. Its efficacy largely depends on the strength and energy of the collective bodies promoting the publicity.

It was probably in 1933 that the Brewers' Society gave the most significant impetus to the policy of advertising drink generally rather than advertising single brands. One of its directors, Sir Edgar Sanders, promoted it vigorously at a trade meeting in that year. He explained how 'wonderful' it was that 'you can educate public opinion, generally without making it too obvious that there is a publicity campaign behind it at all'; he warned his listeners that 'unless steps are taken to say . . . that England's beer is the best and healthiest beverage' they would see the trade on a declining basis; and he insisted that 'we want to get the beer-drinking habit instilled into thousands, almost millions, of young men who do not at present know the taste of beer'.[1] As Mr. Robert Sinclair has appropriately pointed out, 'this cold-blooded argument was formally frowned on by the liquor trade when the report leaked out, and was properly reviled by the newspapers'; and it is difficult indeed to reconcile it with Sir Edgar Sanders' evidence before the Amulree Commission only three years previously, and with his former position as a General Manager of the Carlisle and District State Management Area, from which he had annually issued reports describing the 'progress of the undertaking' in connection with, for instance, the 'abolition of advertisements of intoxicants' and 'the limitation of the sale of intoxicants to young persons'.[2] Nevertheless, the 'Beer is Best' campaign followed that statement; and in the same way as the brewers, the distillers and wine merchants began joint advertising campaigns to publicise sherry, rum and other spirits, without reference to particular trade brands (see *Alliance Yearbook for 1947*, p. 25). The effectiveness of that campaign and of its methods is indisputable. 'Whatever may be the moral aspects of liquor trade propaganda', wrote the United Kingdom Alliance in 1947 (see ibid.), 'we shall be deceiving ourselves unless we are prepared to recognise frankly that it

[1] Circular distributed in the liquor trade and reprinted in *World's Press News*, 14th September 1933, quoted by Robert Sinclair, op. cit., pp. 125 and 338.

[2] See Sinclair, op. cit., pp. 125–6; also Wilson, op. cit., p. 258; also Lord Arnold's speech in the House of Lords, 28th March 1935.

has been organised and carried through by individuals who are experts in the fields of advertising. The concentration of a whole industry in some simple slogan and its constant repetition through every available channel, is the most conspicuous fact of recent Liquor Trade propaganda.'

It seems from Miss Rankin's recent study in Scotland that advertising is considered in some quarters more important than ever before (see Rankin, op. cit., p. 216). In particular she remarks that 'the necessity for advertising has increased since the extension of beer drinking among women'. Women are said to prefer beer from the bottle, since it froths more, sparkles more, and seems generally more attractive. For the individual brewer, the demand for bottled beer may thus extend to more distant markets, but it may contract his market for draught beer nearer home. He is thus more or less forced to advertise and make his product known, so that he may, as it were, gain on the bottle what he loses on the draught.

The whole policy of drink advertising can be severely criticised. As to its general implications it can be plainly said that no public advantage is secured by stimulating further the consumption of drink. It is excessive as it is. Greater consumption may perhaps be in the immediate interest of the Exchequer, but we have already noted that this interest does not seem to conform to the general aims of social policy. This point should be kept in mind in connection with Miss Rankin's observation (see op. cit., p. 218) that the Brewers' Society 'undertakes the advertising of beer in general in order to keep the product before the community and make known the extent to which the Exchequer benefits from its taxation—hence the injunction, "Drink more Beer" and such flashes of alliterative insight as "Beer is Best". On this general score, the Amulree Report left no doubt that it considered the volume of advertising, the 'flow of advertisement', with 'some alarm'.

Certain types of drink advertisement must be subject to even stronger and more justified objection. It is usual to draw distinctions between informative, persuasive and suggestive advertisement. This may not be very logical: as Mr. E. A. Lever has only recently pointed out (see Lever, op. cit., p. 48 sq.), 'all advertising is intended by its originators to be persuasive; it *informs and influences;* it aims at increasing sales by affecting the minds of consumers'. But the distinction is something more than just play on words. The same author rightly emphasises that persuasive advertisement is characterised in general by its stress on certain qualities of the product. It is here that the danger of harmful advertising most generally arises. It may well happen that the advertised qualities do not exist at all. But it is more likely that the advertised 'qualities' do not, in practice, have the effects promised by the advertisement.

Plain deception of these sorts has, in some fields, made it more and more necessary to institute some kind of control.[1] Advertisements in the medical field have evoked the strongest criticism on these grounds. Following earlier disclosures by the British Medical Association, Mr. Hugh Linstead, M.P., the Secretary of the Pharmaceutical Society, recently revealed the most shocking facts: 'Exaggerated claims are made for medicines for chronic conditions ... and hopes are held out which cannot be realised. Many advertisements are couched in scientific or semi-scientific terms, often meaningless, designed to impress and deceive uneducated and credulous people.' (See Hugh Linstead, M.P., *Patent Medicines, An Indictment*, 1947.) Mr. Lever, who does not write against but in favour of advertising, observes (see Lever, op. cit., p. 120) that 'the highly complicated body is most difficult to describe briefly and in simple language. Yet physiological "facts" are often paraded in advertisements with shameless simplicity. This is generally only possible by such over-simplification as for the results to be misleading.'

Exactly the same applies to many drink advertisements. 'Many advertisements', emphasised the Amulree Report, 'contain statements which amount to palpable untruths.' (See Amulree Report, para. 736.) We saw in the first chapter that such 'untruth' must be contained in any assertion that alcohol is good for people's health: the best that might be said for it is that it is not harmful to some people, or generally when taken in small doses; and it may lead immediately to manslaughter when taken even in a small quantity by a motorist; and even if taken only in small quantities, but day by day, it may lead to secondary poverty. Yet drink may be consumed in the belief, created by advertisement, that it improves the worker's performance, that it gives more strength, that it prevents colds and even cures some sorts of sickness, despite the fact that all such suggestions are notoriously the opposite of what medical science and modern physiotherapy have to say on the matter. Even

[1] See for full details Hermann Levy, 'Industrial Law and Quality Control', in *The Industrial Law Review*, May 1948.

the food value of drink is negligible, though the urge of this factor is less harmful than the exaltation of the medical qualities of alcoholic drink.

Criticism has been strong and clear. One can well agree with what Lord Winterton said to the Royal Commission (see Amulree Commission, A. 33,823): 'When I see a bottle of beer standing on an island by the sea with the caption "Good Health", I know that the man who designed that poster had an imagination which exceeded his scientific knowledge. When I hear, for example, that school children are repeating the slogan "Guinness is good for you", I understand that the Trade is deliberately antagonising the efforts of the State when it spends public money to inform these children, as it does in the Health Syllabus, that "Children and young people should not drink beer, wines, or spirits of any kind". Lord Arnold criticised the advertisement 'Gin is the Origin of Good Health' in the House of Lords in similar vein (see Debates of 28th March 1935): 'Gin is one of the most intoxicating liquors. It is one of the main constituents of many cocktails, which are largely condemned by the medical profession. It contains practically no nourishment at all, and the statement in the advertisement is about as far from being the truth as it can be.' Mr. Courtney C. Weeks, M.R.C.S., L.R.C.P., says in a book strongly recommended by Sir Thomas Barlow, M.D. (see Weeks, *Alcohol and Human Life*, 1938, pp. 186–7): 'A recent liquor advertisement says: "It is the sugar in your beer that gives you energy." One asks why buy beer to obtain sugar, and not the most readily available or assimilable sugar either? There is as much real potential energy in threepenny-worth of sugar as is in twenty-two pints of beer.' Sir Frederick Gowland has made the point that the existence of propaganda proclaiming the nutritional merits of beer removes the discussion of the food value of alcohol from the academic or purely scientific field into the arena of everyday life: 'Neither with proteins, nor fat, nor carbohydrate, nor vitamins, can the body dispense. With alcohol we know that it can dispense altogether.... A pint of beer mostly sold today contains some carbohydrate material, with a fuel value only equal to that of about one ounce of bread, but even this material is so much altered by fermentation that we do not know whether it has real value of food.' (Quoted by Weeks, op. cit., p. 187.) Humorous advertising may be a means of increasing cheer and may take a place alongside comic journals. There is no harm when an American poster suggests that Grapenuts are good for the brain—and after all a grain of truth may be found in any sort of joke. But the joke goes perhaps too far when it is suggested to workers that they can lift heavy burdens better after having a pint of beer, or that a tree is hewn with a few strokes if only a glass of beer precedes the work.

'INFORMATIVE' LITERATURE

But drink advertising is designed less to 'enlighten' the public on the physiological and other specific 'values' of alcohol than to attract the attention quite generally to the importance of beer, wine or spirits. As a result, what may at first appear as purely informative publicity can be shrewdly used for suggestive purposes. Perhaps this is the most important field in which, in Sir Edgar Sanders' words, one can 'educate' public opinion 'without making it too obvious that there is a publicity campaign behind it'. The apt observation of Mr. Lever that the line between informative and persuasive publicity is difficult to draw has a clear case example in the propaganda launched by the brewing trade in the form of what must impress the general public as merely instructive enlightenment. For instance, an important firm of brewers has of late produced advertisements which do not urge that people should drink more and that this is good for their health and strength, but simply exhibit in an impressive and artistic way the history, the technique, the economic significance of the brewery and the relationship of the firm with famous research scientists.

This type of publicity need not be, and is not, confined to posters. A book can provide informative matter with a suggestive background. There is, for instance, the Whitbread Library published by Whitbread and Co. Ltd. We have already mentioned *Your Local*, one volume of the series, which includes also a beautifully illustrated volume on *Whitbread's Brewery*, and others on the *Brewer's Art*, *Some Inns of Kent* and *Inn Signs*. These volumes do not differ on the outside from books describing the development, the structure, and the economic and social characteristics of specific trades. But their purpose is mainly the promotion of alcoholic drink. *Your Local* goes so far as to extol the high significance of the 'regular' as against the 'casual' drinker. Of the 'regular' drinker, Professor Zweig reports in his study that he drinks at least four to six pints a night, that he spends the whole evening in the pub, that his first two to three pints go in half-an-hour, that he has 'formed such a strong habit of drinking, and his organism is already used to drink to such a degree, that breaking this habit is dangerous, and often impossible', and that in general, the wives of the regulars are left at home. This, in brief, is the description of the 'regular' given by an experienced economist after close study, the publication of which is prefaced by two of the greatest social reformers of the age, Lord Beveridge and B. Seebohm Rowntree (see Zweig, op. cit., pp. 27–9).

But the writer of *Your Local* thinks differently. For him the 'regular' is the type of drinker to be cultivated, and, indeed, highly praised. This is what he says (see *Your Local*, 1947, pp. 28–9): 'The "regulars" are, of course, the backbone of the local, enjoying certain undefined privileges and being on much more familiar terms with the Guv'nor and his staff. No one can define the qualifications that equip one for promotion: certainly no one will inform you when your probationary period is over. In some locals tankards are reserved for the regulars, and to have your beer served up in one by the Guv'nor may be the first intimation you will receive of your election to membership. Amongst themselves the "regulars" adhere to as intricate a code of rules governing their procedure and behaviour as could be found in any volume of Victorian etiquette. They affect your manner of address to the Chair, the number of drinks you may have to pay for without appearing to be buying popularity, the seats you may not occupy without giving offence, the topics of conversation that are taboo. . . . The wise landlord is naturally courteous, affable and urbane towards his "casuals"—good manners are after all part of his stock-in-trade. But he realises that his regulars claim preferential treatment. If he knows his business, he will grapple them to him "with hoops of steel".' Reading this glowing appreciation of the 'regular' one cannot feel otherwise than that, *inter alia*, it is meant to convey to publicans something of the methods of 'promoting' a mere 'casual' into a 'regular' drinker. The publican is further told that he must rely on the 'regular' because he is 'a financial insurance to him against a rainy day'. It is probably very clever to use a book of informative appearance as a means to incite the 'social' ambition of would-be habitués and as a guide for those who must be interested in the promotion of drink.

THE 'IMPROVED HOUSE'

Of no less importance than advertisement as an attraction is the type of drinking place and its amenities. We saw in earlier chapters how many different factors could increase the desire to drink, e.g., the social amenities of the pub, the personality of the innkeeper, the provision of games.[1] The trade always realises the fact that drinking is not merely a physical but eminently also a social function, and that it must be in its interest to support the latter in order to assist the former.

The type of inn or public house deserves the trade's particular attention. Which type of house, the trade must ask, will best promote the consumption of drink? In our changing times the question has become an issue as between the old-fashioned public house and that of modern style and appearance, and the policy of the trade has been shaped by its views on this alternative. The so-called 'improved house' has thus become a very important problem to the drink trade. The development of this type of public house has been conspicuous since the end of the First World War, and the Royal Commission on Licensing gave it considerable attention (see Amulree Report, pp. 45 sq.). There are two distinct sides to its development; but we are not here concerned with the purely architectural and technical which finds expression in the building of new public houses, and, very conspicuously, also in the modernisation of established public houses (see Mass Observation, *The Pub and the People*, p. 103): it is highly desirable; as a result the modern public house is very different from the old, particularly from those in industrial districts which were, and still are to a large extent, 'poor and cramped in structure, gloomy, often insufficiently ventilated, and sometimes even deficient in standards of cleanliness' (see Amulree Report, para. 196). What concerns us here is rather the question of how far the 'improved' house has been conducive to an increased consumption of drink and how far its possibilities in that respect are exploited by the trade and for a part of trade policy.

There is no doubt that in one way at least, the trade is highly in favour of the modern and 'improved' public houses: it is particularly the young people who are attracted by the features of modern public houses. This was stated before the Royal Commission and has never been refuted. It is to the credit of the young generation that they dislike the old-fashioned public houses, of which the *New London Survey* says that many 'are undeniably squalid—often so to an extent not approached in this country by

[1] For the significance of the latter, see also *Your Local* where all the games played are described in detail; see pp. 31 sq.

anything else save the poorest homes' (see *New London Survey*, op. cit., p. 19). In many cases young people frequent public houses just for their pleasant atmosphere and environment. To create such conditions is therefore an effective way in which the trade can increase their custom. As Cecil Heath puts it in his chapter on the 'improved public house' (see Heath, op. cit., p. 91): 'The Brewers realise only too well that the younger generation cannot be attracted to the old type of tavern.' Sir W. W. Butler, the eminent Birmingham brewer, regarded it as 'certain that the younger generation will not be content with the conditions which satisfied their forefathers. They have been educated up to a higher standard of comfort and will expect to obtain it' (see Wilson, loc. cit., p. 181).

But the improvement of public houses is in the interest of the trade for reasons besides attracting the young. The modernisation of public houses was bound to become a major plank in trade policy also because the modern type of inn or bar offers outstanding possibilities of 'inducement', in particular the installation of all sorts of amenities in line with modern social life. The difference between the improved large house and the old small house resembles that between the modern department store and the small traditional shop. In the same way as the department store, the large modern public house can try to attract custom not merely by the goods it offers for sale, but, as L. E. Neal has expressed it, 'by every inducement open to the store proprietor' (see Neal, *Retailing and the Public*, 1933, p. 17). It is not surprising to find, therefore, brewers readily willing to sacrifice two or three old licences in exchange for one new licence. The new public houses aim at becoming the social centres of the neighbourhoods for which they cater. Many provide on the grounds tennis courts and bowling greens, and occasionally a concert and dance hall, and even a cinema.[1] Without doubt the equipment of some modern public houses is lavishly planned and their artistic features are publicised as special attractions. As the *Brewing Trade Review* put it in describing the Inn Craft Exhibition of May 1948 (cf. May 1948, p. 309): 'Great changes—important changes—have taken place, which have resulted in the "Pub" (whether country inn or urban hotel) becoming more and more a worthy centre of social life.' The influence of brewers on amenities and pleasant surroundings is emphasised: fine beer mugs and claret glasses, knives and forks,

[1] See Heath, p. 91; also *The Licensed House* as quoted above, illustrations, pp. 19–20.

and vases with flowers are shown in photographs, and the furnishing material is given special credit.

The resemblance between the modern public house and the department store in the width of their attraction to the customer should not, however, blind us to an underlying difference between them. The large department store's interests differ clearly from those of small independent shopkeepers. The latter have the advantage of proximity to their customers: large stores rely on attracting crowds of buyers from farther away by offering a greater variety of goods and lower prices, special amenities and other inducements, and a delivery service. The two interests oppose one another (see for details Levy, *The Shops of Britain*, 1948, *passim*) and each has its own trade organisations. Except in the case of the composite establishment producing and retailing at the same time there is not behind both a policy decided on by the manufacturer to favour either the one or the other. In the liquor trade this is different. The drink retailing trade is immediately influenced by the large brewing interests; and it is for these manufacturing interests to decide what policy should govern the potential competition between the modern improved house and the small old-fashioned pub in the side street. If trade in other commodities were in the same position, i.e., were the manufacturers similarly obliged to decide generally between the channels of retail distribution, a distinctive policy of favouring the one or the other type of shop, or an attempt to strike a balance between them might have developed. The brewing trade is in that position. Through controlling the public houses it can develop a definite and effective policy in its choice of retail outlets.

The drink trade has not favoured a policy of promoting the large modern and 'improved' house as a substitute for the local pub. It therefore has not carried out any wholesale policy of concentration. If it had, the Amulree Report would not have found it necessary to emphasise in the very first of its recommendations that a 'much more rapid reduction of licences' was needed (see Amulree Report, para. 110). What the trade really wants is to promote both the modern public house and a great multiplicity of locals. The Amulree Commission was convinced that public-house improvement was really 'only in its infancy'. The decade that followed and the war and post-war periods have not altered this situation. On the contrary, building and repair shortages have made the position more difficult. But the determining factor in the development is the deliberate policy of the trade to keep alive as far as possible all types of public houses, regardless of any consideration of superfluity and overlapping. The late Lord D'Abernon observed (see M. V. Vernon, *The Alcohol Problem*, 1928, preface, p. x) that 'the fundamental truth in this matter is that, under present conditions and in the present state of civilisation in England, a bad public house pays better than a good public house. Competition tempts even the most public-spirited brewer into management that pays best. Competition has a tendency to drive him to favour bad public houses.'

To reduce competition by reducing the number of public houses would mean, the trade is convinced, a reduction in the consumption of alcoholic drink, and not merely a transfer of drinkers from many small places to fewer large ones. We have already noted the contradiction in brewers strongly arguing at one and the same time that fewer public houses would not mean less drink, but that public houses must be situated at short distances from the homes so that 'no one need complain of having too far to walk' (see *Your Local*). To claim that fewer public houses means reduced consumption of drink is, of course, correct, and this is the argument which is embodied in trade policy: proximity increases consumption, while distance from the home reduces it. The trade just does not favour a sharp reduction of the locals. The most it can agree to is, as Mr. Whitbread told the Royal Commission in his Minority Report, that in the development of the improved house, 'progress must be by steps' (see Amulree Report, p. 240, *sub* 34). And this can be interpreted very widely and vaguely.

A recent publication of one of the leading brewing firms makes the position formally clear. This is what it says with reference to 'Tomorrow's Town' (see *Your Local*, p. 43): 'Will there be two more big houses, or several smaller ones? Those who appreciate best [*sic*] the intimate value of the local will say instantly, "Let's have the smaller houses". . . . The real local will forgo snack bars, car parks, white-coated attendants and neon lighting. . . . Furthermore, an overcrowded inn may quite easily lead to over-drinking through reaction against comfort.' The argument that less public houses means over-crowding is frequently used. 'Over-crowding is a social disadvantage' was the headline of one of the sections in the publication of the London Brewers' Planning Exhibition of 1947 (see op. cit., p. 7) and the same publication urges that 'under-licensing does *not* promote sobriety' (see ibid., p. 5). The fact that a more scanty distribution of public houses necessarily reduces the number of potential customers is never taken into account.

The trade policy is then to support simultaneously what the publication of the London Brewers' Planning Exhibition clearly specifies as various types of inns: the 'Social Centre' type of house with facilities for catering and entertainment for as many as 500 to 600 customers at peak hours; the 'intermediate house'; and the 'small', 'intimate' 'local house', which has not more than 100 to 150 peak-hour customers (ibid., p. 17, with typical illustrations) and whose 'real charm lies in its friendly atmosphere', catering for the 'little street' and necessary 'as the street's informal club'—the trade's continued attachment to the small public house is obvious.

The trade is well aware that the improved houses and the old pub are not really straight competitors. To a large extent they do not compete at all, because they tend to appeal to different types of customer. The *New London Survey* noted that the 'so-called Model Public Houses', though an interesting development, 'are not numerically important', because 'there is a tendency among customers to dislike these model houses, and an inquirer will often be told that they are cold, or that no one can feel at home there, or that the people who run them are new and unfriendly' (see *Drink*, as cited above, reprint, p. 20). The trade knows something of the sociological differentiation in the appreciation of the various types of public houses. And this appreciation differs between the old and the young, the poorer and the rich. The difference is not just 'big' and 'small', or 'improved' and 'old-fashioned'. Large and small houses are not simply complementary: a rapid extension of the former may gravely reduce the size of the clientele as a whole and a rapid reduction of the latter might well have the same effect. That is what the trade means by suggesting that the dispersal of licensed houses has 'an additional merit' over any concentration in larger units. (See *Your Local*, p. 43.) The type of public house to be favoured anywhere depends on the type of customer. To discourage one type may mean a weakening of a whole class of customers and a reduction in the consumption of drink, a result which the trade can, after all, only be dead against. The trade's interest in the modern improved public house is, therefore, strictly limited. And this limited interest can be easily reconciled with the admirable technical and hygienic construction of improved houses where they seem to further trade interests; it must merely be remembered that they are designed to compete with luxury cinemas and other places of modern entertainment which, to the great chagrin of the trade, threaten to withdraw too many from the drinking habit.

THE PROBLEM OF GENERAL REFRESHMENT

There remains another feature of public-house improvement to which trade policy might well be directed, possibly to the advantage of all. Indeed, the Amulree Report considered it as a more urgent requirement than the mere reduction in the number of public houses. It is the 'ideal' of transforming the public house from a place where more or less drink may be had, into 'a place where the public can obtain general refreshment, of whatever variety they choose, in decent, pleasant and comfortable surroundings' (see Amulree Report, para. 198). This should be generally desirable for at least two reasons. The first is that drink on an empty stomach leads more easily to intoxication than drink taken together with food. This observation by the customer has been unquestioned fact ever since Sir E. Mellanby made his experiments some twenty-five years ago.[1] Since the liquor trade is averse to intoxication it can on this ground approve of food taken with drink.

But there is another side also to this matter. Drinking without taking food is part of the British habit of 'perpendicular', i.e., stand-up, drinking at the bar, and 'perpendicular drinking' is, as the Amulree Commission stated, undoubtedly the cause of 'much of the present excessive consumption of intoxicants'. (See Amulree Report, para. 208.) It is perpendicular drinking which leads to 'treating' and which indefinitely prolongs the stay of the customer in the public house. If public houses were visited, like restaurants, for the taking of meals, it would be assumed that customers would not stay indefinitely long at the table. Certainly at busy times in the evenings tables would be required by other guests; as in the case of restaurants, the presentation of the bill to the customer shortly after the conclusion of the meal would normally have to be taken as a hint to leave the table. But the customs which have been built round perpendicular drinking are the mainstay of heavy alcoholic consumption. If a customer's consumption is adequate in quantity and regularity, it may, as we have seen,

[1] See for details *Effects of Alcohol on Man*, op. cit., pp. 54–6; also *The Action of Alcohol on Man*, p. 33.

enhance his recognition by the publican as well as by his friends: 'Today's good fellow is the man who drinks up quickly and pays for a fresh round, urging his consorts to be gay this way' (Mass Observation, *The Pub and the People*, p. 181). It is here that the combination of food with drink necessarily meets the opposition of the trade: it would presuppose, in the words of the Amulree Commission, 'the minimum of facilities' for perpendicular drinking.

In view of this basic disadvantage, the trade might naturally have embarked on a policy of wholly discouraging the combination of selling meals with drink. It has done better: it has chosen the policy of running with the hare and hunting with the hounds. Mr. Whitbread's Minority Report to the Royal Commission 'warmly welcomed' what the Report had stated as the 'ideal', and restricted its observations to what was to be considered as the modern model house—and here, as we have seen the author remark, progress could only be slow. Mr. Whitbread contended that 'in many licensed houses there is at present no demand for the supply of food' (see Amulree Report, p. 240). It is a little difficult to see how, conditions in the pubs and drinking habits being what they are, it could be tested whether and to what extent this was really the case. And the member's report altogether refrained from making any suggestions as to how perpendicular drinking could be replaced by some comprehensive requirement for people to have meals with their drink.

The Amulree Report commended the Public House Trust Companies on having given a lead 'in the promotion of a new conception of the public house'. They had already then shown how business in food and non-intoxicating drink could be developed alongside the trade in alcohol. But few Trust Houses are situated in industrial or city areas; they are mostly country houses of the hotel type. In the days of the Royal Commission they represented only one-half per cent of the whole number of on-licensed premises and even now they are limited to a small portion of the field (see Amulree Report, paras. 195, 217 and 368–71).

It would appear to be of possibly far greater importance to extend the scope of the Continental type restaurant at the cost of the traditional type of British public house. The Amulree Report remarked (see ibid., para. 209) that the 'Continental café' had been held up to the Commission as the type of establishment at which reform in this country should aim. But they found that, for all their numerous advantages, the scope for transplanting Continental type cafês was limited 'by racial differences and the vagaries of the weather', and that the conception of the average Continental establishment was easily 'idealised'. But the Royal Commission hardly exhausted the possibilities when it restricted its attention to Continental 'cafês' and ignored the quite general Continental habit of having drink in 'restaurants' and 'beer-gardens' and, connected with this, the almost total absence of perpendicular drinking prior to the arrival of the 'American bar'. The conditions of weather do not adequately explain the difference.

There are also in Britain opportunities in country and suburban pubs for the consumption of drink in the open air, but the tables and other equipment are generally shabby and uninviting, the service almost non-existent, and the choice of meals very small. Such places cannot be compared with the French, German, Austrian, Italian or Swiss open-air restaurants or beer-gardens, with tables neatly covered with linen, their attractive lay-out, their numerous waiters and waitresses and, in normal pre-war days, their highly elaborate menus with numerous 'special' as well as ordinary dishes. When the Amulree Report spoke of 'refreshments', it overlooked that 'refreshment' in the form of what in this country are called 'snacks' is virtually unknown in Continental establishments. It is a meal, and not a snack, that the Continental customer wants and that he consumes along with some alcoholic or non-alcoholic drink. It is important to note this fundamental difference: in British establishments, which the Amulree Report had in mind, what food is offered is complementary to the drink; but in Continental restaurants, beer-gardens and hotels, the drink is complementary to the food. That more public houses on the Continental pattern would be welcomed 'by nine-tenths of the justices of London', was suggested to the Royal Commission by Mr. B. S. Straus, J.P., the Licensing Justice for the St. Marylebone District.

Mr. Straus saw that there would be strong opposition to any such move by the present licence-holders and the brewers who own licences: 'Brewers do not want to spend a lot of money on increasing the size of premises and putting in tables, etc., when they know that it is going to lessen rather than to increase the consumption of alcoholic liquor' (see Amulree Commission, A. 2,493 and 2,520–1). Not surprisingly, therefore, recent developments have shown that what the trade is doing to combine the serving of food with the serving of drink is virtually different from the 'ideal' which the Amulree Report and many of the witnesses of the Commission sought to promote. Publications of the trade are proudly emphasising the endeavour to combine food with drink (see e.g., *The Licensed House*, as quoted above, p. 19). They reprint the 'ideal' postulated by the Royal Commission, as we have quoted it on a previous page. But they wisely omit the observation that it should replace perpendicular drinking; and what continues to be mostly offered by the pub is, indeed, 'refreshment' in the form of some food, but not meals. Cecil Heath describes the type of service in one of these modern public houses as follows (see Heath, op. cit., p. 92): 'There was displayed in large type on the walls of the room a menu which comprised a goodly assortment of various dishes, cooked meats, vegetables, etc. Very little food was available and none of the dishes on the menu could be served. There were one or two waiters going round with trays of sausage rolls, and apart from these only sandwiches could be supplied. . . .' Mass Observation describes in much the same way how in a newly decorated pub the main attraction in food was 'a great pile' of pies displayed on the bar counter, and 'the waiters walk round with a plate of them now and then during the evening'. (See *The Pub and the People*, p. 208.)

Thus drinking, far from being restricted in favour of food, is perhaps if anything increased, since the snack simply serves to cater for long-drawn-out drinking visits. It cannot even be said that such small bites are certain to prevent quick intoxication; and the customers' alleged preparedness to make do with lighter beers when snacks are available[1] may be a temporary condition due to other circumstances. Sometimes the trade press itself cannot avoid confessing that the trade does not really want to provide genuine meals. As one of them complained in connection with a general refusal of the Food Control Committees to grant catering licences to publicans, the publicans do not 'make extravagant demands . . . most of them ask for no more than snacks' (see *A Monthly Bulletin*, June 1948, p. 44). The writer can hardly have realised that it is just in this that the pub is to be distinguished from the restaurant and just this which makes the latter more valuable for public health.[2]

[1] See the Director of the National Trade Defence Association in a letter to *The Times*, 3rd November 1948.

[2] The point also overlooked by Mr. E. H. Keeling, M.P., when he pleads in *The Times* of 14th October 1948 that catering permits should be granted to licensed and

The trade has been somewhat alarmed by the increase in catering facilities during the Second World War and since. British Restaurants, for instance, made their appearance and their competition with the pub would perhaps be even more telling if they succeeded in making their meals more attractive.[1] As it is, works canteens are in many cases even stronger competitors.[2] It may well be that the trade will consider it wise to change its policy. If it should continue to support in the main the provision of food only in the form of 'snacks', it may close to itself a not altogether unfavourable line of development, and one which is supported by the Amulree Commission and by all those who see in the genuinely reformed public house and, in particular, in the reduction of perpendicular drinking, one of the most effective means of preventing the excessive consumption of alcoholic liquor.

---

unlicensed premises without distinction on the grounds that 'people who eat a sandwich with a glass of ale, or drink a glass of ale with their dinner, may work better as a result'. Quite apart from the fact that the serving of meals in licensed premises is not confined to factory working hours, the argument overlooks the fundamental difference that, in the one case, the food is only of secondary significance and the drink all-important, while with a meal the relative importance is reversed. See also Sir Herbert Dunnico in *The Times* of 9th October 1948.

[1] See for this the interesting study *British Restaurants*, an inquiry made by the National Council of Social Service, 1945, p. 70: 'There are notable exceptions, but the British Restaurant service as a whole tends to serve meals of an almost wearisome uniformity both in their quality and quantity.'

[2] See for details as to Works Canteens, Barbara Drake, *Community Feeding in War-time*, 1942, Fabian Research Series, pp. 11 sq.

CHAPTER XV

LINES OF ACTION

'It is unity and diversity which tempts us to frame rules and prescribe specific remedies'; but 'it is infinite diversity amid general unity which tempts us at times to give up the task of reform in despair'. With these words George B. Wilson (op. cit., p. 148) has suggested why diverse types of people have for one reason or another combined great clarity of thought on the problem of drink with deep pessimism about making much progress in solving it. Among supporters of temperance, the late Lord D'Abernon, for instance, voiced the same sentiment in his preface to H. M. Vernon's book on *The Alcohol Problem*, published in 1928 (cf. preface, pp. v-vi). And the people whom we have termed temperance 'purists', who will not be satisfied with anything short of total prohibition, tend to despair through the unlikelihood of prohibition coming about, or human nature being what it is, of its being effective even if it did come about. For scientists the great diversity of aspects of the problem, the inability effectively to use simple causal analysis in this essentially sociological field, and the prospect of being drawn into the debatable and largely non-scientific sphere of social policy—these have the same deadening effect on action.

Then there are those who deny the problem any significance on the basis of the statistically variable incidence of drinking and drunkenness: by all available indices, no less than by general agreement, the evils which result from drinking have declined over many years, and, as we have seen Professor F. Zweig put it (op. cit., p. 30), for them 'drinking is no longer a moral or health problem of great magnitude; . . . the problem of drunkenness in this country has been more or less solved'. The trade finally is, of course, ready to support all contentions of this sort; even though it has little hope to recruit any of these groups for its own aggressive opposition, it may at any rate increase the inertia regarding further measures to reduce the evils of drink.

We have already met and discussed these various attitudes on various pages throughout this book. To answer them briefly in turn, the outlook for abatement is not really discouraging. Real and lasting progress is slow in any social field. The problem of drink is no exception. But progress can undoubtedly be seen to have been made even only over the last few decades. With probably only one exception, on the roads, the incidence of the problem has without doubt declined. It is particularly encouraging to find recent observers noting public-house populations to be made up largely of older men and ascribing this healthy unbalance to 'a more interesting family life' and the existence of other interests on the part of younger people (see e.g., Zweig, op. cit., p. 25). In this advance restrictive legislation has played a valuable part. On several occasions, as we have seen, it had immediate effects. The attitude of all, i.e., prohibition, or nothing, is therefore out of place and not likely to promote the interest its protagonists have at heart.

If the complexity of a problem and the wide gaps in our knowledge were adequate grounds for doing nothing, no action at all could be taken in evolving and implementing policy on any matter of social significance: and there are few matters indeed which have no social significance. Taking calculated risks is the normal condition of social activity: the analysis of social problems is never complete. The perfect must not therefore be allowed to obstruct the good. Politics, and any application of science, is the art of the possible. The very least decision that hesitant scientists and their adherents should feel able to take is to promote further study of the problem of drink. For instance, Mass Observation's gallant attempt to study the problem of drink through the public house might well be repeated with other places as focal points. But it is important also to stress that a good deal of the missing knowledge of social problems and inadequate experience of dealing with them can emerge only in the course of coming to grips with them, that is, in the dynamics of the situation.

Most dangerous is the suggestion that drink no longer presents any serious problem. For that the problem of drink, though it has decreased, is still of considerable magnitude really admits of no doubt: the statistics of convictions indicate this, and they are only a small indication of the total size of the problem. In any case, as long as the effects of drink are severe, even though only occasionally so, the problem of drink remains important; and, as we have seen, the occasional results of drink include death and utter destitution. Averages are valueless in this connection. As Mass Observation remarked in its study of *The Pub and the People* (p. 10): 'The obsession for the typical, the representative, the "statistical sample", has exercised a serious limitation on the British approach to human problems and is largely responsible for the admitted backwardness of social science in this country'; and, they might have added, it is responsible also for many of the deficiencies of social policy.

ARGUMENTS FOR STATE ACTION

It may be true, as Adam Smith pointed out in *The Wealth of Nations* (bk. IV, ch. iii), that 'though individuals . . . may sometimes ruin their fortunes by an excessive consumption of fermented liquors, there seems to be no risk that a nation should do so. Though in every country there are many people who spend upon such liquors more than they can afford, there are always many more who spend less.' Even so, the nation's losses in terms of accidents and reduced efficiency through drink are considerable and, especially at times of scarcity and of need for great and sustained effort, may well be held to be excessive.

Further official action to reduce the consumption of drink and drunkenness would also seem to be a proper function of the emerging welfare state. We have heard much lately about social security and freedom from want—two well-coined phrases. If, with advancing social progress, it is judged desirable that the State becomes the comprehensive provider of social security and the safeguard against many of the usual contingencies of life, it might well become also the comprehensive provider of greater safety to the individual citizen. This would mean that it would have to devote far more attention than it has done to date to the elimination of factors which constantly endanger safety. The principle is well established. Factory legislation has been designed to reduce the risk of accidents and injuries; in this field the interconnection between the moral duty to man and the economic interests of the State has been quite obvious and is generally accepted. The possible effects of alcoholic drink constitute another of the many factors which may endanger the individual's safety. That their economic implications may not be as direct and immediate as in the case of defective machines and dangerous methods of work is no argument against taking action.

Certainly nobody should be deterred by trade opposition to any action which directly or indirectly is likely to reduce the consumption of alcoholic drink. The trade's opposition must be taken for granted and treated as that of an interested party. And it is important not to be deceived by the ingenious way in which it often voices its views. For instance, as we have seen, the trade is naturally against all restrictive legislation. So it combines, as occasion arises, such facts as that drunkenness is much rarer in France than in Britain with an equally true fact, such as that in France legislation is not so restrictive (see e.g., Mr. Frederick Hennessy in *The Times*, 11th December 1948). The suggested cause-effect relationship between these two facts is, of course, to say the least, not proven and hardly plausible.

The Amulree Commission was fully satisfied that the evidence put forward to show the influence of immoderate drinking pointed unmistakably to its 'aggravation of a variety of social evils'. It was convinced that so long as the sale of alcohol was permitted—and it was against prohibiting it—insobriety could not be wholly eliminated. But given this it regarded it as the 'clear duty of the State to take all reasonable action which will assist to reduce excessive drinking to the lowest dimensions possible, and . . . it is our opinion that the possibilities of such action, and the directions in which it can be taken, have not yet been exhausted' (see Amulree Report, paras. 88 and 108). We would add that, in addition to excessive drinking, the abatement of excessive expenditure on alcoholic drink should be a target of further restrictive legislation.

CHANGES IN LEGISLATION AND ADMINISTRATION

Our analysis has thrown up numerous possible lines of action. In the first place, a number of the recommendations of the Amulree Commission which have failed so far to be implemented could usefully be put into effect now. In connection with redundancy, for instance, the Commission made the important proposal that licensing justices in all districts should review their areas and prepare within a short period of time provisional plans for reduction. These surveys were to be considered as supplying the material for reduction on a national scale, carried out possibly by a central authority, the National Licensing Commission (paras. 137–9). It would be useful, further, to divorce considerations of the merits of redundancy in any area and the responsibility for the consequent decisions from the provision for compensation. The latter might well be left to the industry. To help assess the merits of redundancy, it would also be desirable to collect and collate experience to date in order to arrive at criteria for general guidance. It might well be possible now to derive standards of the amount of public-house accommodation to be licensed per so many hundred inhabitants in different types of geographical areas on the lines that G. B. Wilson has suggested. Codification of practice and evolution of standards could also usefully take place in connection with the permitted hours of opening, the granting of occasional licences and licences for clubs, and the regulation of bottle shops.

Other countries' experience with stricter regulations and heavier penalties concerning motorists' consumption of drink may be worthy of emulation. We have already noted that in Norway, for instance, a person is not allowed to have any drink within several hours of driving. Though it is not very clear how this regulation can be strictly enforced, the great majority of law-abiding citizens no doubt comply with it; and it certainly emphasises the danger of driving 'under the influence of drink'. Again, there, as also in some other countries, a person convicted of drunkenness under any circumstances is not allowed to have a driver's licence for several years and prison sentences are considered normal punishment for drunken motorists. In regarding legislation not merely as providing for the necessary punishment of the offender but also as an effective preventive measure, Britain has gone in the right direction. It is further advance rather than fundamental change which would be beneficial.

THE SPHERE OF PREVENTION

It is perhaps unfortunate that the State system of insurance which demands equal premiums from all cannot take immediate account of the relationship between alcoholism and health, in much the same way as life-insurance premiums take account of the publican's occupation, and accident insurance 'merit-rate' higher and lower risks.[1] Such parallels suggest that this is all the more reason, therefore, for the State to adopt other means of counteracting the impact of drink on health, whether by means of elaborating further the existing system of licensing, by expanding State control on the lines of the Carlisle scheme, or by striking out into new directions. The growth of State activities and control should itself

[1] See Sir A. Wilson and Professor H. Levy, *Workmen's Compensation*, vol. ii, 1942, *sub* 'merit-rating'.

increase the possibilities of action. Town-planning and control over building sites, for instance, can prevent a decline in the number of allotments on the same scale as in the inter-war years, which was partly due to the paucity of attempts to compensate allotment holders for the loss of war-time allotments situated on building sites ready for development by offering other plots. As the principal insurer of the nation's health the State again has direct and great opportunities to promote preventive measures. Immediately this depends on the acceptance of the proposition that the object of social insurance is not merely the provision of relief from various contingencies but also the reduction of these contingencies in terms of severity as well as frequency. The abatement of drinking would then have its place alongside the abatement of the many other circumstances which lead to ill-health and destitution. Its significance will not be on the same scale as, for instance, great improvements in housing and the abolition of slums, but may nevertheless have appreciable importance even in connection with the finance of the social insurance scheme.

But the most profitable field for direct preventive action would seem to lie in the field of education, interpreting this term widely as lasting from 'the cradle to the grave'. The first step would be to try to prevent the trade from deliberately misleading the public. Though we have noted a number of examples of this in the last chapter, an additional and particularly subtle example may not be amiss. It is the very use of the term 'medicated wine' to describe certain concoctions of alcoholic drink. We came across the term in the very first chapter of our study. There can be no doubt that its use has done much to instil into people the idea that spirits are something good for their health. The late Sir George Newman gave a straight 'no' as answer to the following question asked by the Royal Commission: 'One set of advertisements which is familiar to us all, dealing with notorious medicated wines, would hardly commend themselves to you as a guide to public health?' We need not, at this stage of our study, delve into the legality of the term; it has been lately much discussed in connection with the Labelling of Food Orders (see *Alliance News*, March-April 1947, p. 20). What interests us here is that the mere existence of such things as 'medicated spirits' and 'medicated wine' have reinforced the popular belief that there must be a close interrelation between the alcoholic or the medicinal or health-giving effect of drink. The Royal Commission recognised this and regarded the term 'medicated spirits' as obscure and misleading. In particular did this apply in their view to the distinction drawn, in licensing law, between 'medicated spirits and spirits made up in medicine'. It suggested that the phrase 'medicines containing spirits' should be substituted (see Amulree Report, para. 768). As to 'medicated wines' the Report was of the opinion that 'a line can be drawn between those varieties which are medicines rather than wines, and those which are wines rather than medicines'.

These classifications are undoubtedly beset with difficulties. But however great these are and whatever classification can be evolved, it should certainly be possible to stop within a short time the purveying of falsehoods. As the Amulree Commission put it, 'Many advertisements contain statements which amount to palpable scientific untruths: and others make use of anonymous medical testimony in a way which seems to us to be open to strong objection. We understand that the British Medical Association shares our view in this matter' (see Amulree Report, p. 156). There is here a general affinity also with medical advertisements encouraging people to select and administer medicines without medical advice. The social reformer's attitude towards this in the field of drink is likely to be the same as his attitude towards self-medication in general: he deplores it. But he does not suggest that the use of patent medicines should be prohibited, that there should be no aspirin or gargling solutions or boil plasters, just because they may be ill-applied or sometimes camouflage more serious illnesses. But we agree with *PEP* when they urged in their Report on the British Health Services (see *PEP*, *The British Health Services*, 1937, pp. 57–58; see also Hermann Levy, *National Health Insurance*, 1944, p. 190) that where self-medication 'for deep-rooted troubles cannot be other than mischievous, irresponsible manufacturers and advertisers should not be permitted to exploit public credulity by spreading the contrary belief in their own interest'.

The trade's very heated opposition to the systematic education of young people in the dangers of drink should be interpreted primarily as a commendation and should promote further efforts in the schools. Trade opposition can in this way be used as a criterion of effectiveness or, at least, of possible effectiveness. Were the trade able to show that the educational measures of enlightenment and dissuasion had failed in their effect, that they had merely resulted, for instance, in increasing young people's eagerness to do secretly what they should not do in the open, they might establish their case against a strong educational policy. But though there is some evidence of that kind of failure, not even the trade contends that this denotes the general failure of anti-drink education. On the contrary, it is furious every time a new educational venture is announced. Proper education helps young people as they grow up to avoid the habits which may entail all the physical evils of excessive drinking and the uneconomic expenditure that often goes with it.

In the field of anti-drink education Britain may also usefully consider the efforts of other countries. Sweden has probably instituted the most comprehensive and effective measures. There it is prescribed that temperance instruction shall be given in all educational establishments which come under the direct supervision of the Central Board of Education. In this way every type of school, with the exception of universities and colleges and certain private establishments, is covered. Temperance instruction is prescribed for all schools controlled by the public authorities where no special conditions, e.g., the youth of pupils, stand in the way. Concerning the contents of the courses and the methods of instruction, the Government circular regarding temperance teaching, which has been in force since 1928, prescribes that the teaching should be 'suited to the pupils' comprehension concerning the effects of alcoholic liquor on the individual and community'. This sound guiding line has not always been evident in this country, and the temperance movements themselves could well follow it more closely in future than they sometimes have in the past. In Sweden the programme is intentionally not associated with any movement. It states that temperance teaching shall be neutral from the point of view of religion, of politics and even of temperance. The scientifically ascertained facts, as it were, speak for themselves.

Finally the increasingly close association of scientists with the educational programme is most beneficial and deserves every encouragement. In the opinion of Sir H. M. Vernon, as of many others, the Central Control Board, which embodied the earliest large-scale efforts on the part of the Government to abate the consumption of alcoholic drink, 'owed its success in no small degree to the fact that it had the advantage of being advised by a committee of eminent scientific men' (see H. M. Vernon, evidence to Amulree Commission). It is the same in the field of preventive education. The forecast of the medico-social classic, *The Action of*

Alcohol on Man—not a propagandist publication but one written by eminent doctors and scientists—concerned industrial drinking specifically but applies no less to the problem of drink in general: 'Industrial drinking will be cured by education and improvement in social conditions of the worker. There is no reason to apprehend that the growth of control and temperance which has been continuous during the last generation will now come to an end—rather may we expect it to proceed at an accelerating pace' (see *Action*, p. 167).

INDEX